THE WORLD OF
THE BACH CANTATAS

JOHANN SEBASTIAN BACH'S
EARLY SACRED CANTATAS

The World of the

BACH

Cantatas

Edited by
CHRISTOPH WOLFF

With a foreword by
TON KOOPMAN

JOHANN SEBASTIAN BACH'S
EARLY SACRED CANTATAS

W. W. NORTON & COMPANY

NEW YORK   LONDON

*This edition was produced with the
sponsorship of Erato Disques.*

Copyright © 1995 by Uitgeverij Uniepers
    Abcoude /The Netherlands
This edition copyright © 1997 by
    W. W. Norton & Company, Inc.
Originally published in Dutch as *De wereld
    van de Bach-cantates*, vol.1.: *Johann
    Sebastian Bachs geestelijke cantates van
    Arnstadt tot Köthen.*

Design and production: Uniepers Abcoude
Photo cover: Marienkirche (St. Mary's),
    Mühlhausen: Thierry Cohen, Paris
Translation: Cees Bakker and Margaret
    Ross-Griffel
Printed by Walburg Druk, Zutphen

Library of Congress Cataloging-in-Publication Data:
Wereld van de Bach-cantates. English.
The World of the Bach Cantatas /edited by Christoph Wolff.
 p. cm.
Includes bibliographical references and indexes.
Contents: v. 1. Johann Sebastian Bach's early sacred cantatas.
ISBN 0-393-04106-9
1. Bach, Johann Sebastian, 1685-1750. Cantatas. 2. Cantata.
I. Wolff, Christoph. II. Title.
ML410.B13W2713 1997
782.2'4'092—dc21   97-2417
                                                CIP
                                                MN

W. W. Norton & Company, Inc.,
    500 Fifth Avenue, New York, N.Y. 10110
http://www.wwnorton.com

W. W. Norton & Company Ltd.,
    10 Coptic Street, London WC1A 1PU

1 2 3 4 5 6 7 8 9 0

CONTENTS

FOREWORD

My dream to play and record all of Bach's cantatas one day has come true. In the course of a conversation with the French label Erato about renewal details of our agreement, I expressed this, my fondest wish. To my utter amazement their reaction was not in the least negative. On the contrary, we had to prepare a solid plan very quickly as the basis for further discussion. And when a sponsor came forward, I was able to start my dream project, which turned out to be a tremendous task, both in size and requirements. The project will encompass sixty-six CDs and forty-four concerts.

We are dealing here with all the cantatas known at this time, both sacred and secular. Gustav Leonhardt and Nikolaus Harnoncourt were the first to record all of the sacred cantatas on authentic instruments, with men's voices and boy's choir. That project was begun in the early 1970s and took nearly twenty years to complete. During the same period Helmuth Rilling recorded all of Bach's sacred cantatas but used modern instruments and both male and female solo voices. As far as we know, however, no conductor has recorded the complete secular cantatas. Our recording project will include, for the first time, all of the sacred and secular cantatas, with a single conductor working with various soloists, his own chorus, and his own orchestra playing on historical instruments. We will, of course, rely on the latest musicological findings. In addition, we will gratefully benefit from the collective experience in instrumental and vocal techniques gained over the past decade by many of our participating musicians who specialize in Baroque music.

Over the next ten years we will present cantata performances in all of the major concert halls in the Netherlands. The Amsterdam Baroque Orchestra and Choir will also give numerous cantata performances in other parts of the world.

I shall conduct The Amsterdam Baroque Orchestra and Choir, with well-known soloists, for all compact disk recordings. The CDs will be brought out under the Erato label, a subsidiary company of Warner.

At the same time we will not ignore the written word. Since CD booklets lack space to include an in-depth study, we have decided to put together this first (of three) volumes on the Bach cantatas. Strange as it may sound, in the history of Bach literature this is the first set of books to deal exclusively with Bach's cantatas. Much research was necessary before we could start recording. Fascinating talks with Christoph Wolff made the world of the Bach cantatas even more intriguing to me.

This first volume deals with Bach's early cantatas and throws more light on the various aspects and background of his life and work during this period. It makes fascinating reading. *The World of the Bach Cantatas*, above all, is not meant for musicologists and specialists although they will undoubtedly discover that it contains much unusual and important information. The principal aim of the book is to bring the spiritual and artistic world of Bach nearer to the reader, to whom I wish happy reading.

Ton Koopman   Amsterdam
                                                                                                    Fall 1996

PREFATORY NOTE

Johann Sebastian Bach's cantatas belong among the great treasures of Western art music but come from a world that is no longer ours. When we hear the cantatas, we may well fall under their spell, but, even if the sound of Bach's music seems somehow familiar, much remains alien to us.

The gap in time and culture between our world and the one of the Bach cantatas is certainly hard to bridge; perhaps the easiest way of doing so would be through a convincing musical performance. However, when we listen to the music or read the scores, questions of the most diverse kind arise constantly: What is the role of the cantatas and their development in relation to Bach's overall output? In what context were they written, and how important were they to the composer? What musical models do they follow, what important comparisons can we draw with pieces by other composers, and what are the specific individual features of Bach's cantatas? How are the texts structured, what is their function, and what are the messages they convey? How are the musical and literary forms related to each other? What is the explanation for the broad spectrum of different compositional settings for chorus, solo voices, and instruments? What difficulties do we come across today in performances because of changed conditions? The attempt to uncover and try to answer such questions can only result in a better understanding of the works in their historical context. This, then, is the purpose of the present book: to provide a companion guide that broadens and deepens one's musical experience.

The idea for this book developed in the course of planning the first-ever recording of *all* of Bach's cantatas, both sacred and secular, by Ton Koopman and his Amsterdam Baroque Orchestra and Choir (for the Erato label). The preparatory discussions with Mr. Koopman not only affected the concept for making the CD recordings but also resulted in an outline for a comprehensive introduction to the world of the Bach cantatas based on the present state of scholarship. We plan to publish three volumes, each devoted to a different subject area (but each complementing the other): (1) the sacred cantatas to 1723, (2) the secular cantatas, and (3) the church cantatas dating from the Leipzig period.

While this division into three parts has been coordinated with the Erato recording schedule, the resulting books must be understood as a largely independent undertaking, a project in its own right. There is no previous introduction to Bach's cantatas comparable to the present one, which comments less on the particular works themselves and focuses more on the wider and deeper context. General historical and biographical aspects, literary and theological points of view, as well as analytical and aesthetic considerations will be mutually complementary in the contributions to this volume and the subsequent two.

It should be noted that while the illustrations in this volume relate, in general, to the theme of Bach's pre-Leipzig sacred cantatas, for technical reasons they are not matched in any direct way with the sections of text near which they appear.

The success of a thematically planned and systematically organized collection of essays hinges on the interest and willingness of the authors taking part in the work. For that reason the editor happily takes this opportunity to express his debt of gratitude to his friends and colleagues. He also wishes to thank Marinus H. van Raalte and Annelies Bouma of Uitgeverij Uniepers and Michael Ochs of W. W. Norton for their unfailing support during the publication and editing process.

Christoph Wolff   Cambridge, Massachusetts
                                                            Fall 1996

x

BIBLIOGRAPHICAL ABBREVIATIONS

BC   Hans-Joachim Schulze and Christoph Wolff, *Bach Compendium. Analytisch-bibliographisches Repertorium der Werke Johann Sebastian Bachs*, vol. 1, parts 1–4 (Leipzig and Frankfurt, 1985–89); vols. 2–4 in prep.

BG   *Johann Sebastian Bachs Werke. Gesamtausgabe der Bachgesellschaft* (Leipzig, 1851–99; repr. Ann Arbor, 1947).

BJ   *Bach-Jahrbuch*, ed. Arnold Schering (1904–39); Max Schneider (1940–52); Alfred Dürr and Werner Neumann (1953–74); Hans-Joachim Schulze and Christoph Wolff (1975–).

BR   Hans T. David and Arthur Mendel, eds., *The Bach Reader. A Life of Johann Sebastian Bach in Letters and Documents* (New York, 1945; 2nd ed. rev. 1966).

BWV   Wolfgang Schmieder, *Thematisch-systematisches Verzeichnis der musikalischen Werke Johann Sebastian Bachs: Bach-Werke-Verzeichnis* (Leipzig, 1950; 2nd ed. rev. and enl. Wiesbaden, 1990).
            BWV 4/3 = BWV 4, movement 3.

Dok I, II, III, IV   Werner Neumann and Hans-Joachim Schulze, eds., *Schriftstücke von der Hand Johann Sebastian Bachs; Bach-Dokumente, I* (Leipzig and Kassel, 1963);
            Fremdschriftliche und gedruckte Dokumente zur Lebensgeschichte Johann Sebastian Bachs 1685–1750; Bach-Dokumente, II (Leipzig and Kassel, 1969); Hans-Joachim Schulze, ed., *Dokumente zum Nachwirken Johann Sebastian Bachs 1750–1800; Bach-Dokumente, III* (Leipzig and Kassel, 1972); Werner Neumann, ed., *Bilddokumente zur Lebensgeschichte Johann Sebastian Bachs; Bach-Dokumente, IV* (Leipzig and Kassel, 1978).

Forkel   Johann Nicolaus Forkel, *Über Johann Sebastian Bachs Leben, Kunst und Kunstwerke* (Leipzig, 1802; repr. Frankfurt, 1950).

HMw   *Handbuch der Musikwissenschaft*, ed. E. Bücken (Potsdam, 1927–).

Mf   *Die Musikforschung*

NBA   Johann Sebastian Bach, *Neue Bach-Ausgabe sämtlicher Werke*, ed. Johann-Sebastian-Bach-Institut, Göttingen, and Bach-Archiv, Leipzig (Kassel and Leipzig, 1954–).

Nekrolog *Carl Philipp Emanuel Bach and Johann Friedrich Agricola* [obituary notice]. In *Dok* III, no. 666; *BR*, pp. 215–24.

Spitta   Philipp Spitta, *Johann Sebastian Bach*, 2 vols. (Leipzig, 1873–80; repr. New York, 1952).

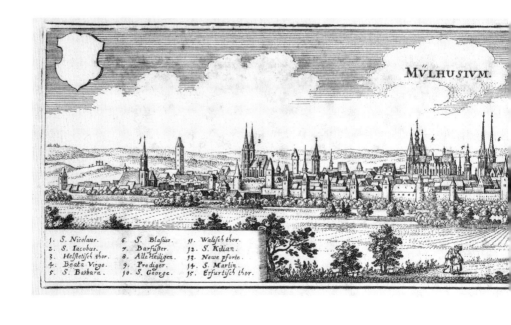

MVLHUSIVM.

1. S. Nicolaus.	6. S. Blasius.	11. Walisch thor.
2. S. Iacobus.	7. Barfusser.	12. S. Kilian.
3. Helstetisch thor.	8. Alle Heiligen.	13. Newe pforte.
4. Beata Virgo.	9. Prediger.	14. S. Martin.
5. S. Barbara.	10. S. George.	15. Erfurtisch thor.

I

THE COMPOSER IN HIS WORLD

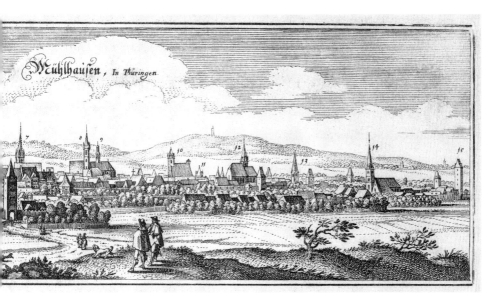

Mühlhausen; engraving by Matthäus Merian, circa 1650.

Mühlhausen, showing the Marienkirche (St. Mary's) (4) and the Blasiuskirche (St. Blasius's) (6); detail from the engraving by Merian.

1

BACH'S PRE-LEIPZIG CANTATAS: REPERTORY AND CONTEXT

Christoph Wolff

Johann Sebastian Bach has left a body of work that is unequaled in its musical diversity, compositional quality, and aesthetic standards. This distinction applies to the creation of instrumental and vocal music alike, although during Bach's lifetime and for a few decades after that, he was known above all as "the world-famous organist" (Obituary, 1750–1754 [*BR*, 215]). In the first biography of Bach, by Johann Nicolaus Forkel (Leipzig, 1802), the vocal works are hardly mentioned at all. Carl Philipp Emanuel Bach, at least, drew proper attention to them in 1786, when he performed the Credo part of the Mass in B minor, which the Hamburg audience considered "one of the most superb musical pieces ever heard" (*Dok* III, No. 911). Nevertheless, Bach's vocal compositions were overshadowed for a long time by his works for clavier and organ, for which a complete edition was planned as early as 1800. Bach as the master of vocal music was first revealed to a wider public in 1829, when Mendelssohn gave his memorable performance of the St. Matthew Passion at the Singakademie in Berlin, a performance that generated a groundswell of far-reaching proportions.

In the nineteenth century the reception of Bach's vocal music was concentrated on the oratorios, except in the city of Leipzig, where the St. Thomas choir had, already under Bach's immediate successors, kept up a steady tradition. The actual extent of Bach's vocal oeuvre, and especially the large number of church cantatas, became generally known only after the complete publication of the cantatas by the Bach-Gesellschaft (*BG*), beginning in 1850. Meanwhile, the crucial importance of both sacred and secular cantatas in Bach's creative output is displayed with impressive documentary evidence in both the old (*BG*) and new complete editions (*NBA*). Within Bach's works the cantata repertory represents by far the most extensive and diverse body, and its unique significance for musical practice has finally been understood only very gradually—a process that is not yet finished.

The *Vierstimmige Choral-Gesänge*, published in 1784–87 in four volumes by Carl Philipp Emanuel Bach and Johann Philipp Kirnberger and reprinted frequently, could have provided an early although greatly abridged insight into Bach's cantata work. It is all the more astonishing, then, that the Berlin critic Johann Friedrich Reichardt felt the need to hail the composer of these chorales as "the greatest harmonist of all times and peoples," in a review that was published in 1781 (*Dok* III, No. 853). But such an assessment—expressed at a time when Haydn and Mozart were still alive—must have totally ignored the actual cantata context, for although the chorales admittedly form a very characteristic element of Bach's skill at writing cantatas, at the same time they are but one of its many components and aspects. The complete dimension of this skill is revealed neither in a single work nor in the totality of cantata choruses, arias, recitatives, and chorales, but ultimately only when one takes into account the musical and historical context of the cantatas as a whole. That is why the chapters of this book are devoted to the traditions of the cantata genre, assumptions and conditions in regard to the compositional technique, poetics and function of cantata texts, and also biographical, local historical, and other perspectives. The essential starting point, however, lies in the questions about the transmission and repertory of Bach's church cantatas.

According to the obituary, Bach left "five full years of church pieces, for all the Sundays and holidays," that is, a series of cantatas for five complete ecclesiastical years—in all, more than three hundred works. Although several contemporaries like Georg Philipp Telemann, Gottfried Heinrich Stölzel, and Christoph Graupner wrote a larger number of similar works, Bach's cantatas stood out especially for their plethora of compositional extravagance and performance demands, which went far beyond well-established conventions and gave them a far-reaching and unique profile. In this respect the corpus of Bach's cantatas, while not the largest in number, is in terms of overall quality the most important creation ever in the history of church music.

What seemed a rather vague idea in 1708, when Bach declared his musical aims to the town fathers in Mühlhausen—his "ultimate goal, namely, a well-regulated church music to the glory of God" (*BR*, 60)—was realized by him in the course of his later activity spanning more than four decades. Thus, in 1750, his musical legacy consisted in large part of works that served "well-regulated church music": a vast repertory of sacred pieces, including, in particular, cantatas for Sundays and holidays during the church year, but also oratorios, passions, masses, and other works that served liturgical purposes. Bach's twenty-seven years as the Thomaskantor (cantor at St. Thomas's church) in Leipzig (from 1723 to 1750), then, left their mark in this respect. Since, by the end of the 1720s, he had prepared five *Jahrgänge* (annual cycles) of church cantatas, the requirements for the 1730s and 1740s could then be met largely by a repertory that consisted of repeat performances.

It is a great pity that this once complete cantata oeuvre has been handed down to posterity in a considerably decimated form. The division of Bach's estate among his heirs resulted in a splitting up of the repertory after 1750, with his widow, Anna Magdalena, and his four musician sons obtaining the principal portions. In any case, Wilhelm Friedemann had "the larger share" (according to Forkel). Nearly two-fifths of the cantatas were lost because the estate was split up, the eldest son was in fact the least careful with his share of the inheritance, and other unfortunate circumstances came into play. Despite this fragmentary transmission and the irreparable losses, there is still a repertory of nearly two hundred church cantatas—more than one hundred hours of music—that offers an abundant wealth of works for voices and instruments, from every period in Bach's life. The extraordinary musical diversity and distinctive character of his cantata output are found not only in the oeuvre as a whole but also, especially, in the individual annual cycles and the smaller and larger groups of works that owe their unmistakably characteristic features to various phases of Bach's creative life.

The church pieces that were written in the pre-Leipzig days, including the entire body of Weimar works, are often described broadly in the literature as the "early" cantatas. This is misleading and ultimately incorrect, for when Bach finally left his post as Cöthen Kapellmeister in 1723 for that as the cantor in Leipzig at the Thomaskirche (St. Thomas's), he was already in his thirty-eight year. True, Bach wrote the bulk of his cantatas during his years in Leipzig, and the consolidation of the essentials of style and composing technique that Bach put into his vocal work also dates from the period after 1723, yet the stage of "early" mastery had ended a long time before that.

Even at his appointment as concertmaster at the Weimar court, which gave him the opportunity in 1714 to produce cantatas regularly, Bach was already in his thirtieth year. By that time there was no doubt about his reputation, and even outside his narrow sphere of activity he was considered an experienced composer. This is proved by the highly significant fact that toward the end of 1713 he was nominated to succeed Friedrich Wilhelm Zachow, Handel's teacher, as director of music at the Marktkirche in Halle. Soon after, in the first reference to Bach in print, Johann Mattheson (*Das Beschützte Orchestre*, Hamburg, 1717) wrote: "I have seen things by the famous organist of Weimar, Mr. Joh. Sebastian Bach, both for the church [vocal music] and for the fist [clavier music], that are certainly such as must make one esteem the man highly" (*BR*, 228).

The expression "early" cantatas and the entire notion of "early work" imply that compositions so labeled lack maturity and mastery. Since we are faced with the loss of compositions and uncertainties of chronology, the definition of early work is especially difficult in Bach's case, and certainly not just in the area of vocal music. The mere fact that one of the most important of Bach's masterpieces for organ, the Passacaglia in C minor, BWV 581, had already been written before 1710 prevents us from including the output of the Weimar period, starting in 1708, in the category of the early works. When Bach brought in his cantata "Gott ist mein König," BWV 71 (written for the Mühlhausen council election), to be printed, he must have been very aware that this piece of civic music left the examples of the older generation, including the master composer Buxtehude, far behind. Although the printing of BWV 71 and its lost twin from the year 1709 (BWV deest/BC B 2) remained a singular event in his cantata output, it underlines Bach's ambition to publish "masterpieces" and his own recognition that he could. Neither Handel, who was the same age as Bach, nor the older Telemann, had as yet put any vocal work into print.

The oldest layer of extant vocal compositions by Bach dates from his short time at Mühlhausen (1707–08) but may in fact hark back to his years at Arnstadt. It demonstrates impressively that the young Bach understood how to operate on the level of the greatest composers of the late seventeenth century, among them, in particular, Buxtehude, Pachelbel, and older members of the Bach family (including, above all, his uncles Johann Christoph and Johann Michael). Moreover, he knew how to introduce new musical elements into composing sacred pieces, which at the time were mostly called "motetto" or "concerto." Eventually, in his continuing confrontation with traditional and modern trends, he lay the foundation for a lifelong and

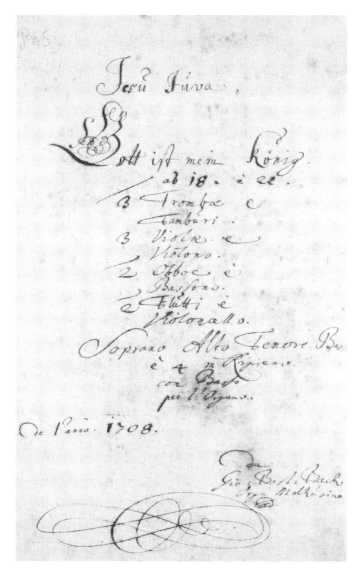

Title page of the cantata "Gott ist mein König,"
BWV 71 (Bach's autograph).

extraordinarily productive occupation with the cantata genre. As early as 1711–12 he was accepted as a composer from whom one could learn something. At that time a certain Philipp David Kräuter set out from Augsburg to Weimar for lessons "from the famous musician Bach" (*Dok* III, 649ff.), and in fact for the express purpose of being instructed in the art of composing cantatas.

Later, at Leipzig, Bach gave repeat performances of many of the cantatas that he had written during his days in Weimar, and he even integrated them into the annual cycles of cantatas there. It is true that he left out the older pieces from the pre-Weimar period, with the exception of the Easter cantata "Christ lag in Todesbanden," BWV 4, and one can understand why. On the one hand, there were not enough appropriate occasions in Leipzig for which the works had been composed; apart from BWV 4, they were not the so-called *Jahrgangsstücke* (annual cycle pieces) that fit into the rhythm of Sundays and holidays of the ecclesiastical year. On the other hand, the compositions, still rooted in many respects in the style of the seventeenth century, belonged—as Bach recorded in his "Entwurf einer wohlbestallten Kirchen-Musik" (Draft for a well-appointed church music) in 1730 (*BR*, 123)—to that "former style of music" that "no longer seems to please our ears." This was meant not as a value judgment of the "former" style of music, but as an indication that it was dated—a reference not only to the works of Bach's predecessors at St. Thomas's but also to his own early output.

As selective as Bach was in reintroducing his older works in Leipzig, he was even more cautious about borrowing from available compositions for works written at Leipzig. However, borrowing music dating from his Cöthen period obviously created fewer problems in view of the greater similarity of style. In this way incidental works written at Cöthen could be transformed easily into church cantatas by giving them new texts, one such example being the birthday serenade "Durchlauchtster Leopold," BWV 173a, of 1722, which was heard in Leipzig in 1724 as the Whitsunday cantata "Erhöhtes Fleisch und Blut," BWV 173. The disparity between the vocal styles in Leipzig and Weimar was definitely too great for such borrowings or conversions, to say nothing of the compositions from the pre-Weimar days. A rare and therefore all the more spectacular exception is the adoption of the choral passacaglia "Weinen, Klagen, Sorgen, Zagen" from the 1714 cantata BWV 12 for the B-minor Mass, nearly forty years later. Transformed into the "Crucifixus," this movement, stylistically the oldest piece of the whole Mass, appears immediately next to the most modern one, the "Et incarnatus est," composed late in Bach's life.

The pre-Leipzig cantata writing can be divided into three main phases: compositions from the pre-Weimar years, the Weimar cantatas, and the works written at Cöthen. Nevertheless, the boundaries remain fluid in their details, particularly because of new versions, alterations, and repeat performances of various works.

PRE-WEIMAR CANTATAS, CA. 1706–1708

BWV	Title	Occasion

Texts taken from the Bible, the hymnbook, and (occasionally) free poetry

150	Nach dir, Herr, verlanget mich	not recorded[1]
196	Der Herr denket an uns	wedding
106	Gottes Zeit ist die allerbeste Zeit	funeral service
4	Christ lag in Todesbanden	Easter Sunday (organist audition?)
131	Aus der Tiefen rufe ich	not recorded[2]
71	Gott ist mein König	council elections
—	[cantata BC B 2]	council elections
223	[Meine Seele soll Gott loben]	not handed down

[] Not preserved, or preserved only in part

We are in the dark about the origins of Bach's composition of cantatas but it seems obvious that we should look for them in the days when he was the organist at Arnstadt. Supplying regular pieces for Sundays and holidays ("cantor's music") was not part of the duties of an organist; normally it was his job to write works for funerals, weddings, and other special occasions ("organist's music"). It is evident that the people of Arnstadt indeed expected Bach, as organist, to perform vocal music, judging from the reproof by the council, in the spring of 1706, that there had been "absolutely no concerted music" (*Dok.* II, No. 16). When the same authorities criticized Bach that November because he had "recently invited a young female stranger into the choir loft and let her make music there" (*Dok* II, No. 17), we may take it as evidence of the woman's participation in a cantata performance as a soloist (see also chapter 4). The style of cantatas BWV 150 and the earlier 196 makes an Arnstadt origin entirely plausible. However, in the absence of original sources, it cannot be verified. And because of the lack of documentation, the identities of the persons for whom these pre-Weimar wedding masses and funeral services were held remains in question.

*First page of the cantata "Aus der Tiefen rufe ich, Herr, zu dir," BWV 131
(Bach's autograph).*

BWV 4 was probably performed on the occasion of Bach's audition for the post of organist in Mühlhausen on Easter Sunday, 1707. In that case it would still have been written in Arnstadt. Later it was the only pre-Weimar work to be included in the Leipzig repertory (in 1724, with a new closing chorale and extended orchestration). As the festival cantata BWV 4 suggests, Bach apparently did not limit himself to writing vocal music at Mühlhausen merely for special occasions. To this end he also supplied himself "not without cost, a good store of the choicest church compositions" (*Dok.* I, No. 1), but he vainly hoped to be able to set up a "well-regulated church music" in the form of regular performances on Sundays and holidays. Obviously, his activity as a composer at Mühlhausen remained restricted, as before, to writing for special occasions. In any case, BWV 71 (1708) belongs in that category; the lost second Mühlhausen cantata for the council election of 1709 was supplied after Bach had left Weimar—indicating the possibility that this kind of composition could also have been intended for use elsewhere.

The liturgical designation of the undated cantata BWV 131 remains unclear. But all pre-Weimar Psalm cantatas (BWV 131, 150, and 223, as well as the oldest version of BWV 21) could be adapted to the most varied occasions, without any regard to the date of the ecclesiastical year. In fact, the written designation of BWV 21 mentions expressly that it is intended "in ogni tempo" (for any time). This multi-functionality of the Psalm cantatas is somehow in keeping with the fact that music for funerals and weddings could also be repeated on similar occasions and suggests that the composer probably made a conscious effort to allow for some latitude and freedom in his arrangements. Ultimately, such repertory pieces could well be written "in preparation," that is, without a specific occasion in mind.

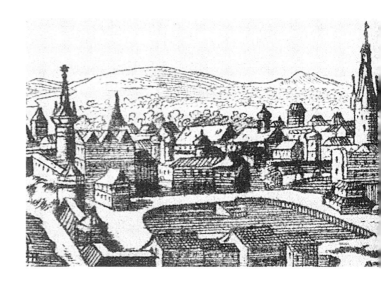

WEIMAR CANTATAS, 1708–1717

BWV	Title	Occasion

Texts from S. Franck, *Evangelisches Andachts-Opffer* (Weimar, 1715)

BWV	Title	Occasion
132	Bereitet die Wege, bereitet die Bahn	4th Sunday of Advent
152	Tritt auf die Glaubensbahn	Sunday after Christmas
155	Mein Gott, wie lang, ach lange	2nd Sunday after Epiphany
80a	Alles, was von Gott geboren	3rd Sunday in Lent
31	Der Himmel lacht	Easter Sunday
165	O heilges Geist- und Wasserbad	Trinity Sunday
185	Barmherziges Herze der ewigen Liebe	4th Sunday after Trinity
161	Komm, du süsse Todesstunde	16th Sunday after Trinity
162	Ach! ich sehe, jetzt	20th Sunday after Trinity
163	Nur jedem das Seine	23rd Sunday after Trinity

Presumably unpublished texts by S. Franck

BWV	Title	Occasion
182	Himmelskönig sei willkommen	Palm Sunday[3]
12	Weinen, Klagen, Sorgen, Zagen	3rd Sunday after Easter (Jubilate)
172	Erschallet, ihr Lieder	Whitsunday
21	Ich hatte viel Bekümmernis "in ogni tempo";	3rd Sunday after Trinity[4]
—	[Was ist, das wir Leben nennen, BC B 19]	Funeral service

Weimar; detail from an eighteenth-century engraving.

BWV	Title	Occasion

Texts from S. Franck, *Evangelische Sonn- und Festtages-Andachten* (Weimar, 1717)

BWV	Title	Occasion
70a	Wachet!, betet! betet! wachet!	2nd Sunday of Advent
186a	Ärgre dich, o Seele, nicht	3rd Sunday of Advent
147a	Herz und Mund und Tat und Leben	4th Sunday of Advent

Texts from E. Neumeister, *Geistliches Singen und Spielen* (Gotha, 1711)

BWV	Title	Occasion
61	Nun komm, der Heiden Heiland	1st Sunday of Advent
18	Gleichwie der Regen und Schnee	Sexagesima

Texts from G.C. Lehms, *Gottgefälliges Kirchen-Opffer* (Darmstadt, 1711)

BWV	Title	Occasion
54	Widerstehe doch der Sünde	3rd Sunday in Lent
199	Mein Herze schwimmt im Blut	11th Sunday after Trinity

Unpublished texts by J.M. Heineccius (?)

BWV	Title	Occasion
—	[cantata, Halle, 1713][5]	organist audition
63	Christen, ätzet diesen Tag	Christmas Day

[] Music not preserved

After serving since the middle of 1708 as organist and chamber musician at the Weimar court, Bach was appointed concertmaster by the duke at the beginning of March 1714 with the specific assignment to "perform new works monthly." Even before 1714, Bach surely conducted and composed sacred music at the Weimar court while working alongside the old Kapellmeister Johann Samuel Drese (according to the latest research, BWV 18 and 199 date from 1713). Bach's appointment as concertmaster gave him his first opportunity to realize his expressed "ultimate goal toward a well-regulated church music." He had achieved his objective as a result of having refused to succeed Friedrich Wilhelm Zachow, the late organist of the Marienkirche (St. Mary's) at Halle. This post had been offered to Bach in December 1713, after a successful audition that included a performance of a cantata now unfortunately lost.[6] The first piece of the new monthly Weimar cantata cycle, heard on March 25, 1714, was the cantata "Himmelskönig sei willkommen," BWV 182.

In contrast to his works for special occasions dating from the pre-Weimar period, Bach now followed the modern custom of setting the music for his Sunday and holiday cantatas mostly to texts from printed collections, understandably giving preference to the Weimar court poet Salomon Franck. The exact chronological order of the compositions in Weimar is not altogether clear. Only the cantatas BWV 21 (1714), 61 (1714), 185 (1715), and 132 (1715) are dated in the autograph scores. Yet the texts by Franck (1715 collection), Lehms, and Neumeister are essentially spread over the years 1714–16. In this respect a certain turning point is provided by BWV 31 (Easter 1715), the last work based on a five-voice (French) scoring for strings (see also chapter 10). After Easter 1715, BWV 132, 155, 161, 162, 165, and 185 were written in this way. The compositions to texts by Franck (1717 collection)—soon discontinued—started only during Advent 1717.

It is unlikely that Bach set to music much more from Franck's 1717 collection, apart from the three extant Advent cantatas. The conditions at Weimar, which at that time had gone from bad to worse for Bach, would hardly have encouraged him. On the other hand, it is likely that some cantatas from the period 1714–16 were lost—primarily works based on Franck's 1715 volume. On a four-week production cycle, they could hardly have numbered more than a half dozen cantatas. In the end, how many vocal pieces were written at Weimar remains an open question. That Bach had already composed cantatas before his appointment as concertmaster has in any case been documented by his audition piece for Halle in December 1713 and is altogether plausible, even if there is no direct supporting evidence.

Included among works performed outside Weimar (for instance, the secular cantata BWV 208, composed for 1713/16 in Weissenfels) may well have been the Christmas cantata BWV 63, with its particularly extravagant orchestration (including four trumpets). The same may apply to later repeat performances of BWV 21 in Hamburg and BWV 199 in Cöthen. There is evidence that most of the cantatas were performed again in Leipzig, BWV 12, 61, 63, 155, 162, 163, 165, and 185 with only slight alterations (including some transposition). More drastic changes in orchestration were made in BWV 18, 21, 31, 161, 172, 182, 185, and 199. Bach made considerable changes to the structure and form of BWV 80a, 70a, 186a, and 147a.

CÖTHEN CANTATAS

BWV	Title	Occasion
(Leipzig) author of text unknown		
22	Jesus nahm zu sich die Zwölfe	Quinquagesima
23	Du wahrer Gott und Davids Sohn	Quinquagesima

At the Calvinist court of Cöthen the Kapellmeister was not required to write any music for religious services. Nor was Bach officially responsible for church music at the Lutheran Agnuskirche. Compositions of vocal music were therefore restricted, on the whole, to regular performances of congratulatory cantatas, on the one hand for Prince Leopold's birthday and on the other for New Year's Day. As far as we can judge from the surviving bits and pieces of the relevant compositions (BWV 66a, 134a, 173a, 184a, and 194a, as well as BWV Anh. I/5, 6, 7, and 8), Bach already tried early on in Leipzig to integrate many, if not most, of his secular occasional works into his

Cöthen; engraving by M. Merian, circa 1650.

The Jacobikirche (St. Jacobi's) in Hamburg; detail from an engraving by Peter Schenk, Amsterdam, circa 1700.

repertory of church cantatas. To this end the librettos were reworded, so that the available music could be given a new sacred text and a more lasting purpose. The cantatas BWV 66, 134, 184, and 194 from Bach's first year of service in Leipzig support this decisively.

Repeat performances in Cöthen of the Weimar cantatas "Ich hatte viel Bekümmernis," BWV 21, and "Mein Herze schwimmt im Blut," BWV 199, are supported by source references, which does not necessarily mean that these works were also heard in Cöthen itself. In the case of BWV 21, it is much more likely that the reason for its performance was connected to Bach's audition for the post of organist at the Jakobikirche (St. Jacobi's Church) in Hamburg in November 1720. Little more than two years later Bach was invited to audition for the post of cantor in Leipzig (February 1723) with the special privilege of being allowed to play two cantatas, one each before and after the sermon. To that end Bach brought one completed work (BWV 23) with him from Cöthen; the other one (BWV 22) he apparently wrote only in Leipzig. The solo style of BWV 23 clearly follows the model of the Cöthen congratulatory cantatas. However, shortly before auditioning for the cantorate, Bach decided in Leipzig to lengthen this cantata by adding a new final movement, "Christe, du Lamm Gottes." He did not have to write this as a new piece; rather, he took it from a Passion composition dating from his time in Weimar (*BC* D 1) that he probably kept in his baggage—perhaps in order to be able to offer an example of a large concerted work, should the occasion arise. Leipzig, at least, was given a sample in 1723 in a performance on Quinquagesima Sunday. No one then would have known how promising it was. At any rate, newspapers in Leipzig and elsewhere (*Dok.* II, No. 124) reported on the audition for the cantorate by the "Capellmeister of his Serene Highness at Cöthen, Mr. Bach," saying that his "music was highly praised by all who judged it."

Notes

1. The character of the text suggests a service of repentance.
2. Ibid.
3. Coinciding in 1714 with the Annunciation of the Virgin Mary (March 25).
4. It cannot be completely ruled out that the cantata BWV 21 was played at the audition for the post of organist in Halle. In all probability Bach also played BWV 21 in 1720, when he auditioned for the position of organist at the Jakobikirche (St. Jacobi's) in Hamburg.
5. See note 4.
6. Ibid.

The Blasiuskirche (St. Blasius's) in Mühlhausen; engraving by J. Poppel.

2

GENRES AND STYLES OF SACRED MUSIC AROUND AND AFTER 1700

Peter Wollny

Johann Sebastian Bach's earlier cantatas were not composed independently of the traditions of the genre or the inspiration of his own musical environment, even if their uniqueness and incomparable quality sometimes suggest such a premise. Bach's familiarity with the sacred vocal music of his day is borne out from the start by his "supply of the choicest church compositions" that he had built up in Mühlhausen, which—in his own words—he had acquired "from far and wide" and "not without cost" (*BR*, 60). Undoubtedly, this collection of works served to gather "well-regulated church music" at Bach's place of employment at the time, the Blasiuskirche (St. Blasius's) in Mühlhausen. It also provided the young composer with special material for study. Unfortunately, not a single composition from this collection has survived, nor is anything else known about it, so that we do not have any actual reports of his dealings with contemporary composers of vocal music.

The first tangible evidence of Bach's enthusiasm for collecting comes from his Weimar period. Dating from that time are personal transcripts or copies owned by him of Reinhard Keiser's St. Mark Passion, the Latin solo cantata "Languet anima mea" by Francesco Conti, the full-scale cantata "Auf Gott hoffete ich" by the Dresden court Kapellmeister Johann Christoph Schmidt, and arrangements of Mass Ordinaries by Johann Christoph Pez, Marco Gioseffo Peranda, Johann Baal, and other composers not yet identified. Despite the careful handing down of a truly wide spectrum of collected masters, we can hardly get an idea about the styles Bach may have preferred, and we should certainly not form any hasty hypothesis about the character of the missing repertory in Mühlhausen. Nonetheless, the Weimar material allows for some careful conclusions. Keiser's Passion music points to Hamburg, a city with which Bach remained in touch following his school days in Lüneburg. The names Peranda and Schmidt suggest the court of the Elector of Saxony and Polish King August the Strong in Dresden, whose display of splendor, particularly where music was concerned, must also have have attracted attention in Weimar. Works by Viennese composers such as Conti also reached central Germany by way of Dresden's connections with the Roman Catholic South. Regarding the favorite composers of the Weimar period, Bach knew and perhaps owned some compositions in Mühlhausen by Peranda, who at the time had the reputation of being a "conqueror of the affections" and whose vocal works were to be found in practically every central-German catalogue or collection.

Considering the predominantly North German orientation of Bach's youth (his schooling in Lüneburg, his journeys to Hamburg and Lübeck, and his contacts with Georg Böhm, Jan Adam Reinken, and Dietrich Buxtehude), we might speculate that works by North German composers had a strong impact on Bach's musical thinking from early on. In addition, Bach must certainly have noted the numerous prints of works by Italian composers that were widely disseminated in northern Germany through trade relations between the Hanseatic city of Hamburg and Venice. Moreover, it is likely that Bach was well acquainted with works from his Thuringian family circle, as, for instance, compositions by his father-in-law Johann Michael Bach or Johann Michael's brother Johann Christoph. Furthermore, one may safely assume that Bach found stimulating examples in the widespread and celebrated compositions by Agostino Steffani and Johann Rosenmüller, works that served, at the same time, as models for the young Georg Philipp Telemann for his "future church and instrumental music."[1]

The works of the composers named above represent the most important genres and styles of religious vocal music around and after 1700. At the center of Protestant vocal music stood the cantata in its various forms and types. In addition, there was a fondness for Latin settings of the Kyrie and Gloria, as well as *a capella* motets set to biblical texts and usually combined with chorale tunes; and on major feast days large-scale oratorios were performed.

The Marienkirche (St. Mary's) in Lübeck, where Dietrich Buxtehude performed his "Abendmusiken"; engraving, 1749.

The best way for Bach to learn about setting portions of the Mass to music was to study Italian and South German composers. Around 1700 there were two different traditions that continued well into the eighteenth century. The older one was to compose in strict *stile antico*, following the rules and ideals of classical vocal polyphony without obbligato instruments. The other tradition, which began in the middle of the seventeenth century and became equally popular, consisted of composing mixed vocal and instrumental settings in modern *concertato* style, the Mass text being divided into a large number of shorter sections.

Bach's ancestors were recognized masters in composing motets. The brothers Johann Michael and Johann Christoph Bach, especially, left a large number of ambitious and representative works in this genre. A typical Thuringian motet of those days was written mostly for double choir and was moderately polyphonic. In the final section a chorale in the top voice was normally sung as a cantus firmus in long note values simultaneously with the text in the lower voices.

As for oratorio works, Bach would have known, above all, the large-scale "Abendmusiken" by Dietrich Buxtehude, works that often came close to sacred opera. Oratorios and oratorio-like Passion settings were also widely known in Hamburg and other North German cities beginning in the latter part of the seventeenth century.

By far the greatest stimulus undoubtedly came from the cantata, which proved to be a most variable field for experimentation and whose numbers, around 1700, surpassed all other genres. It is therefore hardly surprising that the sacred cantata of the time is imprinted with an almost boundless stylistic pluralism that blurs the boundaries of the genre and makes it nearly impossible to come up with an exact definition. The extremely varied structure and form of the cantata came about because right from the outset very few limitations had been placed on this genre. As it is, polyphonic church music with obbligato instruments and singing voices, which first appeared in Italy in psalm settings of the Venetian school and of Claudio Monteverdi, and a little later in Germany in the chorale concertos of Michael Praetorius, was primarily marked by the abstract and genre-crossing concertato principles and much less by well-defined formal rules regarding content and scoring. Even in its simplest form—as a setting of a biblical verse—the early cantata, with its varied types of composition and textures, could be classified only with difficulty within the styles of the seventeenth century that were intended primarily for didactic purposes. In the end, the mixed forms used in the latter part of the century by cantors and organists were no longer comprehended by contemporary musical theory.

Such problems of terminology are also found in Bach's early cantatas. Titles include the terms "motetto" (BWV 71), "actus" (BWV 106), and "concerto" (BWV 61), whereas the term "cantata" seldom appears (BWV 54, BWV 199). Often there is no indication at all of the genre, and the title must make do with the opening words and the instrumentation. The habit of Bach's contemporaries of using the deliberately vague colloquial indication "Kirchenstück" (church piece) or simply "Music" (music) is also typical of their indifference toward any precise terminology. The present-day concept "cantata" was then generally reserved for Italian secular solo cantatas.

The difficulties that theorists experienced with the terminology were caused, first and foremost, by the stylistic diversity of the individual works as well as their general variations of structure. For that reason Johann Mattheson denies that the "so-called church pieces" have a genre of their own; instead, he calls them "a creation patched together from many different styles" and substantiates his opinion as follows:

> The characteristics of the cantata [i.e., the succession of recitatives and arias] that are found in it belong to the madrigal style, polyphonic choruses and fugues to the motet style, accompaniment and ritornellos to the instrumental style, and finally, the chorales to the melismatic style. Faced with such procedures, we have hardly anything systematic to go by.[2]

Adopting elements from outside the genre took place at both the textual and musical levels. Whereas a sacred concerto in the early seventeenth century still had a homogeneous textual basis (with a preference either for biblical verses, such as psalms, or for chorales), soon after 1650 mixtures of text were increasingly favored. At first these mixtures were limited to a combination of chorale and biblical verses, but soon free poetry began to appear, mostly in strophic form. Toward the end of the seventeenth century, internal verses were frequently replaced with rhymed paraphrases. The didactic and graphic claims of the cantata led to frequent use of texts in dialogue form. The ususal types of text would be divided among various *personae* who came together only in a "conclusio" at the end of the composition. Around 1700 the possibilities for mixing texts were almost unlimited.

The musical side of the early cantata is even less defined than the textual one, since more than any other genre of the seventeenth century it could incorporate foreign elements—whether sacred or secular, vocal or instrumental, contrapuntally strict or free. What started out as a unified sacred concerto of one movement soon turned into a sequence of subdivided, mostly brief sections that tended to be arranged by contrasting principals. The choice of a chorale text often, but not always, required the use of its corresponding melody as a cantus firmus. Free poetic interpolations created an opportunity for strophic arias interspersed with instrumental ritornellos. Central German cantors, particularly when they were producing a series of cantatas or annual cycles, preferred a certain "standard form" consisting of biblical verses and an aria with several stanzas. If passages from a Gospel were inserted as narrative elements, the composer often set these sections as recitatives, heightening their dramatic aspect and bringing them close to the oratorio or even the opera. The adoption of operatic elements, first noticable around 1680, gained importance around and after 1700. Many arias and ritornellos were from then on notable for their cheerfully playful, even dancing tone, which was often juxtaposed with more solemn choral movements.

Overall, the cantata incorporates elements of all sacred and many secular genres. The range of stylistic possibilities stretches from *stile antico* of classical vocal polyphony to the French opera chorus in the style of Lully. Occasionally, longer sections—in extreme cases even whole cantatas—are shaped as chaconnes with an obbligato bass. Another special form, the cantata accompanied by a virtuoso solo violin (and, sometimes, a solo viola da gamba)—as in pieces by Heinrich Ignaz Franz Biber, Dietrich Buxtehude, Nikolaus Bruhns, or Daniel Eberlin—verges on the solo sonata.

Just as the various stylistic possibilities were almost unlimited, so were the possibilities for scoring a cantata. Every conceivable combination can be found, from solo cantatas accompanied only by a basso continuo to full-scale works with vocal and instrumental accompaniment and even, occasionally, several choirs. If there was ever anything like a standard orchestration for cantatas, it would most likely have consisted of a vocal ensemble for four voices (mostly with a reinforcing ripieno) and a five-part group of strings with divided violins and violas. But strings were used in all other possible combination as well. Sackbuts and trombones were the preferred wind instruments; trumpets and drums could be added for festive compositions. Occasionally, recorders or flutes also appeared. With the growing popularity of the French style, beginning around 1690 in the Protestant regions of Germany, the oboe also found its way into sacred vocal music. While it is frequently found in typically French trio scoring, it is sometimes set as a solo part opposite a group of strings, as in Bach's cantata from his Mühlhausen days, "Aus der Tiefen rufe ich," BWV 131.

It is hardly surprising that as early as the seventeenth century certain trends toward standardizing the cantata form began to appear, even if these were rather hopeless from the outset and resulted only in forming new sub-types that hardly influenced the cantata's overall development. In one such subtype, the chorale setting *per omnes versus*, using the complete set of stanzas of a hymn provided a unified textual basis and the treatment of its melody guaranteed a homogeneous musical realization. Such chorale set-tings were frequently modeled on the genre of the chorale partita that was

Renaissance and early Baroque woodwind and brass instruments; after a series of engravings by M. Praetorius.

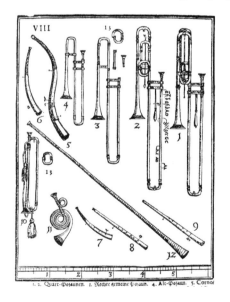 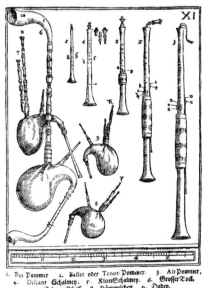

common in organ music. The Leipzig Thomaskantor (St. Thomas's cantor) Johann Schelle wrote a complete cycle of such cantatas for the church year 1689–90 and matched them with the "hymn sermons" delivered that year by the preacher Johann Benedikt Carpzov, who took "a good, beautiful old, Protestant Lutheran hymn"[3] as the subject for his meditation. Johann Pachelbel also wrote representative works of a similar kind; Bach may have modeled his early chorale cantata "Christ lag in Todesbanden," BWV 4, on these compositions.

The most important stimulus for standardizing Protestant church music was provided by the theologian Erdmann Neumeister, who in 1700 published a complete year's cycle of cantata texts under the provocative title *Geistliche Cantaten statt einer Kirchen-Musik* (Sacred Cantatas instead of Church Music). These texts consisted exclusively of free poetry with alternating recitatives and arias, abandoning biblical dicta or chorale verses altogether. Coming after various timid and tentative approaches to secular models, Neumeister's innovation was quite revolutionary, since the form of his cantatas corresponded with the structure of Italian solo cantatas or opera scenes—with the one difference that he worked with religious subjects.

It could hardly be a coincidence that the musical protagonists of this new form were Kapellmeisters at the Saxon and Thuringian courts, such as Johann Philipp Krieger in Weissenfels and Philipp Heinrich Erlebach in Rudolstadt, who were both very much at home with the operatic music of their time. Only at a later stage was the new type of cantata taken up by municipal cantors and organists, more often than not only after Neumeister and other librettists in his wake had found a compromise: although the real novelty of Neumeister's reform—alternating recitative and aria in free poetry—continued, biblical dicta and the chorale made their reappearance in the cantatas, mostly as the introduction and closing movements. To be sure, this compromise did not change the heterogeneity of cantata poetry, yet it enabled the composer of sacred music to keep up with the stylistic and formal innovations that were developed in secular vocal genres. This mixed form proved most durable and remained in use for the larger part of the eighteenth century.

Understandably, the change from old to new was not always straightforward and without conflict. A cantata cycle composed by Johann Kuhnau for the 1709–10 ecclesiastical year gives the impression of being intended as a counterpoise. In his extensive foreword to the published text, the composer writes:

This time I wanted to try out how scriptural verses could be composed that relied on their own beauty, without any external embellishment, not accompanied by any arias or other poetical paraphrases. . . . I must admit that. But when impassioned words are confined by meter and rhythm, the arias provide the music with tremendous *grace*, which does not happen so easily when words are sung in prose. Nevertheless, I have stuck to my resolution, especially since I believe that, by showing nothing of the style of the madrigals, which consist of arias and recitatives, I can easily avoid any suspicion of having anything to do with theatrical music.[4]

However, that by 1711 he was already setting texts by Neumeister shows that Kuhnau's attitude toward what is deemed proper church music was ambivalent.

Detail of the title page of the "Arnstädtisches Gesangbuch,"
1700.

We do not have Bach's own views on these questions nor do we know whether he even followed the debates about writing cantatas. Probably he would have been more interested in the musical prospects opened up by the new form than in theoretical and theological discussions. In particular, he would have been impressed positively by the opportunity to compose extended and separate movements that the new type of cantata poetry made possible. (Around 1710 this was a matter of importance in other musical genres as well, as, for instance, in organ and harpsichord music and in chamber and ensemble pieces.) At the same time, Bach may have valued the flexibility adopted from the old type of cantata, which enabled him to transfer to the cantata some forms and textures from other areas of vocal and instrumental music. The masterly way in which Bach used the new compositional freedom is borne out, among other things, by the variety of chorale settings in the Weimar cantatas. For example, whereas in the cantata "Nun komm, der Heiden Heiland," BWV 61, the first chorus is modeled on the French overture, the opening movement of the cantata "Christen ätzet diesen Tag," BWV 63, is based on the principle of polychoral writing. The ninth movement of the cantata "Ich hatte viel Bekümmernis," BWV 21, is constructed as an elaborate choral fugue with a chorale cantus firmus. In addition, the second movement of the cantata "Weinen, Klagen, Sorgen, Zagen," BWV 12, presents in its outer sections a passacaglia with a basso ostinato.

To what extent Bach was inclined to get involved with the theatrical style in his church music at Mühlhausen and Weimar is still debatable. The opening movement of the cantata "Nun komm, der Heiden Heiland," BWV 61, with its adoption of the French overture form, clearly points to opera. We can even identify Bach's most likely model, since, in the operatic literature of the seventeenth and early eighteenth century the combination of overture and choral movement is found—as far as we know—only in *Henrico Leone*, written by Agostino Steffani in 1689 for the opening of the opera house in Hanover. The work stayed in the repertory of North German opera houses well into the 1720s, and it is perfectly conceivable that Bach got to know it during one of his early visits to Hamburg. In spite of its affinity to opera, the opening chorus of BWV 61 is still strongly stamped by the transformed chorale, since the beginning of the chorale melody already appears in the continuo part of the instrumental introduction.

In general, we notice that compared to his contempararies, Bach was remarkably cautious about adopting secular forms into his sacred music, at least at the time preceding his period in Leipzig. These were almost always adjusted to fit their religious context, or they were justified by some under-lying significance (thus the French opera overture, which originally supplied the musical backdrop for the entrance of the king, serves in Bach's Advent cantata to herald the entry of the divine Lord of Hosts). Altogether, Bach's systematic exploration of given models for form, style, and genre, coupled with the integrating power of his personal style, produced a fusion of dis-parate elements at a higher musical level.

When trying to understand the historical and aesthetic qualifications of the extraordinary artistic skill expressed in Bach's early church cantatas, one should not ignore the sociological aspect either. Bach's teachers and mod-els were all organists in the northern and central regions of Germany, and since his early years he had also wanted to become an organist himself, not a cantor. The organists in most cities in Thuringia and northern Germany clearly had a higher status than cantors in matters of salary and social standing. They were indeed respected nearly as much as Kapellmeisters at court. Among the organists were important virtuosos and great composers who frequently made public appearances with ambitious compositions. Cantors, on the other hand, were first and foremost employed as teachers and choirmasters and rarely came to the fore as artists. Bach's own reser-vations about accepting the appointment as the St. Thomas cantor in Leipzig ("Though, at first, indeed, it did not seem at all proper to me to change my position of Capellmeister to that of Cantor" [BR, 125]) alludes unmistakably to this social hierarchy, although in Saxon Leipzig the cir-cumstances were precisely the opposite, since the cantor, in his capacity as *Director musices*, was the town's central musical personality and there-fore also "directed" the organists.

Organists in northern Germany and Thuringia were usually not compelled to compose and perform concerted music. If, nevertheless, they occasionally played their own work, they did so for self-promotion. Such personal initia-tives could assume an importance beyond their own region. Famous exam-ples are the annual "Abendmusiken" by the organist of the Marienkirche (St. Mary's) in Lübeck, Dietrich Buxtehude, or the performances by the Hamburg Collegium Musicum under the direction of the organist of the Jakobikirche (St. Jacobi's), Matthias Weckmann. Thanks to their relative independence, these organists wrote music that was distinguished by its "individual styling, unschematic presentation, and committed expression of affections."[5] It was often decidedly modern or unconventional in its choice of stylistic means, had altogether high artistic aspirations, and sometimes even tended toward elitism. In contrast, the compositions by the cantors, written in

CASTRUM DOLORIS,

Dero in GOTT Ruhenden

Römiſ. Käyſerl. auch Königl.

Majeſtäten

LEOPOLD

Dem Erſten/

Zum Glorwürdigſten Andencken/

In der Käyſerl. Freyen Reichs-Stadt

Lübecks

Haupt - Kirchen zu St. Marien/

Zur Zeit gewöhnlicher Abend-Muſic/

Aus Aller - Unterthänigſter Pflicht

Muſicaliſch vorgeſtellet

Von

Diterico Buxtehuden/

Organiſten daſelbſt.

LÜBECK/

Gedruckt und zu bekommen bey Sehl. Schmalhertzens Wittwe/

Anno 1705.

TEMPLUM HONORIS,

Dero Regierenden

Römiſ. Käyſerl. auch Königl.

Majeſtät

JOSEPH

Dem Erſten/

Zu Unſterblichen Ehren/

In der Käyſerl. Freyen Reichs-Stadt

Lübecks

Haupt - Kirchen zu St. Marien/

Im Jahr Chriſti 1705.

Zu beliebter Zeit bey der gewöhnlichen Abend-Muſic/

Aus Aller - Unterthänigſter Pflicht

Glückwünſchend gewidmet

Von

Diterico Buxtehuden/

Organiſten daſelbſt.

LÜBECK/

Gedruckt und zu bekommen bey Sehl. Schmalhertzens Wittwe/

Title pages of Dietrich Buxtehude's "Abendmusiken," 1705.

fulfillment of their duty, were often formulaic and simple, and devised for mass production.

Cantatas by North German organists like Weckmann, Bruhns, and Buxtehude, whose example Bach followed in his own early vocal works, show a whole range of characteristic features. They include a choice of strongly expressive yet rarely used texts, mainly from the Bible, a mostly unconventional arrangement of the accompanying instruments, and a suggestive, unmistakable, yet inimitable transposition of the text, usually at a high technical level of compositional technique. Because of their musical quality, such compositions were valued by contemporaries as works of art of the highest order. As late as 1740—eighty years after its creation— Johann Mattheson reported on a cantata by Matthias Weckmann that the latter had made known under the name of his friend Christoph Bernhard. According to Mattheson, the reputation that Bernhard achieved in this way was responsible for his appointment in Hamburg. Weckmann's composition, a setting of "Weine nicht, es hat überwunden der Löwe" that is fortunately extant, in fact meets all criteria mentioned above. In very much the same way Georg Philipp Telemann, then a law student, made his reputation in 1701 as a composer in Leipzig with a setting of Psalm 6. Following the formal and stylistic conventions of the Hamburg opera, the sacred oratorios that Buxtehude performed each year at his "Abendmusiken" gained importance outside the region. The two large-scale oratorios of 1705, *Castrum doloris* and *Templum honoris*, demonstrate each of the vocal forms of his day (according to the libretto, which is all that has been preserved) and require an instrumentation that had never before been seen: a double choir of trumpets, as well as French horns, oboes, and twenty-five violins that are mentioned specifically. Apart from his oratorios, in the domain of his sacred cantatas (for instance, his cantata cycle *Membra Jesu nostri*, dated 1680) Buxtehude has also left a large number of works that in their great individuality stand apart from the traditions of the genre.

Bach's early cantatas fit very well into this context. Direct examples or compositions that compare with works like the "Actus tragicus," BWV 106, or the Psalm setting "Aus der Tiefen," BWV 131, can be found only insofar as Bach adopted, from the exquisite vocal works of these North German organists, their individuality and obvious lack of tradition as decisive criteria. Bach apparently liked to place himself in the elite circle of North German organists; this is shown in the reaction of the venerable Jan Adam Reinken to Bach's playing the organ at the Katharinenkirche (St. Catharine's) in Hamburg in 1720, a reaction undoubtedly handed down to posterity by

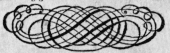

The pages 3 and 4 from the original libretto of Buxtehude's oratorio "Templum honoris."

Bach himself: "I thought that this art was dead, but I see that it still lives in you" (*Dok*. III, No. 66, p. 84). These distinctive features are, of course, insufficient to constitute an all-embracing aesthetic that governed the cantatas of the North German organists. However, one could maintain that the abstract principle of high quality also forms a consistent feature of Bach's later cantatas, as it does indeed of his total output. In this respect he can be said to have preserved the mentality of the North German organists at the end of the seventeenth century.

Notes

1. Autobiography of 1740, quoted from Georg Philipp Telemann, "Singen ist das Fundament der Musik in allen Dingen" in *Eine Dokumentensammlung*, ed. Werner Rackwitz (Leipzig, 1981), 198.
2. J. Mattheson, *Der Vollkommene Capellmeister* (Hamburg, 1739), 215.
3. Quoted from *Denkmäler deutscher Tonkunst* (*DDT*), 58–59, xxxiii.
4. Ibid, xlii.
5. F. Krummacher, *Die Choralbearbeitung in der protestantischen Figuralmusik zwischen Praetorius und Bach* (Kassel, 1978), 163.

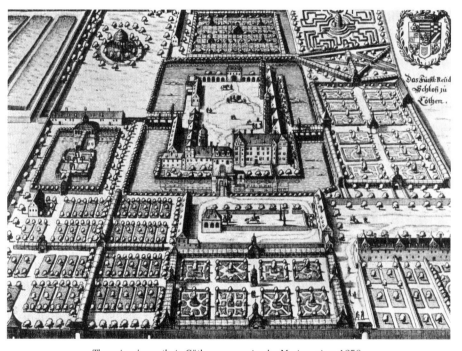

The prince's castle in Cöthen; engraving by Merian, circa 1650.

3

MUSICAL LIFE OF THE TOWNS AND COURTS
IN CENTRAL GERMANY AROUND 1700

Claus Oefner

Where better could Bach have gotten to know Martin Luther than in Eisenach, Bach's birthplace? Luther and Bach had attended the same school, though admittedly some 190 years apart. But Luther had not just been a pupil at the Georgenschule (St. George's School); two decades later he started his work as a reformer that, among other things, set the course for some important stages in the development of Protestant church music. Then again, it may not have been necessary to contemplate this coincidence of locality at all, for Luther's ideas had not merely entered the curriculum at schools in the Central German Lutheran states through the Smaller and Larger Catechisms.[1] His views also dominated collections of music and the repertory of church music, as we can see from the *Eisenacher Kantorenbuch* (Eisenach Cantional), compiled around 1535.[2] They are also found in the preface by the Lutheran pastor Johann Günter Rörer to the Eisenach Hymnal of 1673, which was in use when the young Bach went to school in Eisenach.[3] Finally, Luther's conception of music in praise of God becomes very obvious when one views the beautifully carved organ façades in the towns and villages of Thuringia. Quite often complete choirs of angels can be seen on the organ cases or above them on the church ceilings. This leads us effortlessly to 2 Chronicles 5:13: " . . . and when the song was raised, with trumpets and cymbals and other musical instruments, in praise to the

Some pages of the Eisenach Hymnal, 1673.

Lord / For He is good / for His steadfast love endures for ever,/ the house, the house of the Lord, was filled with a cloud." Bach himself even wrote a note that is characteristic of him next to this very passage in his own copy of the Calov Bible: "N.B. In   pious *musique* God's merciful presence is always there" (*Dok.* III, p. 636).[4]

But painted or carved representations of angel choirs are not the only record of Luther's influence. Equally significant are the music galleries installed for assistants, which wind closely around the organ and organ benches in many Thuringian village churches. In harmony with Luther's idea of a general ministry made up of all believers, the country people stood here during services with violas, French horns, or double basses, whereas during the week they were busy working in stables and barns or in the fields. To this day important parish libraries bear witness to the activities of these adjuvants.[5] The example of Einhausen, near Meiningen, shows that similar practices were still in operation until the middle of the nineteenth century. At this point we are almost forced to quote Georg Michael Pfefferkorn, who wrote in 1685 in his *Merkwürdigen und auserlesenen Geschichte von der berühmten Landgrafschaft Thüringen:*

> Because even the farmers in these places also know their instruments, they make all sorts of string music in the villages with violins, violas, viola da gambas, harpsichords, spinets, and small zithers, and often we also find in the most modest church music some works for the organ with arrangements and variations that are astonishing.

Pfefferkorn's observations can easily be broadened through similar comments by Michael Altenburg or Wolfgang Carl Briegel. Both of them point out the abundance of village church organs, some of which remain, unchanged to this day. They evidence the imagination and skilled craftsmanship of numerous organ builders or entire families of organ builders, such as the Wenders, Trosts, Stertzings, Volklands, Schröters, and others. The importance of organ building in Thuringia has only recently caught the attention of the scholarly world.[6]

School Choirs

Finally, and not least important, Luther's ideas were also reflected in singing at schools. While in rural areas the adjuvants' choirs fulfilled the role of the *Kantorei* (the cantor's church choir), this task was taken over in the cities by school choirs from the Latin schools. In short, they performed concerted music during services that included a sermon. In addition, there were also boys' choirs through which the pupils earned a modest living by singing in the streets and squares. The order of service for Saxe-Weimar in 1664, which was also in force in Eisenach, could still in many ways be defended strongly 130 years after the Reformation. It speaks of the "misuse by the papacy of singing and the organ" but also mentions that "concerted music and organs stir up heart and mind of preacher and congregation alike to praise the Lord our God even more joyously." In general, "such pieces that have an appropriate dignity and are not made for dancing but rather for a religious service should be used as church music."

The Eisenach *Chorus musicus* (sometimes also *Chorus symphoniacus*) was founded in 1629 by Jeremias Weinrich, headmaster of the Latin School. The choir pupils had to complete a considerable curriculum. Choir rehearsals took place after classes, between 12 and 1. The cantor rehearsed with the advanced pupils on Monday and Tuesday, and the beginners were drilled on Wednesday and Thursday. The curriculum statutes of 1705 for Saxe-Eisenach even set aside three hours a week for learning polyphonic music. If a particular holidays lay ahead, an extra rehearsal was then scheduled, so that the choir pupils "would be even better prepared for the festival." The statutes demanded that the pupils would "not only understand clefs, times, and rests," but could also sing at sight "a fugue, motet, and concerto." We can infer from sources at Eisenach that music was made "vocally and with instruments." There is evidence of the use of instruments in 1672–73 and in 1711. Of course, precautions were taken against any misuse of the instruments, and the statutes insisted that "whoever desires to provide commoners with instrumental music, which is the prerogative of the town musicians, will be cashiered for one month."[7] This meant that as punishment, the pupil concerned would be passed over for one month when the proceeds from singing were divided. The choir pupils had to supply polyphonic music in the Georgenkirche (St. George's Church) and the vesper service on the eve of festivals (and, conducted by the prefect, at the Nicolaikirche [St. Nicholas's] and the Annenkirche [St. Anne's]), as well as the "regular services" on Fridays. At funerals "a polyphonic motet suitable for mourning should be sung at the home of the deceased, but, when the body is lowered into the grave . . . in general the well-known funeral songs should be sung in counterpoint, if possible, or otherwise in plainsong." In accordance with the aforementioned liturgy,[8] polyphonic music had its place in services as follows: during Saturday's vesper service the "Magnificat" was "sung or played"; during the main service on Sunday the "Veni sancte spiritus" as well as the "Kyrie" were "played." Furthermore, after the reading of the Scripture and the Gospel, and following the sermon, polyphonic music was

Interior with organ of the Georgenkirche (St. George's) in Eisenach
before the restoration.

scheduled, as it was during the holy Communion. In the afternoon service there was room for a motet after the opening hymn and following the sermon. The greatest celebrations (i.e., with morning, main, and afternoon services) were on the first and second days of Christmas, the Circumcision of our Lord Jesus Christ (January 1), the Feast of the Epiphany (January 6), the Purification of the Blessed Virgin, Conception of the Virgin Mary, Easter Sunday and Easter Monday, Ascension Day, Whitsunday and Whitmonday, Trinity Sunday, St. John's Day, the Visitation of the Virgin Mary, and St. Michael's Day. "Half celebrations" (i.e., only morning services) were held on the "third holy days" at Christmas, Easter, Whitsun, Maundy Thursday, and Good Friday, as well as on August 19, the day "on which in the year 1650 a general remembrance day for peace was most ceremoniously observed and celebrated in these lands."

Today only the repertory gives evidence about the quality of the singing. In any event, much importance was attached to quality, since the entrance auditions held by the cantor were attended by the headmaster as well. The boys also had to be used as soloists, "so that everyone would improve little by little." "Whoever is not willing to do so is free to seek his *dimissa a choro* [dismissal from the choir], to which he will be perfectly entitled."[9] It appears that participating in the school choir was of fundamental importance to developing and structuring the personality of the young singers. Musical impressions received during their own childhood may have contributed to motivating many a choir pupil to want to become an organist, cantor, court musician, organ builder, virtuoso on some instrument, or even Kapellmeister later in life, as we can tell from official Eisenach documents. The *Eisenacher Kantorenbuch* then still in use contained a repertory—"standard" for the time—of works by Johann Walter, Ludwig Senfl, Josquin des Pres, Jacob Obrecht, Thomas Stolzer, Antonius Musa, Conrad Rein, and others. At the same time the repertory was also very "contemporary," since it included works by cantors then in office. There are also works written for Eisenach, by Ambrosius Profe of Breslau, and by Adam Schadaeus, Samuel Scheidt, Melchior Franck, Heinrich Grimm, Andreas Hammerschmidt, Hieronymus Praetorius, Heinrich Schütz, Michael Praetorius, and Daniel Selich. Town pipers or town musicians had been in evidence in Eisenach since 1566. If around 1700 one had asked the inhabitants what they thought of music, very likely they would immediately have mentioned the town musicians, who could be found everywhere. At certain times of the day the musicians had to "supply" music at public places in town. They performed music for wind instruments from the towers of city and town halls, they played the instrumental parts of concerted music at church services, they were asked to celebrate with festive music on the occasion of changes in the council, and of course, they also played for fun. The towns had consciously given them privileges and thereby lifted them deliberately above the social status of street musicians.

Town Pipers

The name *Stadtpfeifer* (town piper) stems from the fact that this group came from the ranks of the tower watchmen and warders. In order to stand out from warders, the most experienced among them called themselves *Kunstpfeifer* (skilled pipers). As we might expect, they had mastered string instruments as well. Sources in Eisenach show that the Ohrdruf town piper Hofmann received a certificate declaring that "in addition to playing the violin decently, he could also entertain with a beautiful cornet, trombone, violone, and an extraordinarily pleasant trumpet."[10] When there were court orchestras, close contact obviously existed between the *Capellisten* (court musicians) and the town musicians. The latter were always on hand if the court musicians needed reinforcement. They even assisted when comedies were staged.[11] But we should not get the wrong idea: their most important function was playing at christenings, weddings, and the like.

Eisenach in the seventeenth century; detail of an engraving by Merian, circa 1650.

Less agreeable for the pocketbook was the fact that the town musicians always had to be on the lookout for competition, especially when they were playing. For a start, they knew that playing music was altogether forbidden by court order at times of official mourning. They struggled therefore all the more bitterly against unpleasant competitors, who always disputed the rights of the town pipers and tried to play without authorization at weddings and other festivals. The city council supported its musicians and, when such instances of unfair competition were reported, handed out stiff penalties to these musicians to whom the town pipers contemptuously referred as "Bierfiedler" (beer fiddlers).

COURT ORCHESTRAS

During the last four centuries the maps of Thuringia and Saxony resembled a bright patchwork quilt. Small and even smaller principalities sprouted up as a result of constant divisions. The division of 1485 separated the Wettin lands into Albertine and Ernestine duchies. Further divisions constantly produced new centers. Each duke made a point of providing castles, parks, and theaters for his court. Naturally, the court included an orchestra, since the entire ensemble was supposed to look like a Baroque stage set. The scenery became magnificent, with silhouettes of castles in Rudolstadt, Sondershausen, Weimar, Meiningen, Dresden, Weissenfels, Merseburg, Gotha, Wittenberg, Torgau, and Meissen. Nor did smaller courts like Arnstadt or even Marksuhl forego either castle or court music. The character of the court orchestra was determined to a very large extent by the Kapellmeister, who decided on the repertory. The Kapellmeister's responsibility was not yet limited to leading the music. Being in charge of the repertory, he usually turned out his own work but also resorted to other modern pieces. Music, in contrast to that of the twentieth century, bore a very "contemporary" stamp forming part of the Baroque *Gesamtkunstwerk* (total artistic scene). At the courts it had to serve as exalted entertainment and also pay special homage to the current ruler. But the court musicians also participated in church services, and, of course, here they had the most involvement with the town musicians, the organist, the *chorus musicus*, and its cantor.

Performing at court; detail of an eighteenth-century engraving.

The certificate of appointment of the Eisenach Kapellmeister Daniel Eberlin, dated July 4, 1685, gives a job description for the leader of an orchestra in its growing stage:

> Above all, he shall be loyal and diligent in the service entrusted to him and always be unfailingly available for all things for which we consider him competent. At any time and at our pleasure he shall perform his musical duties with loyal diligence both at our royal dining table as well as on every Sunday and feast day in church prior to the morning and afternoon sermons, and not neglect anything. Also, he shall devote himself to giving musical instruction to two choir boys per year, whom we or our people have recommended, training them in music and teaching them to play those instruments that he has mastered himself or may have some affinity with, instructing and teaching them diligently as follows: He shall carry out with them and other servants that have been assigned to the music all specific rehearsals in those rooms that have been allotted to him in our royal castle, and see to it that, in order to provide the best service to ourselves, they derive therefrom the greatest benefit and improvement without any waste of time or expense. Moreover, he shall take care that music books and instruments are available or procured, and that at all times they are properly catalogued and kept in good condition.[12]

Many churches in Central Germany served as both court and parish church. This must have led to constant controversies between the court Kapellmeister and town cantor but also to some productive and friendly cooperation when they worked together. The following commemoration of the funeral ceremony of Duke Johann Georg I of Eisenach mentions only the Kapellmeister's tasks:

> Right from the beginning the Capellmeister plays polyphonic music and after that the choir will sing "Herr Jesu Christ, mein Lebens Licht." Thereafter, the Capellmeister plays polyphonic music again, which will be concluded with the chorale "Alle Menschen müssen sterben" and followed by the sermon. After the sermon and the reading of the personal details and achievements, the Capellmeister plays music once more.[13]

Let us look at two more Kapellmeister appointments at the Eisenach court. In 1717 Georg Philipp Telemann was rehired as Kapellmeister having left Eisenach around Easter 1712. The certificate of appointment required him to supply a year-long complement of cantatas every two years, "the text of which will be given to him," and to provide the orchestra "with enough notated material both for music at dinner and for birthdays and other solemn occasions that may occur." At the same time he was ordered "to communicate the music here delivered to no one within two years and at all times to submit newly composed pieces that are not otherwise known."[14]

The certificate of appointment of November 25, 1730, issued to Johann Adam Birckenstock, stipulated that "at all happenings and events he should conduct our vocal and instrumental music, and that in addition he should also look after our customary music at dinner and supply the necessary compositions for festivals and other occasions, but then he should be excused from supplying the usual complement of church music."[15]

The most important personalities headed the Central German court orchestras, including Johann Sebastian Bach at Cöthen, Georg Philipp Telemann and Johann Melchior Molter at Eisenach, Gottfried Heinrich Stölzel and Georg Benda at Gotha, and Johann Ludwig Bach at Meiningen, among others. And the virtuoso soloists playing with the orchestras were not bad, either, for example, the violinist Pantaleon Hebestreit or the viola da gamba player Ernst Christian Hesse at Eisenach.

Members of the court orchestras were frequently recruited from the ranks of town musicians, since, understandably, their most capable members always looked for secure employment at court. Often, other court servants were enlisted for musical duties as well. It was also customary to use one and the same musician for two different jobs. Telemann, for instance, having been commissioned to expand court music at Eisenach, took on "the necessary singers" who could also "be used as violinists."

Between 1690 and 1700 many "corps of hautboists" were founded at the courts. According to the records, these oboists behaved in a rather military fashion, undertook independent musical tasks, and, of course, also worked together with the court orchestra on special occasions. The same goes for the "royal trumpeters and drummers." In the treasurers' accounts they were listed first, so their social standing was higher than that of court orchestra members. They were also entrusted with especially representative assignments, such as escorting princely visitors. Their "release" upon completion of their training appears to have been something of a social event.

Where did all those musical talents of Thuringia and Central Germany come from? Located in the middle of Germany, Thuringia was always a territory

Georg Philipp Telemann; engraving by G. Lichtensteger.

for transit. Travelers going from Warsaw to Paris or from Copenhagen to Rome passed through the area. Outside musical influences probably mixed with the population's innate musical skills. Thanks to Luther, Thuringia became the heartland of the Reformation. Ideal opportunities became available for the development of church music and organ building, and early opera was also cultivated. Nearly every musical skill had the possibility for further development. It is no exaggeration to say that from the sixteenth until well into the eighteenth century the cradles of composers in Central Germany stood closer to each other than anywhere else. Occasionally the limited space could not nourish these skills, so that not a few of them left for other German territories or even went abroad.

Notes

1. Martin Petzoldt, "Ut probus & doctus reddar." See "Zum Anteil der Theologie bei der Schulausbildung Johann Sebastian Bachs in Eisenach, Ohrdruf und Lüneburg," *BJ* 71 (1985): 7–42.
2. Municipal archives at Eisenach.
3. Copy at the Bachhaus in Eisenach.
4. Compare Petzoldt & Petri, *Bach—Ehre sei dir Gott gesungen, Bilder und Texte zu Bachs Leben als Christ und seinem Leben für die Kirche* (Berlin, 1989), 9.
5. For instance at Udestedt near Erfurt or Goldbach near Gotha.
6. Felix Friedrich, *Orgelbau in Thüringen—Bibliographie* (Kleinblittersdorf, 1994).
7. Municipal archives at Eisenach, 10–B.XXVI.C.11, vol. 6, *Gymnasialmatrikel 1713*, 97.
8. Municipal library at Eisenach, *Derer Durchleuchtigen, Hochgebohrenen Fürsten . . . Kirchen-Ordnung* (Weimar, 1664), unsigned.
9. See note 8.
10. Municipal archives at Eisenach, B.XXV.C.1.
11. Municipal archives at Eisenach, municipal accounts 1684/85, 67.
12. Main Thuringian public records at Weimar, Eisenach archives concerning domestic staff 17, 166.
13. Herzogin-Anna-Amalia Library at Weimar, folio 5a.
14. Main Thuringian public records at Weimar, Eisenach archives concerning domestic staff 3431, 12.
15. Main Thuringian public records at Weimar, Eisenach archives concerning domestic staff 582.

Arnstadt; engraving by Pius Rösel van Rosenhoff, circa 1720.

4

STAGES OF BACH'S LIFE AND ACTIVITIES

Andreas Glöckner

Organist of the New Church at Arnstadt, 1703–1707

At the beginning of the eighteenth century, Arnstadt had approximately 3,800 inhabitants and had developed into an important commercial and industrial town, undoubtedly because of its favorable location for travelers at the northern edge of the Thuringian Forest. For a long time it had been a central place for the widely dispersed Bach family. Among those who worked here as town musicians or organists were Caspar Bach (born around 1570, died after 1640), Johann Bach (1602–1632), Melchior Bach (1603–1634), Heinrich Bach (1615–1692), Johann Christoph Bach (1645–1693), Johann Sebastian Bach's father Johann Ambrosius Bach (1645–1695), and Johann Michael Bach (1648–1694).

The actual main church of the town was the Oberkirche (also called the Barfüsserkirche). There, Ernst Dietrich Heindorff served as town cantor and Christoph Herthum as town and court organist, alongside superintendent Johann Gottfried Olearius. Services were attended predominantly by members of the royal household (court officials and servants) and privileged citizens of Arnstadt. The church had a spacious organ loft for putting together a considerable number of performing musicians. Concerted music

Arnstadt; detail of an engraving by Merian, circa 1650.

was regularly played on major church festivals. However, the largest and most impressive church building in town was the Liebfrauenkirche, or Frühkirche. In Bach's time, mainly secondary services (morning services) were held there. In contrast to both other town churches, the Neue Kirche (New Church) looks like an unpretentious building with modest artistic furnishings and was of relatively minor importance. The narrow organ loft offered poor facilities for placing a choir and instruments. This house of God (first called Bonifatiuskirche, later the Sophienkirche or Kirche zur Heiligen Dreifältigkeit) burned down in 1581 and was rebuilt only between 1676 and 1683, because the town's citizens—as reported in 1701 by town chronicler Johann Christoph Olearius—could no longer find sufficient room in the main church. Thereafter the citizens of Arnstadt referred to this church as the Neue Kirche or Neukirche.

The reconstructed church did not at first have an organ. On October 17, 1699, a contract was made with the organ builder Johann Friedrich Wender of Mühlhausen to build an organ with twenty-one stops, two manuals, and pedal. Completion of the new organ, which according to the agreement should have been done on St. John the Baptist's Day, June 24, 1701, was delayed. The organ was not finished until the beginning of July 1703; up to then only a few stops could be used during the service to accompany the choir. On January 1, 1702, Andreas Börner was appointed organist of the New Church, after he had already performed musical duties there at a modest salary. Börner led the school choir, which apparently was often called on to reinforce and support the congregation's singing. Accounting entries dating from that time provide evidence that music was bought for the church library, which also contained motets by Senfl, Obrecht, Isaac, Josquin des Pres, Hammerschmidt, and others.

Börner's appointment was merely temporary. Perhaps before the organ was even finished, the council already had its eye on the young Johann Sebastian Bach to become the future organist of the New Church. In any case, we have no evidence that other candidates made it onto any short list. It is not known whether Bach applied for the position of organist, and if so, in what manner. Anton Günther, the ruling Count of Schwarzburg-Anstadt and Bach's principal employer beginning in 1703, had long had a high opinion of the Bach family and its long tradition, was therefore interested in seeing a member of that family fill the post of organist.

Until July 3, 1703, the organ built by Wender was tested out by various organists and found to be "in good order," but the organ was officially accepted and dedicated on July 13, 1703, by the young Bach, who had been brought over from Weimar especially for that purpose. In addition to the usual travel and accommodation expenses, Bach received the considerable amount of 8 florins and 13 groschen. The title of "royal Saxon court organist at Weimar," given to him on the pay order, does not correspond with the facts, since in the court accounts of Weimar for 1703 Bach is referred to only as "Laquey" (lackey). It remains uncertain whether the inspector of hospitals and part-time chief mayor Martin Feldhaus registered him under that title or whether Bach had perhaps introduced himself as such. The council had put Feldhaus, a member of the Wedemann family and thereby related to the Bach family by marriage, in charge of supervising the building of the organ.

The question still remains why Bach was given the chief responsibility for the final inspection of the organ. He was only eighteen years old and had no experience to speak of as an organist, nor had he acquired any special reputation as an authority on organ building. Perhaps influential relatives, in particular the aforementioned Feldhaus, proposed Bach as organ inspector and put up his name for the about-to-be created position of organist.

On August 14, 1703, Bach received his first certificate of appointment, and a handshake sealed the deal for him to become organist of the New Church. When he moved to Arnstadt cannot be exactly determined. Until May 30, 1703, he remained, officially, violinist ("Laquey") in the private orchestra of the co-ruler Duke Johann Ernst of Saxe-Weimar and was paid as such. Upon Bach's appointment as organist at the New Church, his predecessor, Andreas Börner, was promoted to organist at the Frühkirche and had to take over from the town organist Christoph Herthum at the Oberkirche when the latter was called away to the court orchestra.

Bach's duties as organist were few. He had to play the organ at the main service on Sunday, during the hour of prayer on Monday and at the early service on Thursday. He did not seem to have any other fixed tasks. Since for various reasons he did not lead the school choir and was not obliged to do so according to his contract, he had ample time available to improve further artistically.

Bach received a fixed annual salary of 84 guilders and 6 groschen for his services as organist. This sum consisted of 25 florins from the church treasury, 25 florins from the breweries' tax fund — so-called beer money—and 30 thaler from the budget of St. George's Hospital (the "rich hospital"). The certificate of appointment stipulated that the latter sum was intended to cover Bach's expenses and accommodations. All the same, it appears that this "special bonus" for the young organist was not quite legal. At any rate, the hospital's inspector was none other than Bach's relative Martin Feldhaus, who in 1709 and 1710 not only had to stand trial for "much incorrectness and embezzlement" but was also suspended from all his functions. Looking at Bach's length of service and taking into account the prevailing standards of those days, this bonus seems to be above average, to say the least. In any event, the salary of his successor, his cousin Johann Ernst Bach (1683–1739), was reduced to 40 guilders and half a measure of corn. In view of the fact that from August 1706 to August 1707 this additional allowance for room and full board was paid directly to Feldhaus, it is conceivable that during his last year of office, and possibly in the preceding years, too, Bach lived at the "Steinhaus" or at the "Golden Crown." Both guest houses were owned by the hospital inspector and ex-mayor.

The court music at Arnstadt, whose flowering had come to a temporary halt as a result of the Thirty Years' War, was revived and reorganized after 1850. Its fortunes rose when, in 1671, Ludwig Günther II appointed Johann Christoph Bach (1645–1693) as court musician. At that time the court orchestra not only recruited from the ranks of musicians at court, but also from the Elector's servants. Reinforcements were also drawn from local and out-of-town musicians, together with their students. When necessary, the ensemble had a maximum of twenty-two members at its disposal. Soon after coming to the throne Anton Günther appointed the experienced Adam Drese (ca. 1620–1701) as the new Kapellmeister. Drese had led the Weimar court orchestra since 1652. Thanks to two stays with Heinrich Schütz in Dresden he had acquired further valuable experience on how to build a decent court music program. When Bach arrived at Arnstadt in 1703, the court orchestra had been led for two years by Paul Gleitsmann. In 1701 the latter had become Drese's successor; his official appointment as the "Capell-Direktor" (court orchestra director) did not come until a few years later. Gleitsmann conducted the court orchestra until his death in 1710.

Unfortunately, we do not know about Bach's relation to the theatrical and musical scene at the court of Arnstadt. There is no indication that he may have taken an active part in court music, for instance as harpsichordist or violinist. Concert and theater performances given by the capable court ensemble, which played a prominent part in the capital's cultural life, may nevertheless have had a lasting effect on the young organist's musical development. The few available sources dating from Bach's time at Arnstadt record only a few arguments he had with the council. The main reason was Bach's refusal to perform with his church's school choir. On the one hand, he thought his contract did not oblige him to do so; on the other, personal conditions and musical requirements for good vocal music in the New Church did not meet Bach's standards. The young organist seemed to lack the necessary patience, pedagogical experience, and diplomatic skill required for making music with the available material, i.e., poorly trained instrumentalists and choir pupils. This may also have been the basis for the quarrel with Johann Heinrich Geyersbach on the night of August 4, 1704. Because of his allegedly having insulted the pupil—Bach is supposed to have called him a "Zippel Fagottist" (greenhorn bassoonist), perhaps in connection with a performance—they came to blows. Geyersbach hit Bach in the face, and Bach defended himself with his sword. One of the students who had accompanied Geyersbach had to intervene and separate them.

Bach complained to the council and the case was investigated. As a result of various hearings Bach was advised to come to terms with the students in the future. Furthermore, he was expected not just to play the organ, but also to participate in vocal music. Bach's reply was that he would be prepared to do so only if a music director were appointed.

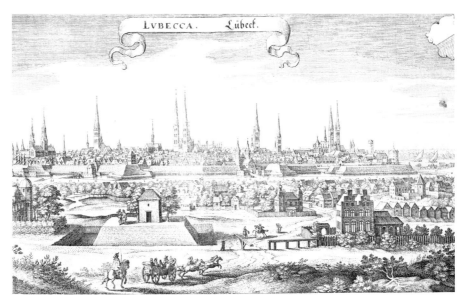

Lübeck; eighteenth-century engraving.

Instead of giving in, Bach asked for four weeks' leave and in mid-October 1705 traveled to Lübeck "on foot"—according to his obituary notice—to meet Dietrich Buxtehude. The reason for this journey and the required traveling time raise some doubt as to whether he had indeed planned to be away for only four weeks. To all appearances it looks as if the young Bach had set off with the intention of exceeding his period of leave. The "Abendmusiken" (evening concerts) that he apparently wanted to attend at the Marienkirche (St. Mary's) in Lübeck did not start until after November 15, by which time he should have been well on his way back to Arnstadt. It is also possible that Bach wanted to find out about his chances of succeeding Buxtehude in Lübeck. Bach did not stay away from his post for four weeks—as he had told the council—but for sixteen. Only on February 7, 1706, did he participate at communion again at Arnstadt. Presumably, he had returned from his study trip only a few days earlier.

The Arnstadt council was annoyed. On February 21 Bach was summoned and rebuked for his long absence. Moreover, his way of playing the chorales was criticized for its many "curious variations," which "confused" the congregation. After the superintendent had reprimanded Bach for his overlong chorale preludes, the organist went to the other extreme and made them much too short. Finally, the old reproach, that the organist still did not perform with the choir students, was raised again. Bach's reaction was sullen rather than conciliatory. He was asked to "explain himself" within eight days. This requested explanation failed, of course, to materialize and the entire matter was left open for more than eight months. Bach was summoned again only on November 11. He then made it known that he would comment on the remonstrations in writing. A further reproach by the council that Bach had performed in church with a "young female stranger" was refuted by him on the grounds that this had happened with the pastor's permission.

The records at Arnstadt do not tell us whether a compromise was ever found for the clashes with the council. In the meantime the city fathers presumably realized that in due course they would not be able to keep the young organist in his post. In Lübeck he had collected new and marvelous artistic experiences, so that he would have understood more than ever that the opportunities in his current position were limited. His reputation as an outstanding organist spread quickly, and, according to his biographer Forkel, he received job offers from various quarters.

Bach's reaction to his employers and to the choir pupils of his church make it clear that his artistic intentions were not entirely compatible with his official duties. Perhaps he still had visions at that time of becoming a virtuoso, relieved of the responsibilities attached to the position and tasks of an organist. In any case, Bach gave priority to his artistic and technical development as an organist and harpsichordist. Consequently, he concentrated first of all on writing for the keyboard. Carl Philipp Emanuel and Johann Friedrich Agricola told about the productivity of this first creative period in the obituary notice of 1754:

> Here [in Arnstadt] he really showed the first fruits of his application
> to the art of organ playing, and to composition, which he had
> learned chiefly by observing the works of the most famous and pro-
> ficient composers of his day and by the fruits of his own reflection
> upon them. In the art of the organ he took the works of Bruhns,
> Reinken, Buxtehude, and several good French organists as models
> (*BR*, 217).

Organist of St. Blasius's Church at Mühlhausen, 1707–1708

When Johann Georg Ahle, the Mühlhausen councilor and organist at the Blasiuskirche (St. Blasius's), died on December 2, 1706, the city's musical life—which had flourished in the days of his father, Johann Rudolph—

showed signs of decline. Various candidates applied for the vacant post of organist, among them the future lexicographer Johann Gottfried Walther. He had already submitted two trial compositions for Sexagesima Sunday, 1707 (February 27). Walther withdrew those works when it was pointed out to him that his application stood hardly any chance of success. Apparently the choice of organist had already been made unofficially, since the church council's representatives preferred the young Bach for this new post. The Mühlhausen records do not show how this came about, nor does any application letter by Bach survive.

On Easter Sunday 1707 (April 24) Bach gave his trial performance, and on this occasion he may have performed the Easter cantata "Christ lag in Todes Banden," BWV 4. Exactly one month later, on May 24, the Mühlhausen council decided to give him the post of organist. No other applicants were considered. On June 14 Bach turned up for a contractual meeting. His demand for the same remuneration he had received at Arnstadt was granted, and the council accorded him a fixed annual salary of 85 guilders—some 20 more than had been paid to his predecessor, Ahle. His pay also included allowances for free wood and grain. On June 15 Bach received his certificate of appointment and on June 29 he gave official notice to leave his post as organist in Arnstadt. A few days earlier his cousin Johann Ernst Bach and Andreas Börner had already applied for the post that was to become vacant.

We know from the certificate of appointment that Bach's only requirements were to play the organ at St. Blasius's on Sundays, feast days, and other holidays. For an additional salary he also served as organist at the church of the Augustinian convent, the so-called Brückenkirche. This church had an organ with only seven stops and no pedal that had been built by the Mühlhausen organ builder Johann Friedrich Wender in 1702. Compared with the splendor of the main church of St. Blasius and the Marienkirche (St. Mary's), the Brückenkirche had rather modest architectural features. For the most part, weddings and funerals were celebrated here, with normal services taking place only irregularly. Bach and the organists from St. Mary's and the Nicolai-Kirche (St. Nicholas's) shared the organ-playing duties.

Bach's duties as organist at St. Blasius's did not include leading cantata performances, which were assigned to the cantor, Johann Bernhard Stier. This explains why the few vocal compositions dating from Bach's period at Mühlhausen were all written for special occasions. Bach composed the can-

*Interior of the Blasiuskirche (St. Blasius's) in Mühlhausen,
with choir screen and present-day organ.*

tata "Gott ist mein König," BWV 71, for the council election on February 4, 1708, and the psalm cantata "Aus der Tiefen rufe ich, Herr, zu dir," BWV 131, was created for a penitential service. Their performance may also have taken place in connection with the devastating fire of May 30, 1707, that destroyed 360 houses in the lower part of town, very close to St. Blasius's. Bach did not receive this commission from the pastor of St. Blasius's, Johann Adolph Frohne, but—as he noted in his own hand at the end of his score—"Set to music at the request of Dr. Georg Christian Eilmar." Georg Christian Eilmar (1665–1715) was pastor at St. Mary's and was on friendly terms with Bach. He and his daughter became godparents to Bach's first two children. We cannot establish if there were any special reasons for the performances of the other cantatas from this period.

Large-scale vocal works were seldom performed in the imperial city of Mühlhausen. For one thing, there was a shortage of musical talent; for another, there were hardly any necessary means after the 1707 fire in the city. The tradition of giving a special concert of festive vocal music for the annual changeover of the council membership had already started during the term of Johann Rudolph Ahle. That the city fathers had the performing parts of Bach's 1708 music for the town council election printed in addition to the libretto is not only proof of the extraordinary standing accorded to this event, but even more, of the great esteem in which the young Bach was held. In the following year, 1709, he was asked once again by the city fathers to compose and perform the cantata for the election of the council, although in the meantime he had become organist at the Weimar court. Unfortunately, neither music nor text survives.

Bach had spent scarcely twelve months at his new post when plans for his leaving Mühlhausen again had developed. In the early summer he traveled to Weimar and auditioned before the reigning Duke Wilhelm Ernst. The Duke offered him the post of court organist, which the previous organist Johann Effler had to give up for reasons of age and health. Bach accepted, not only because of the considerably higher salary, but because he realized that in the long run he could not stay at Mühlhausen. He mentions the reasons for this in his discharge request of June 25, 1708, addressed to the Mühlhausen council. Decisive for Bach's leaving were, for one, the city's poor conditions for music and, for another, the difficult economic situation after the catastrophic fire of the previous year. Quarrels and social tension among musicians as well as their worsened standard of living did not provide a sound basis for "well-regulated church music," which Bach had tried vainly to promote, as he emphasises in his request. Bach's efforts to give regular performances of vocal compositions apparently came to nothing, as they were frustrated by the existing organizational structure of musical life in the city. Since his certificate of appointment did not stipulate that leading vocal music performances fell within his duties as organist, there could have been clashes of jurisdiction when he wanted to perform such music.

In his request Bach also mentions that the situation in the townships was much more favorable for church music than in the city itself. Nor could he make much use of a "good store of the choicest church compositions"—i.e., an extensive library of vocal church music that he had purchased over the course of time. Bach would hardly have been bothered by the religious controversy between the orthodox and the Pietists that is always quoted and largely overrated. It does not seem to have had a detrimental effect on musical life in Mühlhausen. Bach's request to be discharged was already discussed by the council on June 26. The city fathers granted his request, but only reluctantly. They asked him, however, to continue to keep an eye on repair work for the organ.

Court Organist and Concertmaster at Weimar, 1708–1717

In July 1708 Bach moved to Weimar with his wife, Maria Barbara, with whom he had been married on October 17, 1707. Right from the start of his employment at the Weimar court, Bach was appointed "Chamber Musician and Court Organist" (*Dok.* II, no. 42). He took over this post from the court organist Johann Effler, who had retired for reasons of health but received his full salary until his death in 1711. Initially, Bach was ranked next-to-last on the roster of the court orchestra, just above the town musician Valentin Balzer. Bach's salary, which he received for the first time on the day of the Exaltation of the Cross in 1708 (September 14), originally amounted to 150 florins, 20 florins more than that of his predecessor Effler. This salary was augmented by an allowance of four cords of timber and 2 florins from the so-called "Wilhelmsstiftung" (Wilhelm's fund). At Michaelmas in 1711, Bach's income was increased to 200 florins and in June 1713 to 215 florins. Upon his promotion to concertmaster in March 1714, his salary was raised to 250 florins. The following year he was even put on the same financial level as the court Kapellmeister Johann Adam Drese and his son, when he participated on special occasions.

An eighteenth-century engraving of Weimar.

Soon after Bach had taken up his post, some far-reaching changes took place in his family circumstances. At the end of December 1708 his first child, Catharina Dorothea, was born. Before that, Maria Barbara's unmarried sister Friedelena Margaretha had been taken into the family, and she continued to live there until her death in 1729. Six more children were born in Weimar. Three of them died soon after birth, and only four reached adulthood: Catharina Dorothea, Wilhelm Friedemann (born in 1710), Carl Philipp Emanuel (born in 1714), and Johann Gottfried Bernhard (1715–1739?). Among the many godparents who appeared at the font of Weimar's town church, including friends and relatives from Erfurt, Ohrdruf, and Mühlhausen (Pastor Eilmar), were well-known personalities from the courts at Weimar and Cöthen. The most prominent among them was Georg Philipp Telemann—C. P. E. Bach's godfather and a family friend—who had been working at Frankfurt-am-Main since 1712 as *Director musices*.

During the first few years at Weimar, Bach and his family lived near the market in the "Freyhaus," which belonged to the falsetto singer Adam Immanuel Weldig, master of the pageboys. Weldig, however, sold the building in August 1713, having left for the court at Weissenfels at the beginning of the year. But he continued his friendship with Bach and may even have taken the initiative for Bach's guest performance at Weissenfels on the occasion of Duke Christian's birthday. In February 1713 Bach stayed at this court for a few days and probably gave the premiere of his Hunting Cantata, BWV 208. It is not known where Bach lived in later years.

When Bach arrived in Weimar in July 1708, Johann Gottfried Walther had been working as organist for one year in the Stadtkirche of St. Peter and St. Paul. The two musicians were almost the same age and were related (Walther's grandfather and Bach's mother had been half-brother and sister), which from the outset made for a close friendship that united Bach and Walther for the rest of their lives. Numerous copies of works by Bach have survived in Walther's handwriting, including a copy, prepared together with Johann Tobias Krebs, of the cantata "Widerstehe doch der Sünde," BWV 54, perhaps composed in 1714.

After Bach had instructed some students at Arnstadt and Mühlhausen, his teaching activity began in earnest at Weimar. In addition to Johann Tobias Krebs (1690–1662), mentioned above, some of the many students from those years worth mentioning are Johann Martin Schubart (1690–1721), Johann Caspar Vogler (1696–1763), Johann Gotthilf Ziegler (1688–1747), Johann Lorenz Bach (1695–1773), Philipp David Kräuter (1690–1741), Johann Bernhard Bach (1700–1743), and Samuel Gmelin (1695–1752). According to Heinrich Nicolaus Gerber (*Dok.* III, no. 950), Vogler was "the greatest master on the organ" trained by Bach. The estate of this organ virtuoso and former pupil contained a great many sources of Bach material (part of which has been preserved). In addition to Krebs and Walther, Vogler is among the most reliable early collectors and custodians of Bach's works for clavier and organ.

Philipp David Kräuter studied with Bach from 1712 to 1713 as the recipient of a scholarship from Augsburg. In his report on the court at Weimar, he draws special attention to his having learned about Italian and French music during the summer of 1713, after Prince Johann Ernst's return from Holland. Kräuter also worked as a copyist for Bach, and under Bach's guidance composed cantatas of his own.

The Weimar Schlosskirche, Bach's workplace as court organist, was located at the southeastern end of Wilhelmsburg Castle. It was built on the spot where the Stiftskirche had stood before its destruction by fire in 1618. Reconstruction of the church started in 1619 and was completed in 1630. In 1658 the church was renovated and enlarged, and in which space was

The Wilhelmsburg in Weimar with the Schlosskirche (left); gouache.

created for the first time for the chapel musicians and the organ. From 1711 until 1713 further alterations and repair works were carried out, particularly to the area reserved for the orchestra. Both the church and the Wilhelmsburg were destroyed by fire in 1774.

The organ, which had been built by Ludwig Compenius in 1657–58, was enlarged and equipped with a sub-bass by the Weimar organ builder Johann Conrad Weisshaupt in 1707–8, before Bach took up his post. We lack precise information about a further reconstruction, probably carried out at Bach's initiative in 1712–14 by the organ builder Heinrich Nicolaus Trebs. Further major alterations to the organ followed in 1719–20. As a result, the specifications we have from the year 1737 do not necessarily refer to the organ that Bach had at his disposal during his years at Weimar, and we are left rather in the dark about its layout and the specifications of its manuals and pedal. According to information contained in his obituary notice, Bach composed most of his organ works at Weimar: "The pleasure His Grace took in his playing fired him [Bach] with the desire to try out every possible artistry in his treatment of the organ. Here, too, he wrote most of his organ works" (*Dok* III, no. 666).

The principality of Saxe-Weimar had been ruled since 1629 by two dukes. In 1683, after the death of Johann Ernst II, government matters were taken over by his sons Wilhelm Ernst and Johann Ernst, with Wilhelm Ernst, as the eldest, obtaining predominance in accordance with the statutes. The subsequent system of joint rule thereafter produced continuing disputes about competence, since the authority and privileges of either ruler had been defined unclearly (in an agreement), especially in respect to domestic politics. The situation became even more critical after Johann Ernst's death, when his son (and Wilhelm Ernst's nephew) Ernst August acceded to the position of co-regent in 1709. The initial controversies escalated into bitter power struggles, during which time both rulers frequently got carried away and acted despotically. (For instance, in 1710 Wilhelm Ernst had Ernst August's councilors arrested on the spot).

At that time the court orchestra was at the peak of its development. Major musicians had worked there, among them the concertmaster Johann Paul von Westhoff (1656–1705), one of the best-known violinists in Germany, and Kapellmeister Georg Christoph Strattner (d. 1704). When Bach stayed in Weimar for the first time in 1703, he had the opportunity to meet Westhoff personally. We do not know if he became a pupil of the widely traveled virtuoso. In 1708 the court ensemble had fourteen musicians. A drummer and seven trumpeters could be brought in for special events. As in other smaller courts, the musicians had to perform additional duties, including, for instance, those of servants, secretaries, or huntsmen. During Bach's term of office in Weimar, the membership roll of the court ensemble remained mostly unchanged.

A sore point during the abovementioned quarrels between the rulers was the right of control over joint servants, which therefore included the musicians of the court orchestra. Already in 1707 (i.e., at the time of his younger brother Johann Ernst's co-regency), Wilhelm Ernst issued a decree that the musicians of the court ensemble were allowed to supply music at the residence of the co-regent only after he himself had first given special permission. When he realized that this order was not treated with due respect, he saw fit to issue more severe sanctions in 1719. Wilhelm Ernst spelled out his decree more precisely, and in the future musicians could be fined or arrested if they violated his orders. He had already used these measures occasionally in the past when similar offences had occurred. It is obvious that such sanctions could not be complied with in practice and that Ernst August was even less inclined to put up with them. Without telling his uncle, he continued to order the musicians to play at his residence and

threatened them with reprisals if they tried to be exempted from this obligation on the strength of the 1707 decree.

Wilhelm Ernst stuck to his position of supremacy stubbornly and inflexibi-
ly, whereas Ernst August did not miss a single opportunity to pursue his
claim to power as co-regent and tried to undermine his uncle's governmen-
tal program. Court employees and, more particularly, the joint servants and
court musicians, were torn apart by regulations, commands, orders,
threats, insults, and punishments. Some sought to resign. The turmoil led
inevitably to a split in the ducal household between supporters of Wilhelm
Ernst and followers of Ernst August. Most court employees took the path
of least resistance and chose the side of the reigning duke, for which Ernst
August took revenge with legal proceedings and dismissal notices when he
assumed absolute power in August 1728. Hardly any of the joint servants
managed to stay neutral in the face of these plots and power struggles.

As a member of the court ensemble, Bach was also a "joint servant" and
therefore found himself in the employment of both dukes. His close links
with Duke Ernst August and his half-brother Prince Johann Ernst could
not help but affect his relations with the reigning Duke Wilhelm Ernst. Even
Forkel referred to Bach's warm relationship with Ernst August, on the basis
of a remark by Carl Philipp Emanuel Bach in a 1775 letter that "Prince
Leopold in Cöthen, Duke Ernst August in Weimar, and Duke Christian in
Weissenfels particularly loved him and rewarded him appropriately" (*Dok*
III, no. 803).

Of the two Weimar dukes, Ernst August was without doubt the one more
interested in music. This is shown by extensive purchases of instruments
and acquisitions of written music, as well as by his own musical activities,
especially on the violin and the trumpet. Members of the joint court chapel
frequently had to come to his residence to make music, which the reigning
duke tried to curb as much as possible. Bach's active participation in looking after the music for the younger regent is borne out by the fact that his
salary increases in 1716 and 1717 came out of Johann Ernst's budget and
not from Wilhelm Ernst's treasury. A letter to August Becker dated January
14, 1714, provides proof of Bach's direct participation in musical performances at the Rote Schloss (Red Castle), the co-regent's residence (*Dok* I,
no. 2). In addition, Bach enjoyed very close links with the highly talented
Prince Johann Ernst, some of whose concertos he transcribed for clavier
and organ.

At the end of November 1713 Bach traveled to Halle. The church board there had invited him for an audition, since he had expressed interest in the post of organist at St. Mary's. After the death of Friedrich Wilhelm Zachow on August 7, 1712, who had for many years been music director, the position of organist had been vacant for more than a year, and negotiations about filling the post had dragged on for various reasons, among them a period of public mourning. The post seemed worth applying for; moreover, the organ was to be enlarged, eventually to have three manuals with a total of sixty-five stops. Bach remained in Halle for two weeks, staying at the town's most fashionable inn. On the second Sunday of Advent, December 10, he presented a test cantata based on a libretto by the chief pastor of Halle, Johann Michael Heineccius. He received a fee of 12 thalers for this composition, which is not extant. Only a few days after this performance he was selected as organist, and the following day he was officially offered the job. Bach behaved in such a way that the board believed he had accepted the post, and on December 15 he traveled back home. Four weeks later, after another meeting of the Board, the certificate of appointment was drafted and forwarded to him at Weimar. In a delaying letter of January 14, 1714, addressed to August Becker, chairman of the church board, Bach explained that he had not yet received his dismissal from Weimar and informed Becker that he would write again in a week's time. On February 1, the Board advised him that a further increase in his salary would be hard to effect. Thereupon Bach turned to the reigning duke in Weimar and asked for a promotion. On March 2, 1714, Wilhelm Ernst officially appointed him concertmaster "at his most humble request" (*BR*, 67). At the same time, his salary was increased to 250 florins. Only then did Bach inform the church board at Halle that he was turning them down.

Bach, who certainly used his application in Halle for tactical purposes in his dealings with the Weimar court, already had ambitions to leave in 1713, because of conditions there. Not without reason did he apply for a municipal position and not one at court. Only his appointment as concertmaster may have persuaded him to delay, for a while, his plans to move. Then again, it could be that the duke had turned down Bach's request for dismissal already in 1714, as he was to do four years later as well.

Upon his appointment as concertmaster, Bach was charged with performing "new pieces each month" in the castle church. The reigning duke's order to compose motivated Bach at first to write large-scale works for the church, as demonstrated by the 1714 cantatas "Himmelskönig, sei willkommen," BWV 182, "Weinen, Klagen, Sorgen, Zagen," BWV 12, "Erschallet, ihr Lieder, erklinget ihr Saiten!," BWV 172, and "Ich hatte viel Bekümmernis," BWV 21. But soon, after Easter 1715—i.e., twelve months later—his initial enthusiasm to produce seemed to have cooled off. The amount of work put into the subsequent church cantatas and the display of instruments were kept to a minimum. Henceforth, the choir, for whom Bach had planned big undertakings through Easter, receded into the background. Usually, they were now called upon only for singing a four-part chorale at the end of a cantata. Only further investigation will tell if this cutback was due to the reigning duke's reservations vis-à-vis concerted church music.

After the death of Prince Johann Ernst of Saxe-Weimar on August 1, 1715, at the age of 18, a "full public mourning" was proclaimed on August 11 for the entire principality of Weimar. All musical activities, including performances of cantatas in the castle church, were immediately prohibited. However, after some thirteen weeks, the first steps were made to lift public mourning gradually, and on November 10 music was allowed to be played once again in the churches. Apparently following the cycle that had been used for a long time, performances of the cantatas began once more in the castle church with Kapellmeister Drese, his son, and Bach having to lead the music in turn. Public mourning was completely lifted only on February 2, 1716. Two months later, on April 2, a memorial service for the deceased prince was held in the castle church at Weimar. On that occasion a two-part mourning cantata in twenty-two movements was performed, of which only the printed text has survived. Bach apparently wrote the music, since two days later he and Salomon Franck, poet laureate at the royal court of Weimar, were granted a special bonus of 45 florins and 15 groschen, surely as recompense for this mourning music.

On December 1, 1716, Kapellmeister Johann Adam Drese died. Filling the now vacant post apparently led to lengthy negotiations with one or more candidates to succeed him and was further complicated because there did not seem any likelihood of an early agreement between the reigning dukes. Nearly nine months passed before Johann Wilhelm Drese was appointed as successor; during this time Bach, who had not appeared on the short list, looked for new job possibilities.

In March 1717 Bach apparently traveled to Gotha to substitute Christian Friedrich Witt, for many years the Court Kapellmeister for Friedrich II. Witt lay on his deathbed and could not conduct the forthcoming Passion performance on Good Friday (March 26) in the church at Friedenstein Castle. Since other commissions were not forthcoming from the Weimar court,

Bach must have relished the opportunity to take over the commission to compose and perform this Passion music. The particular Passion in question is mentioned only once in the literature. Just a few movements have been preserved in later works, primarily in the second version of the *St. John Passion*, BWV 245, and in the solo cantata for tenor, BWV 55. On April 12, a few days after Easter, Bach received a bonus of 12 thalers for the presentation of the Passion.

After Johann Adam Drese's death, Bach apparently stopped providing the court at Weimar with further church pieces. He used the last year of his tenure for his own composing projects. It is quite likely that during this period he already wrote some preludes and fugues for the *Well-Tempered Clavier*, Part I. In any case, Bach must have tackled this series of works no later than toward the end of 1717 (during his arrest), as we can gather from information provided by the lexicographer Heinrich Nicolaus Gerber. It seems that he first tried in the early part of 1717 to find out about opportunities for leaving the Weimar court. The co-regent Ernst August helped him pave the way. In the summer Bach decided on Cöthen, where on August 5 he accepted the post as Kapellmeister at the court of Prince Leopold in Anhalt. Immediately thereafter he must have requested his release from the reigning duke, who refused.

In the meantime, Johann Wilhelm Drese had been promoted to Kapellmeister at the Weimar court. Possibly encouraged by his triumph in Dresden over the French virtuoso Louis Marchant, Bach felt compelled to demand his discharge with ever more tenacity, leading on November 6, 1717, to his arrest. Because of his "forcing the issue of his dismissal too stubbornly," he was "confined to the county judge's place of detention" (*BR*, 75) and finally, after four weeks in custody, received an unfavorable discharge from his position with Duke Wilhelm Ernst of Saxe-Weimar. This was a harsh final note to a creative period for Bach that, according to his obituary notice, had started out so promisingly in 1708.

Hofkapellmeister at Cöthen, 1717–1723

After the death of Prince Emanuel Leberecht of Anhalt in 1704, his wife Gisela Agnes, née von Rath (1669–1740), took over the reign as guardian for their son Leopold, who was still underage. The prince's widow belonged to the underprivileged Lutheran minority. She was therefore at loggerheads all her life with the ruling dynasty of her principality, where, in 1596,

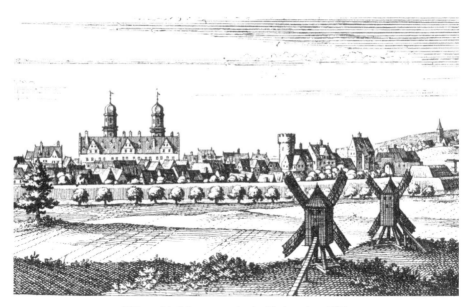

Cöthen; detail from engraving by Merian, circa 1650.

Calvinism had already been adopted as the state religion, according to the "cuius regio, eius religio" principle of law, resulting from the religious Peace of Augsburg. When Leopold came of age and took over the reign in May 1716, she was in constant conflict with her son, who, like his father belonged to the Calvinist Church, as did the majority of the reigning princely family.

The history of the court orchestra at Anhalt began in April 1702, when Prince Emanuel Leberecht first hired two musicians and soon after engaged four more at a fixed salary. The cultivation of music at court, highly praised by Telemann in later years, came to an abrupt end after two years. After the ruler's death, the court musicians (probably for reasons of economy) were dismissed again by Gisela Agnes.

It was not until August 1707 that the crown prince, who was twelve years old by that time, could induce his mother to hire some musicians again for music at court. While he attended the Ritterakademie in Berlin from 1707 until 1710, he met Augustin Reinhard Stricker, Kammermusicus at the royal court of Prussia. In October 1710 Leopold set out for a two-and-a-half year study trip that took him to Holland, England, and Italy as well as Vienna, Prague, and Dresden. When he returned to Cöthen in April 1713, he had developed his musical talent on the violin, viola da gamba, and harpsichord, and insisted on the further expansion of music at court. At the request of her son, Gisela Agnes asked a few members of the disbanded Berlin court orchestra to come to Cöthen,[1] including the aforementioned Stricker as Kapellmeister and his wife, the singer and lute-player Katharina Elisabeth. The reorganization of the court ensemble, begun under Stricker in 1714, continued until around 1720 although, for no apparent reason, Stricker and his wife left Leopold's service at the start of his fourth year of office. The young ruler, who was characterized by contemporaries as unsettled and unpredictable, dismissed Stricker apparently after he had had some negotiations with Bach about taking over the post of Kapellmeister. On August 5 Bach was officially appointed to the new post. Two days later, he received a gratuity of fifty thalers to mark the occasion. However, the start of his term was delayed, since the Duke of Weimar refused to grant him his discharge.

Around the beginning of December Bach moved with his family to Cöthen. Perhaps his release was effected through some diplomatic bargaining, so that he would be available for the musical program to celebrate Prince Leopold's birthday on December 10 at Cöthen. But the music that Bach presumably performed that day as a tribute has not survived. Within a week of his assuming office, he went to Leipzig for the acceptance of the organ built by Johann Scheibe at the Pauliner-Kirche (Universitäts-Kirche).

With a total annual income of 450 thalers, Bach ranked fourth in earnings among the court employees[2] and had as a supreme employer, as he himself judged, "a gracious Prince who both loved and knew music" (BR, 125) and who played music himself at a level far above that of an amateur. Perhaps the conditions for living and doing creative work were in fact so free of trouble—at least during the first few years in Cöthen—that Bach thought that he might stay there for the rest of his life, as he reported later in retrospect. Thanks to thorough and continuous rehearsing, the court ensemble was able to perform at a remarkable level. In particular, the Brandenburg Concertos, BWV 1046–1051, which were part of the concert repertory in Cöthen, are definite proof of the virtuoso ability of the instrumentalists who played under Bach's direction.

In contrast, the organ at the Jakobikirche (St. Jacobi's), with its 13 or 14 stops, was in a deplorable state, although church music at the Protestant court was of only minor importance. Bach would certainly not have accepted a post here that involved just looking after the music in church. However, the Lutheran Agnuskirche—named to recall Princess Gisela Agnes, who had put all her resources into building this house of God—had an organ with two manuals, pedal, and a total of 27 stops.

Bach's move to the Cöthen court inevitably led to a new orientation in his creative work. In the preceding years he had composed mostly organ music and church cantatas—which, of course, did not exclude other genres—but from now on he had to give priority to writing chamber music, concertos, and overtures for the lively musical scene at Leopold's court. Apparently, secular cantatas were performed in the residence only on special occasions, such as the New Year celebrations on January 1 or the prince's birthday on December 10, and Bach had to provide the appropriate compositions every year. Assuming that performing one cantata was sufficient for each occasion, he would then have had to write at least twelve musical works of tribute during the period from December 1717 to the beginning of 1723. Yet we know that on December 10, 1718, two cantatas by Bach were heard. For now, we cannot be certain whether this was an exception. The congratulatory cantata "Der Himmel dacht auf Anhalts Ruhm und Glück," BWV 66a, and the church cantata "Lobet den Herrn, alle seine Heerscharen," BWV Anh. 5, were "performed at the divine service" on that day, as the surviving reprint states. With this background it is difficult to estimate how many new cantatas Bach actually wrote at Cöthen.

Only two works of tribute dating from that period have survived in full: "Die Zeit, die Tag und Jahre macht," BWV 134a, and "Durchlauchster Leopold," BWV 173a. We know of another six cantatas, either because the printed text survives or because they were borrowed from for later church cantatas; their music, then, can be reconstituted only in part.

The loss of original manuscripts from the Cöthen period, which affected the instrumental music even more, may be due to the following. In accordance with the usual practice at various absolutist courts, musicians leaving their employment had to leave behind all compositions that they had written during their term at court. For instance, the concertmaster Johann Pfeiffer, Bach's successor at the Weimar court, had to return—by order of Duke Ernst August—all "Italian and other musical works that he has composed during his service here" when he was dismissed in April 1735.[3] Even if Bach and Prince Leopold parted on good terms in 1723, it does not follow that one could bypass a rule that prevailed at the time. Since that was the case, one may well wonder if Bach did not have to leave behind all, or at least most, of his performance scores (perhaps parts as well?). This would explain the loss of most of the original sources for Bach's instrumental compositions in Cöthen.

First page of the "Serenade" written on the occasion of
Prince Leopold's birthday. (Bach's autograph)

During his time in Cöthen Bach occasionally performed church cantatas, although as Kapellmeister he was not obliged to do so. This is borne out not only by the printed text of Cantata BWV Anh. 5, referred to above, but also by the survival of performance parts for some of the church cantatas in Weimar, suggesting that Bach used them again in Cöthen. These cantatas are "Ich hatte viel Bekümmernis," BWV 21, "Erschallet, ihr Lieder, erklinget, ihr Saiten!," BWV 172, "Bereitet die Wege, bereitet die Bahn!," BWV 132, and "Mein Herze schwimmt im Blut," BWV 199. Nevertheless, it remains uncertain on which occasion and in which circumstances these works were heard.

Bach had been working in Cöthen for exactly two years when his youngest son, Leopold August, died (he was buried on September 28, 1719). Nine months later he was hit by an even worse blow: after nearly thirteen years of marriage he lost his wife, Maria Barbara, to whom he could not even pay his last respects. She was buried in Cöthen, in his absence, on July 7, 1720. According to his obituary notice, Bach happened to be in Carlsbad at the time on a lengthy trip with Prince Leopold. He received the news of Maria Barbara's death, after a short and serious illness, only when he returned home. He was left with his four children, Catharina Dorothea, Wilhelm Friedemann, Carl Philipp Emanuel, and Johann Gottfried Bernhard, all of them underage. For the time being they were probably looked after by Friedelena Margaretha, the aforementioned sister-in-law who lived in the Bach household.

Maria Barbara's death hit Bach so hard that he no longer wished to stay in Cöthen. That very November he applied to the Jakobikirche (St. Jacobi's) in Hamburg for the post of organist, which had become vacant upon the death of Heinrich Friese on September 12, 1720. For one thing, he would certainly have been fascinated by the organ, built by Arp Schnitger in 1688–93, with its four manuals and sixty stops. For another, the free Hanseatic city of Hamburg offered a musical perspective totally different from that of the Cöthen court and the provincial town of Anhalt, which had only 2,000 inhabitants. Apart from Bach, seven other candidates had turned up, and on November 21 the "church trustees" decided on the selection procedure and composition of the jury. An audition was set for November 28, but five days before that Bach departed with the message that he had to return to his prince.

On December 19 the selection of the organist took place, and—since Bach had in the meantime declined—Johann Joachim Heitmann was chosen.

The reasons for Bach's refusal are not known. Perhaps Prince Leopold did not want to release his Kapellmeister from his duties just like that, or Bach did not want (or was unable) to pay the sum of 4,000 marks that Heitmann would donate to the church's treasury following his selection. Erdmann Neumeister, as chief pastor of St. Jacobi's, had openly but unsuccessfully protested against selling the post of organist to the highest bidder, for when Heitmann died, such payment indeed became a basic requirement for obtaining the post again.

Bach's sensational concert at the Katharinenkirche (St. Catherine's) may have tipped the balance for the church council to push so hard for his candidacy. According to the obituary notice, Bach, in the presence of Jan Adam Reinken, the 97-year-old organist of the church, "was heard for more than two hours playing the fine organ of the Katharinenkirche before the magistrate and many other distinguished persons of the town, to their general astonishment." His improvisation on the chorale "An Wasserflüssen Babylon" for almost half an hour prompted the aged Reinken to make the well-known compliment: "I thought that this art was dead, but I see that it still lives on in you" (*BR*, 219).

It had been more than a year since the sudden death of his wife, Maria Barbara, when in September 1721 family changes were again in the offing for the widowed Kapellmeister and his four children, who were still unprovided for. He stood at the font of the castle chapel at Cöthen as godfather to Johann Christian Hahn together with the royal chamber singer Anna Magdalena Wilcke. Engaged couples were often asked to be godparents in those days. Three months later, on December 3, 1721, their wedding took place in private, "by royal command." Widowed persons frequently married in private, in order to avoid attracting public attention. Bach's second wife, a daughter of Johann Caspar Wilcke, court trumpeter to the Duke of Weissenfels, had already made some guest appearances as a singer with her father at the Anhalt residence. Prince Leopold employed her for the impressive annual salary of nearly 200 thalers.

When Bach took over the court orchestra at Cöthen in December 1717, the ensemble consisted of seventeen musicians on a fixed salary. Between then and the summer of 1722, the number was reduced to twelve or thirteen members. The main reason for this reduction was the death of several musicians, not any cutback in musical forces ordered by Leopold. The final reductions apparently took place only after Bach had left. In any case, it is clear that from the summer of 1722, music no longer ranked as high at the court as it had at the start of Leopold's reign. In 1722 the expenses for the orchestra were reduced for the first time. The music budget, which until then had stood at nearly 2,300 thalers per year, was reduced steadily so that in 1728, the year of the ruler's death, it amounted to only 1,459 thalers. One of the reasons, certainly, was a long-standing quarrel within the ruling royal family of Anhalt which climaxed in August 1722 but in fact had cast a shadow over all of Leopold's reign. The family dispute about sharing power and feudal pensions led to compromises in 1716 and 1722, as a result of which Leopold's authority was undermined and the court had to accept a considerable loss of income. The ruler was forced to make out a new budget, which also resulted in reduced spending on court music. In the meantime, he had perhaps come to attach more importance to musical entertainment and variety than the continuous cultivation of music of the highest order. At any rate, after Bach left, the ruler did not bother to appoint a successor. From then on the court ensemble was conducted by the concertmaster.

Leopold's waning commitment to court music—apparently influenced as well by a princess who was not interested in music and seemed to be "without an appreciation of art" (*Dok* I, no. 23)—undoubtedly contributed to Bach's decision, toward the end of 1722, to leave the Cöthen court. Another reason may well have been the difficulties he had with the education of his sons. Far-reaching obstacles erected for the Lutheran school system by the Protestants were part of everyday life at the Anhalt residence and therefore had an immediate effect on the basic way of life of the Bach family.

Already in December 1722 Bach applied for the position of cantor at the Thomaskirche (St. Thomas's) in Leipzig. The post had become vacant following the death of Johann Kuhnau. Five months later, on April 13, 1723, Prince Leopold and his Kapellmeister officially parted ways, by mutual agreement.

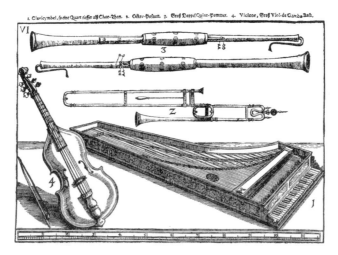

Musical instruments, from M. Praetorius, Syntagma musicum, *1619.*

Notes

1. Immediately after the death of Frederick I (d. February 25, 1713) all musicians of the Berlin court ensemble were dismissed by his successor (Frederick William I, the "Soldier King").
2. The highest salary was drawn by court councilor and chamberlain Johann Christoph Laurentius, with an annual total sum of 540 thalers.
3. Public Records, Weimar, B 26436, folio 126 recto/verso.

*"Fantasia" for organ, BWV 562, circa 1712; the depiction shows
the first page of a copy that Bach made later.*

5

BACH THE ORGANIST

George B. Stauffer

In the world of the "early" cantatas, the figure of Bach the organist looms large. Bach's early training was that of an organist, his first important jobs were organist positions, he first attracted public attention through organ playing, and his earliest significant compositions were organ works. It is not altogether surprising, then, that when he faced the task of writing sacred vocal music for the first time, in Mühlhausen and Weimar, he drew heavily on his experience as an organist.

BACH THE ORGANIST: FROM EISENACH TO CÖTHEN

Although Bach may have been inspired in the first ten years of his life by the organ playing of his second cousin at the Georgenkirche (St. George's) in Eisenach, he seems to have begun his formal training only when he moved to Ohrdruf in 1695 to live with his older brother Johann Christoph. According to the obituary of 1754, it was under Christoph's guidance that the young Sebastian "laid the foundations for his playing of the clavier" (*BR*, 216). Christoph was organist at the Michaeliskirche (St. Michael's) in Ohrdruf and had studied with Johann Pachelbel. He was well versed in Middle German organ music. His clavier book that the young Sebastian—

The Bach organ in the Bachkirche (Neue Kirche) in Arnstadt.

Console of the old organ from the Neue Kirche in Arnstadt, where Bach was organist.

according to family tradition—copied surreptitiously by moonlight was said to have contained pieces by Froberger, Kerll, and Pachelbel. A recently discovered manuscript of Buxtehude's Praeludium in G minor, BuxWV 148, in the hand of Christoph and Johann Sebastian, suggests that Buxtehude's works were also part of the Ohrdruf family tutorial. Two other fraternal copying efforts, the Möller Manuscript and the Andreas Bach Book, contain a still wider selection of keyboard music, including North German works by Reinken, Buxtehude, Böhm, and Bruhns, and French works by Dieupart, Le Bègue, and Marchand. Thus Johann Sebastian Bach may have come to know much of this repertory, too, through Christoph.

When Bach left Ohrdruf in 1700 for three years of study at the Michaelisschule (St. Michael's School) in Lüneburg, he came into contact with two of the most prominent organists of the day, Georg Böhm and Johann Adam Reinken. Bach probably studied with Böhm, a fellow Thuringian who served as organist of the Johanniskirche (St. John's) in Lüneburg and was a much-admired composer of chorale preludes and partitas. Bach did not have the opportunity to study with Reinken but ventured to Hamburg several times to hear him play on the large organ of the Katharinenkirche (St. Catherine's).

In the summer of 1702 Bach competed successfully for the post of organist at the Jakobikirche (St. Jacobi's) in Sangerhausen—a striking accomplishment for a seventeen-year-old. However, the Duke of Weissenfels, whose jurisdiction extended to the church, intervened and appointed an older man. A year later, in July 1703, Bach was paid to test and inaugurate the new Wender organ in the Neukirche (New Church) in Arnstadt. His performance must have been impressive, for the next month the church council invited him to become the New Church organist, even though the post was occupied at the time by Andreas Börner. Bach accepted the offer, and Börner was shifted to another position.

Although we cannot be certain which works Bach wrote in the years leading up to Arnstadt, the winning of the Sangerhausen job and the invitation to test and dedicate the New Church organ suggest that he was a skilled player and improviser by the age of eighteen. The partitas "Ach, was soll ich Sünder machen," BWV 770, "Christ, der du bist der helle Tag," BWV 766, and "O Gott, du frommer Gott," BWV 767, were probably worked out in Lüneburg under Böhm's watchful eye. Free pieces such as the Canzona in D minor, BWV 588, the Praeludium in A minor, BWV 551, the fugues after Legrenzi and Corelli, BWV 574 and BWV 579, and chorale preludes such as those in the recently discovered Neumeister Collection may date from this early period as well. They show Bach imitating contemporary models with drama and finesse—if not disciplined mastery—and exploring contrapuntal procedures (in the Legrenzi and Corelli fugues, especially) that appeared later in a more refined form.

Bach's duties at the New Church were relatively light, giving him ample time to practice and compose. The obituary tells us that the four years in Arnstadt, 1703 to 1707, were the time Bach "truly showed the first fruits of his application to the art of organ playing, and in composition." The most notable event was the four-month pilgrimage to Buxtehude in Lübeck in the winter of 1705–06. Although Bach was surely acquainted with Buxtehude's organ works before he left, the trip gave him the opportunity both to hear the North German master improvise on the Marienkirche (St. Mary's) organ and to attend the Advent "Abendmusik" concerts of church music. On returning to Arnstadt, Bach nevertheless resisted the council's suggestion that he perform concerted works in the New Church, possibly because he considered the local student players too amateurish, at least compared to Buxtehude's professionals. The council also chided him for preluding too elaborately before hymns; Bach responded by going to the opposite extreme. In the winter of 1706 he served as an examiner for a new organ in Langewiesen.

The Capriccio "sopra la lontananza del fratello dilettissimo," BWV 992, illustrates the ambitious but still highly derivative nature of Bach's compositional style toward the beginning of the Arnstadt years. The organ works "Wie schön leuchtet der Morgenstern," BWV 739, "Gott, durch deine Güte," BWV 724, the Prelude and Fugue in G major, BWV 550, and the Toccata in E major, BWV 566, appear to have been written a few years later, around the time of the Lübeck trip, and show Bach working on much the same plane as Buxtehude.

When Bach moved to his next organist post, in Mühlhausen, he gained the opportunity to compose cantatas as well as organ music. Although the town council supported Bach's endeavors, commissioning cantatas and asking him to draw up plans for rebuilding the organ in the Blasiuskirche (St. Blasius's), dissention in the congregation seems to have moved him to seek a position elsewhere. This he found within a year, in Weimar.

The Weimar years are best described in the obituary:

> In the following year, 1708, he undertook a journey to Weymar, had the opportunity to be heard by the reigning Duke, and was offered the post of Chamber and Court Organist in Weymar, of which post he immediately took possession. The pleasure His Grace took in his playing fired him with the desire to try every possible artistry in his treatment of the organ. Here, too, he wrote most of his organ works (*BR*, 218).

For Bach the organist, life at the Weimar court was ideal. His employer, Duke Ernst August, was devoted to organ music and championed Bach's playing. August encouraged concerts in the "Himmelsburg" Chapel and funded extensive alterations to the organ, which were carried out by Heinrich Nicolaus Trebs in 1713–14 under Bach's supervision. Bach's reputation grew rapidly, and he began to attract a large number of students, including Johann Martin Schubart, Johann Caspar Vogler, Johann Gotthilf Ziegler, and Johann Tobias Krebs. All became respected organists in their own right. Another student, Philipp David Kräuter, who came to Bach in 1712, asked his sponsors to extend his stay in the spring of 1713, explaining that when the renovations on the chapel organ were complete, he would be able to see, hear, and copy down "wonderful things." The "wonderful things" were probably Bach's extraordinary organ transcriptions of concertos from Vivaldi's *L'estro armonico*, which August's nephew Prince Johann Ernst seems to have brought back from Amsterdam in the spring of 1713. But they could also have been chorale preludes from the *Orgel-Büchlein* or

*The "Himmelsburg" Chapel in Weimar; gouache by Christian Richter,
circa 1660.*

"Great Eighteen" Collection (which Bach assembled only in Leipzig), or large free works such as the Toccata, Adagio, and Fugue in C major, BWV 564, or the Toccata and Fugue in F major, BWV 540. All of these pieces were "wonderful" indeed and represented new vistas in German organ music. Without question, for Bach the organist, Weimar was—as his biographer Philipp Spitta later put it—"the golden time."

In December 1713, about midway through his Weimar tenure, Bach was invited to become organist at the Liebfrauenkirche in Halle, a demanding position whose requirements were outlined in considerable detail by the church council. After several months of deliberations, Bach decided to stay in Weimar when the duke named him concertmaster. The new title brought more salary and the opportunity to write church cantatas once again. Bach remained on good terms with the Halle officials, however, and returned to the Liebfrauenkirche in the spring of 1716 to serve as an examiner for its new organ. In Weimar he continued to hold the title of court organist, and his rate of producing cantatas was approximately one per month—not nearly as demanding as the cantata-per-week pace he later set in Leipzig. One suspects that during his years as court organist/concertmaster Bach composed sacred vocal works and organ pieces in equal measure. Johann Mattheson, writing in *Das beschützte Orchestre* in 1717, described him as "the famous organist of Weimar" and composer "of things both for the church and for the fist [i.e., the keyboard] that are certainly such as that must make one esteem the man highly" (*BR*, 228).

During the early Weimar years, Bach appears to have labored to bring his writing under tighter structural and contrapuntal control. The Fantasia in G major, BWV 572, and the Prelude and Fugue in D major, BWV 532, represent ingenious solutions to the problem of creating a cohesive, multisectional praeludium. In the *Orgel-Büchlein*, whose origins are now thought to extend back to at least 1710, we see Bach ironing out matters of part writing and motivic unification. The encounter with Vivalid's music around 1713 produced a decisive change: the organ and clavier transcriptions were soon followed by original pieces in Vivaldi's style—free works such as the "Dorian" Toccata and Fugue in D minor, BWV 538, chorale fantasias such as "Komm Heiliger Geist, Herre Gott," BWV 651, and trios such as "Herr Jesu Christ, dich zu uns wend," BWV 655.

In his next post, Kapellmeister at the Cöthen court, Bach was responsible for providing secular vocal works and instrumental pieces for Prince Leopold's professional ensemble. The prince was a Calvinist and showed little interest in church music. The chapel contained a small organ of fewer than fifteen stops, and the instruments in the neighboring Agnuskirche and St. Jacobi's were unmemorable. Under these circumstances Bach's interest shifted away from organ composition. After serving as an examiner for the new Scheibe organ in the Paulinerkirche in Leipzig in December 1717, Bach turned his attention to writing celebratory cantatas, chamber music for solo instruments (the unaccompanied violin sonatas and partitas of 1720, for instance), ensemble pieces (the Brandenburg Concertos, dated March 24, 1721), and, increasingly, harpsichord works.

The purchase in January 1718 of a fine two-manual harpsichord built for Leopold by Michael Mietke in Berlin may have served as a catalyst for Bach, nudging him to change his interest in keyboard music from the organ to the harpsichord. While we can assign very few organ works to Cöthen—the incomplete Fantasia in C major, BWV 573, and the Prelude and Fugue in C major, BWV 547, perhaps—we can observe a host of new harpsichord pieces after the arrival of the Mietke instrument: the *Clavier-Büchlein für Wilhelm Friedemann Bach*, Brandenburg Concerto No. 5 (the first harpsichord concerto in Western music), the first volume of the *Well-Tempered Clavier*, the French and English Suites, and the Inventions and Sinfonias (in early draft, at least). These undertakings replaced the great organ compositions of Weimar.

In November 1720 Bach traveled to Hamburg to perform one of his sacred vocal works and "to be heard" on the organ in conjunction with the vacant organist post at St. Jacobi's. Following a local tradition, Bach improvised on the chorale "An Wasserflüssen Babylons" on the organ for a full half hour. Reinken, who was still alive, attended and made his famous remark (*BR*, 219): "I thought that this art was dead, but I see that in you it still lives." Bach apparently withdrew his candidacy when he learned that a bribe was required to win the job. He would go on to write additional organ works in Leipzig and to present highly acclaimed organ concerts in Berlin and Dresden. But his most important years as an organist were behind him, and the flirtation with the St. Jacobi's audition was the last time he seriously considered an organist position. The tenure as Kapellmeister in Cöthen had changed his status and outlook. It pointed forward to the positions of Thomaskantor (St. Thomas cantor) and *Director musices* in Leipzig, where organ music would play a secondary role to vocal, instrumental, and harpsichord music.

*Jan Adam Reinken; engraving
by Joannes Bambinius.*

*The Schnitger organ in the Jacobikirche
(St. Jacobi's) in Hamburg,
before the most recent restauration.*

THE ORGANIST AS CANTATA COMPOSER

It is against the backdrop of Bach's extraordinary accomplishments in the field of organ playing and composition that we must view the early vocal works. It is quite symbolic that during the Mühlhausen and Weimar years Bach performed his church cantatas in *Chorton* (or *Cornet-Ton*, as it was also called)—that is, at the pitch of the organ. The surviving performance parts show that he notated the strings, brass, and vocalists in the same key as the organ and treated the woodwinds, which were normally pitched in *Cammerton*, a major second or minor third lower than the organ, as transposing instruments. Later, in Leipzig, he adopted the more progressive approach of his predecessor as cantor at St. Thomas's, Johann Kuhnau, and performed concerted church music in *Cammerton*, the pitch of the woodwinds. The organ thus became the transposing instrument (it is written out a major second lower than the other parts in the performance materials), yielding its role as the determining member of the ensemble.

Bach's early concern for making the organ an integral part of the sacred music ensemble is evident from his plans for the reconstruction of the St. Blasius's instrument in Mühlhausen (see *BR*, 58–60). The new *Brust-*

werk division that he proposed was ideal for continuo playing: its location in the breast of the organ case placed it in close proximity to both the player and the instrumental ensemble. Bach stipulated that the Brustwerk should contain a "gentle 8' Gedackt, which blends perfectly with concerted music." He went on to say that the stop should be fashioned from wood rather than metal, because wood produces a better tone. To request a good Stillgedackt for thoroughbass playing was not at all out of the ordinary (Walther, for instance, in the *Musicalisches Lexicon*, pointed out that the stop was ideal for continuo). Bach's second cantata-related concern was more unusual: he asked that the Oberwerk 8' trumpet be replaced with a "16-foot Fagotto . . . which will serve for all kinds of new experiments ('inventionibus') and in which the music will sound very delicate ('sehr *delicat*')." What Bach had in mind by the phrase "sehr *delicat*" is not entirely clear, but most likely he meant that a 16' Fagott could be better and more easily used to reinforce bass lines in concerted works than the 16' Posaune of the pedal division.

Bach submitted his recommendations to the church council toward the end of February 1708. It is not surprising that the role of the organ in sacred vocal music was much on his mind, for earlier that month he had completed the cantata "Gott ist mein König," BWV 71, a brilliantly innovative work in which he gave the organ a new, obbligato role. This is most apparent in the second movement, "Ich bin nun achtzig Jahr," an aria for soprano, tenor, and organ alone (the cello and violone are *tacet*). For the first six measures the organ functions in the expected fashion, as a continuo instrument. But in measure 7 it begins to echo the vocal lines with motives played on the "Positivo." As the aria proceeds, the organ's interpolations become more substantial, and by the end it takes over and brings the movement to a close with an elaborate *fioritura* melody. In the "Friede, Ruh und Wohlergehen" section of the final chorus, the organ again inserts a "Positivo" motive. Elsewhere in the finale the organ sounds a four-part C-major chord in the bottom octave, an unorthodox technique that produces a unique, drum-like sound. One searches in vain for similar passages in the vocal works of his predecessors or contemporaries. Here we see Bach the organist bringing his keyboard playing to bear on his early cantata writing.

Bach again called on the organ to play an obbligato part in "Komm, du süße Todesstunde," BWV 161, a Weimar work dating from 1715. In the opening aria the organ intones "Herzlich tut mich verlangen" with a Sesquialtera stop as the alto and recorders weave a rich web of counterpoint derived from the same melody. Bach returned to this procedure in the opening chorus of the St. Matthew Passion, where the organ sounds the cantus firmus "O Lamm Gottes unschuldig" (again on the Sesquialtera, according to the performance part) with the *soprano in ripieno* chorus, amid a sea of polyphony. And of course in a number of Leipzig cantatas, mostly from the third Jahrgang of 1725–27, Bach featured the organ as an obbligato instrument in a wholly new and ambitious way.

But if Bach's use of the organ as a solo voice was tentative in the early cantatas, his reliance on organ technique as a basic compositional tool was not. Certain scorings closely resemble organ settings. The unison string writing in the arias "Er segnet, die den Herrn fürchten" from the cantata "Der Herr denket an uns," BWV 196, "Doch bin und bleibe ich vergnügt" from "Nach dir, Herr, verlanget mich," BWV 150, or "Mein Seelenschatz ist Gottes Wort" from "Gleichwie der Regen und Schnee vom Himmel fällt," BWV 18, reminds one of an organist drawing several stops on a single keyboard to produce a distinctive tone. In "Nur jedem das Seine," BWV 163, the closing chorale in *simplice stylo* greatly resembles the sparse notation of "Wer nur den lieben Gott läßt walten," BWV 690a, and other figured-bass chorale harmonizations jotted down by Bach's organ students Johann Tobias and Johann Ludwig Krebs. And the affected echo passages in the final choruses "Israel, hoffe auf den Herrn" from the cantata "Aus der Tiefen rufe ich, Herr, zu dir," BWV 131, "Glorie, Lob, Ehr und Herrlichkeit" from "Gottes Zeit ist die allerbeste Zeit" BWV 106, or "Das neue Regiment" from BWV 71 are reminiscent of the rapid alternation between *forte* and *piano* manuals in the closing variations of the chorale partitas "Ach, was soll ich Sünder machen," BWV 770, and "O Gott, du frommer Gott," BWV 767.

The thematic similarities between the Fugue in A major, BWV 536/2, and the opening instrumental fugue of the cantata "Tritt auf die Glaubensbahn," BWV 152, and between the Fugue in G major, BWV 541/2, and the fugue of the opening chorus of the cantata "Ich hatte viel Bekümmernis," BWV 21, have been noted frequently. Whether or not these represent direct borrowings, they point to Bach's way of thinking in the early cantatas—that organ motives can provide a rich store of melodic invention for vocal works. The generic source for the "Ich hatte viel Bekümmernis" theme, for example, can be found in the playful *repercussio* figures that were highly popular among North German organists. One can see a logical—if astonishing—progression from Buxtehude's Praeludium in G minor, BuxWV 148, to Bach's Toccata in E major, BWV 566, to the cantata BWV 21:

Fragment of the second part of the cantata "Gott ist mein König," BWV 71,
with obbligato organ beginning in measure 7.
(Bach's autograph.)

Buxtehude, Praeludium in G minor, BuxWV 148:

Bach, Toccata in E major, BWV 566:

Bach, "Ich hatte viel Bekümmernis," BWV 21, opening chorus:

Bach also appropriated the *suspirans* rhythmic motive ♪♫, that appears ubiquitously in his early chorale partitas, chorale preludes, and free organ works, where he commonly uses it to create rhythmic incisiveness in dense, contrapuntal passages. The *suspirans*-laced texture of the Variatio section of "Als Jesus Christus in der Nacht," BWV 1108, from the Neumeister Collection, is mirrored, for instance, in the violin writing of Verse 1 of the cantata "Christ lag in Todesbanden," BWV 4:

Bach, "Als Jesus Cristus in der Nacht," BWV 1108:

Bach, "Christ lag in Todesbanden," BWV 4, Verse 1, violins and continuo:

In keyboard works the *suspirans* commonly assumed the guise of a leaping bass figure. Buxtehude, for example, used such a motive in the dramatic opening of his organ Prealudium in C major, BuxWV 137. Here, too, we can follow Bach trying out a well-established keyboard motive in his early organ works—the chorale prelude "Herzlich lieb hab ich dich, O Herr," BWV 1115, to take one example—before utilizing it in his early cantata writing, as he does in the aria "Wer bist du?" from "Bereitet die Wege, bereitet die Bahn," BWV 132:

Buxtehude, Praeludium in C major, BuxWV 137:

Bach, "Herzlich lieb hab ich dich, O Herr," BWV 1115:

Bach, "Bereitet die Wege, bereitet die Bahn," BWV 132, 3rd movement, "Wer bist du?":

The *corta* rhythmic motive ♪♫, that pervades Bach's youthful organ and clavier music (we find it in abundance in the Capriccio "sopra la lontananza del fratello dilettissimo" of 1704 or the Passacaglia in C minor, BWV 582, of a few years later) surfaces repeatedly in the Mühlhausen cantatas, in pieces such as the aria "Er segnet, die den Herrn fürchten" from the cantata BWV 196, the duet "So du willst, Herr, Sünde zu rechnen" from BWV 131, or the chorus "Glorie, Lob, Ehr und Herrlichkeit" from BWV 106.

Besides providing a ready supply of thematic and motivic ideas, organ music armed Bach with procedures for elaborating material. Consider the quasi-ostinato variation, for instance, in which an ostinato-like bass is repeated, with some alterations here and there, under a chorale tune. We find it, as we might expect, in Bach's chorale partitas, in "O Gott, du frommer Gott" (Partita II) and "Sei gegrüsset, Jesu gütig" (Variation I). But it also crops up in the early cantatas, where Bach employs it in cantus firmus arias such as "Ich bin nun achtzig Jahr" from the cantata BWV 71 and "So du willst, Herr" from BWV 131. Another traditional keyboard method of varying a chorale called for surrounding or decorating the melody with a rapid, running treble figure, as in the opening of "Gott ist mein Heil, mein Hilf und Trost," BWV 1106, from the Neumeister Collection or Partita IV of "O Gott, du frommer Gott." Bach utilized this technique in his early cantatas, too, in Verse III of the cantata BWV 4, for instance.

Perhaps the most important procedure Bach adopted from the keyboard is the *permutation fugue*. The permutation fugue is so named because the voices enter in canon-like fashion, with two or three countersubjects appearing after the main theme, as beads on a string, in each voice. After the initial exposition, the order of entries can be altered, and the entire structure can be transposed to another key, in order to produce different permutations of the original material. The result is a tightly constructed— if somewhat mechanical—fugue. The permutation fugue was Bach's own invention, a remarkably innovative approach to strict counterpoint that he first worked out in early keyboard pieces such as the Corelli and Legrenzi fugues and the Reinken transcriptions and then brought to a high degree of refinement in the Fugue in G minor, BWV 568, the Passacaglia in C minor, BWV 568, and other ambitious works.

In the early cantatas the permutation fugue is perhaps the most conspicuous and consistent sign of Bach's hand. We find it repeatedly, in choruses from Mühlhausen ("Dein Alter sei wie deine Jugend" and "Muss täglich von neunen" from the cantata BWV 71 or "Und er wird Israel" from BWV 131) and Weimar ("Daß er meines Angesichtes Hülfe" and "Lob, und Ehre, und Preis, und Gewalt" from the cantata BWV 21 or "So lasset uns gehen in Salem der Freuden" from "Himmelskönig, sei willkommen," BWV 182). In these concerted works Bach often enhanced the permutation fugue through additive scoring, writing the first exposition for voices and continuo alone and then gradually introducing the instruments one by one in a second long exposition. Most significantly, during the pre-Leipzig years he frequently employed the permutation fugue to bring his vocal compositions to a climactic close (the cantatas BWV 21, 71, 131, 182, and others). In so doing he appropriated not just the technique but also the design of the large organ preludes and fugues that had first brought him fame.

Finally, it was probably organ music that helped define the difference between the Mühlhausen cantatas on the one hand and the Weimar and Cöthen cantatas on the other. The later works, in addition to showing a distinct shift from North German to Italian models, display a far greater mastery of part-writing and counterpoint. Between 1708, the year Bach left Mühlhausen, and 1714, the year he became concertmaster in Weimar, his skill as a vocal composer grew considerably. Yet only a handful of vocal pieces seem to date from that six-year period. How do we explain the change?

One suspects that the innovative organ projects of the initial Weimar years served as a testing ground for ideas and idioms that blossomed on a grander scale in the concerted vocal music that Bach wrote as concertmaster in Weimar and Kapellmeister in Cöthen. It was Bach the organist, then, that paved the way for Bach the cantata composer.

Detail of the organ clavier on which Bach played in Arnstadt (Bach Museum, Arnstadt).

6

BACH THE COMPOSER

Hans-Joachim Schulze

In his 1802 biography of Bach, Johann Nikolaus Forkel retells an anecdote in which Bach had already during his Weimar period (1708–17), developed such an exceptional proficiency in sight reading at the clavier that he considered himself capable of giving a faultless rendition on his first attempt of anything that was put in front of him. It took a friend to change his mind. As if by chance he handed Bach a specially prepared piece that contained an unplayable passage, at which point Bach duly got stuck. In spite of this one failure, Bach remains renowned for his incomparable ability to play at sight. Apparently this also applied to performing ensemble music on the clavier, whether from a score or from individual parts arrayed next to one another.

These kinds of achievements require not only a highly developed playing technique, but also a thorough knowledge of composition. The biographical accounts give only vague information on when, where, and from whom Bach may have acquired this ability. The few indications that are available point to self-education, combined with singular talent that was developed early on. His models for composition were North German masters like Reinken, Buxtehude, Bruhns, and Böhm, as well as some French organists, and also Froberger, Kerll, Pachelbel, Frescobaldi, and others from Central and South Germany. Bach's encounters with creations by other composers was often limited early on to his merely receiving the written music. This applies in particular to music from Italy, for he never had the privilege of traveling in that country. Everything else he could become thoroughly familiar with in context: music by organists and cantors in Eisenach, Ohrdruf, and Lüneburg, the French manner of court music in Celle, the prestigious polyphonic organ playing by Reinken at the Katharinenkirche (St. Catherine's) in Hamburg, and the *Abendmusiken* staged by Dietrich Buxtehude at the Marienkirche (St. Mary's Church) in Lübeck. We do not know when and how Bach decided to emulate these examples, not only as a keyboard virtuoso but also as a composer in his own right.

Family tradition places his first attempts at composing during his time in Arnstadt (1703–7). It remains uncertain if this was limited exclusively to works for the organ and the clavier. Nothing has been reported about compositions for ensemble or his writing cantatas. His appointment as organist in Arnstadt did not obligate him to do so, and therefore the young Bach declined to participate in any performances of vocal music. Whether this attitude advanced his work as a composer of vocal-instrumental church music remains to be seen.

In any event, Bach must have thought better of it by the time he moved from Arnstadt to Mühlhausen. Although his certificate of appointment in Mühlhausen did not mention anything either about performing or writing cantatas, it did not prevent Bach, now twenty-three years old, from indulging in such activities. In the space of just one year he amassed a highly valuable—but unfortunately lost—collection of works by other composers and enlarged it with some few but masterly contributions of his own. As far as we know, they were all written for special events: a wedding ceremony (BWV 196), a funeral service (BWV 106), a town council election (BWV 71), an unspecified commission from pastor Georg Christian Eilmar (BWV 131). We do not know what induced Bach to align himself with the stylistic development of the late seventeenth century by writing these compositions— including the original version of the Easter cantata BWV 4, which also belongs in this category—and to ignore the trend of using recitatives and da capo arias. It is unlikely that he would of his own accord have tried to swim against the tide. More probably he was following the advice or carrying out the orders of his superiors in Mühlhausen in conforming to the musical traditions of his predecessors. In contrast to his lack of discipline, which was criticized in Arnstadt—mostly his improvised organ playing, which was now too long, now too short, and full of capricious harmony when accompanying the congregation's singing—his Mühlhausen cantatas show a perfect mastery of form and composition. The filigree pattern of chamber music goes hand in hand with the exuberant magnificence of the polychoral style—perhaps following the example of Buxtehude's concerts in Lübeck—and alongside the smaller dimensioned texted motets one also finds large-scale homogeneous chorale elaborations. Bach's sure treatment of fugues with more than one theme is a notable feature of his Mühlhausen cantatas, particularly in the fugue form—developed in Hamburg around 1680—in which four or more voices imitate each other, taking into account the systematic register changes of contrapuntal lines (also referred to in more recent times as a *permutation fugue*).

The decisive factor for Bach's move to Weimar after only one year may have been that the job of organist at St. Blasius's in Mühlhausen did not offer him a basis for planning his life and creative activities in the long term. Regular cantata performances were apparently out of the question in Mühlhausen, so there was no call for writing a repertory of cantatas. True,

Pastor Georg Christian Eilmar.

this situation did not change when he first took over the position of court organist in Weimar. As far as we know, Bach directed his attention initially to refining his skills at playing the organ and improving his writing of organ music. Indeed, there are no extant vocal works from the period 1708 to 1711, and only sporadic ones from 1711 to 1714. These include the Hunting Cantata, BWV 208, the motet "Ich lasse dich nicht, du segnest mich denn," the solo cantatas BWV 199, and—perhaps—BWV 54, the older sections of cantata BWV 21, of which a second or third version was performed in 1714, and possibly one or other earlier version of Weimar cantatas that, in any case, can be traced only to 1714 or even later. We should also add the cantata, unfortunately lost, that Bach performed for his audition in Halle on the second Sunday of Advent 1713 and that he seems to have composed on the spot and without any preparation.

Although so little has survived from the period between June 1708 and February 1714, and regardless of the fact that this was a time when the supply of vocal works was not very large anyway, we must assume, nevertheless, that during these years Bach underwent an astonishing development as a composer. His appointment as concertmaster in Weimar on March 2, 1714, required him to perform a newly written cantata in the castle church every four weeks. This made him draw on his abundant resources immediately and effortlessly, without any apparent hint of having to grow into his new tasks or even to overcome any difficulties. On the contrary, thanks to the inexhaustible abundance of his inventive talent, his secure sense of form, and his superior skill, he created a repertory of astonishing variety within the space of just three years that demonstrates both a musician's verve and a depth of textual exegesis. Once again, we cannot tell whether the great diversity he demonstrated here was aided by an unprecedented concentration on the genre of the church cantata, that is, whether Bach the organist had to defer to Bach the concertmaster and cantata composer. Still, we should not forget that Bach's oeuvre lacks certain genres altogether, such as opera, which had caused a sensation of the first order in Europe. Bach had regarded opera with benevolent tolerance during his time in Leipzig—and maybe even when he visited Hamburg around 1700–1702—but had not made any personal contributions. Similarly, his creative work includes few, if any, odes and songs, Italian solo cantatas, sinfonias, virtuoso concertos with a spectacular solo part and easy-to-play accompaniment, chamber music for popular ensemble combinations, and clavier pieces "à l'usage des dames" (for use by ladies).

Bach probably found it relatively easy to do without compositions of this kind. Writing music as a daily routine was not at all to his liking. In this respect, his charge at Weimar, requiring one cantata per month, offered favorable conditions for him to reach and maintain a high level of quality. If Bach had intended to combine this activity with eventually putting together a complete annual cantata cycle, the unpleasant termination of his stay in Weimar thwarted these plans. The "annual cycle of Weimar cantatas" would remain as incomplete as the set of organ chorales in the *Orgel-Büchlein*. Many other projects were to follow this path later on.

The move from Weimar to Cöthen signified a new orientation for Bach as both composer and virtuoso. He gave up the profession of organist for good, and the composition of church cantatas, to which he had devoted much of his energies for at least three years, played only a minor role thereafter. Concertos, chamber music, and works for clavier came to the fore at this point, with an occasional cantata thrown in as a tribute to some member of the princely family of Anhalt-Cöthen, fashioned, as it turned out, more like chamber music both in scoring and compositional style.

His tour to Hamburg for guest performances in the autumn of 1720—no matter whether or not he seriously considered applying for a job playing the Schnitger organ in the Jakobikirche (St. Jacobi's)—gave him the opportunity to fall back once more on the output of his Weimar years. Bach attracted much attention as an organ virtuoso and earned praise for an extensive, if somewhat old-fashioned improvisation from Jan Adam Reinken, nearly one hundred years old but still the leading organist at St. Catharine's. His colorful but also heterogeneous cantata "Ich hatte viel Bekümmernis" was, nevertheless, much misunderstood. Recognized as a virtuoso but misunderstood as a composer—that was a situation Bach often had to put up with both then and later in his career. This is partly explained by the fact that, in the unanimous opinion of his contemporaries, Bach was an unequaled interpreter of his own work—by chance, not out of necessity—but that for his ensemble works, especially the cantatas, he rarely had performers at his command who were able to translate his intentions. His compositions were a challenge—true in his day as well as in ours.

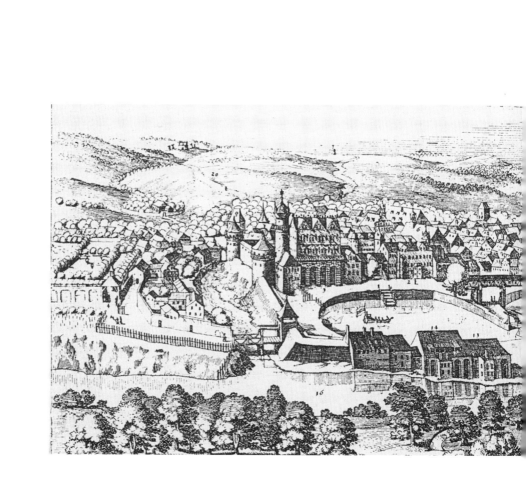

II

THE WORKS AND THEIR WORLD

View of the town and castle of Weimar; detail, engraving by Merian, circa 1650.

Erdmann Neumeister; copper engraving by C. Fritzsch.

7

POETRY AND POETS

Hans-Joachim Schulze

From our current perspective the "Bach cantata" is associated with a mixed textual form consisting of quotations from the Bible, chorale verses, and free poetry in the shape of both recitative and (da capo) aria. At present, a definitive statement on the origins of this more or less classical text model is not possible. However, the authorship of the church cantatas that were written in free text and limited to recitatives and arias can be attributed to Erdmann Neumeister, who later became chief pastor in Hamburg. Neumeister (1671–1756), who at that time was a clergyman in Eckartsberga near Naumburg-Saale, began in 1700 to provide the court chapel at Weissenfels with sacred poetry for every Sunday and feast day. This was all then set to music by the Hofkapellmeister in charge, Johann Philipp Krieger (1649–1725). Four years later, having meanwhile been appointed minister of the church at Weissenfels, he was able to arrange for a reprint of his librettos under the title *Geistliche Cantaten statt einer Kirchen-Music* (Sacred cantatas instead of church music). A preface added to this new edition tells us the reason for these poems and their appearance: Neumeister wanted the essential contents of his private meditation after each of his Sunday sermons to appear in the shape of rhymed verse and, at the instigation of several artists and music lovers, to have the result published—"sometimes odes, sometimes poetic oratorios, and, furthermore, present-day cantatas too." In his opinion a "cantata" looked no different from a piece of an opera, assembled in "the style of recitative and aria." Iambic meter could not be used exclusively, although it would have been preferable, and as far as the length of the verses and rhyme scheme were concerned, the same freedom applied as in a madrigal. Arias were to contain one to three strophes and, if possible, one affect, a "moral," or something else of a special nature. An excellent musical effect could be obtained by coming back to the first part at the conclusion of the aria.

The roots of this so-called "madrigal cantata" go far back into the seventeenth century. Caspar Ziegler (1621–1690), a theologian at Leipzig and later a councilor of the court of appeal and a council member at Wittenberg, should be mentioned in this respect because of his epoch-making treatise *Von den Madrigalen, Einer schönen und zur Musik bequemsten Art Verse* (About madrigals, a wonderful and musically most fitting type of verse; Leipzig, 1653), which was warmly welcomed by Heinrich Schütz. This method of writing, as outlined in the treatise, had in the meantime earned great respect. An early attempt was made by Constantin Christian Dedekind (1628–1715), a pupil of Christoph Bernhard in Dresden, to use it for spiritual matters and to link it with the sequence of recitative and aria. This is shown by the ten cantata texts he published in 1670 as a supplement to his *Neue geistliche Schauspiele* (New spiritual plays). Probably Dedekind was ahead of his time with this ambitious poetry, since his efforts apparently drew no response. David Elias Heidenreich (1638–1688) was more successful with his *Geistliche Oden auf die fürnehmsten Feste und alle Sonntage des gantzen Jahres* (Spiritual odes for the most important feasts and all Sundays in the entire year), printed in 1665 at Halle (Saale). Samples of these texts were set to music by David Pohle, Sebastian Knüpfer, Johann Schelle, and others. By mixing biblical text with free poetry, Heidenreich's textual model—modest in its literary pretensions—aimed at what is nowadays commonly called a "concerto-aria cantata," which can be set to music as a large-scale concerto and solo (strophic) aria. What we have here is, apparently, a Protestant "counterproject" to similar compositions in the Roman Catholic tradition that had become familiar in and around the Dresden court, thanks to the students of Giacomo Carissimi. The "concerto-aria cantata" held the stage for several decades. However, the influence of German and, more particularly, Italian opera, as well as, presumably, the Italian and French chamber cantata, gradually marked a change. And it is certainly no coincidence that Erdmann Neumeister, specifically, played such a leading role toward the end of the seventeenth century in bringing about a new ideal of form. In those crucial years

Title page of Erdmann Neumeister's Fünffache Kirchenandachten *(Fivefold church devotions)*.

Neumeister worked in the central German region encompassing Leipzig, Weissenfels, and Naumburg that had become famous for its opera performances. He therefore had a perfect fertile soil for his innovations. In all likelihood his endeavors were supported by the Duke of Weissenfels, Johann Georg (1677–1712).

This stimulus (referred to at the beginning of the chapter), which began at Weissenfels, must have been taken up in the surrounding area and been developed still further. Thus, funeral music by Georg Österreich (1664–1735) that was performed at the end of 1702 for the interment of Duke Friedrich IV (who resided at Gottorf Castle near Schleswig) contained both chorale verses and biblical texts, as well as strophic arias and recitatives. Dietrich Buxtehude's text for his "Castrum Doloris," one of the two "extra-ordinary" *Abendmusiken* performed in Lübeck at the end of 1705, features recitatives, multi-strophic arias, and chorale verses. A complete annual volume of cantata librettos in the "mixed textual form," which became customary from then on, was already brought out in 1703, in Meiningen. The form combines Bible quotations, a chorale verse, recitatives, and arias. Cantata texts from this successful and frequently reprinted collection were set to music in 1705 by Georg Caspar Schürmann (1672/73–1751), later also by Johann Ludwig Bach (1677–1731) and, in 1726, even by Johann Sebastian Bach. Maximilian Dietrich Freisslich (1663–1731) in Danzig (in a text volume for 1708–09), Friedrich Wilhelm Zachow (1663–1712) in Halle, and others all made occasional or constant use of this newly developed form. A remarkable exception was Johann Kuhnau (1660–1722), cantor at the Thomas-Schule (St. Thomas's School) in Leipzig, who declared his intention—in the preface of a collection of texts for church music, printed in 1709—to dispense this time with recitatives and arias, and therefore with the madrigal style, and so avoid any suspicion of getting too close to theatrical music.

We do not know to what extent the "collection of the most select church pieces," compiled by Bach up to 1708, reflected the latest development in the realm of cantata librettos. His own compositions, insofar as they belong definitely or probably to the period leading up to 1708, do not show any traces of the modern method of writing. Rather, they follow older models from the seventeenth century, with their restriction to one Lutheran chorale for all movements (BWV 4), their concentration on a Psalm text (BWV 196), and their combination of a biblical quotation with a chorale verse (BWV 131 and, according to a traditional "formula," BWV 106) or with a simple aria composition and a chorale verse (BWV 71) or without the latter (BWV 150).

We do not yet know if Bach's approach of going back to the past was his own idea or resulted from special practices in Mühlhausen or even specific orders.

Recitatives and arias of the madrigal type do not appear in Bach's work until he came to Weimar. An early example can be found in the Hunting Cantata, BWV 208, from around 1712 or 1713, a musical tribute to Duke Christian of Saxe-Weissenfels to a text by Salomon Franck (1659–1725), first secretary of the council in Weimar. The solo cantatas BWV 54 and 199 can be traced back to a volume printed in 1711 (*Gottgefälliges Kirchen-Opffer*) and originally intended for Christoph Graupner in Darmstadt, from the pen of Georg Christian Lehms (1684–1717), born in Silesia, who worked in Darmstadt until his early death. The former—probably written before 1715—with its sequence of aria-recitative-aria, follows the type created by Erdmann Neumeister; the latter (around 1712 or 1713) also includes a chorale verse.

In 1711 Erdmann Neumeister also endorsed the "mixed" textual form, which had been established no later than 1704, with a volume of texts that was printed in 1711 at Gotha for Georg Philipp Telemann in Eisenach. The cantata BWV 18, possibly written before 1714, harks back to this. Another volume intended for Telemann, this one printed in 1714 in Frankfurt-am-Main, provides the text for the cantata BWV 61. On the whole, Neumeister, whom Telemann referred to in a letter at the end of 1714 as "the most famous and only good poet in sacred matters," is relatively underrepresented in Bach's cantatas.

One need not explain Bach's falling back mainly on the creations of the "competent" librettist Salomon Franck when he "officially" began to produce cantatas in 1714. Franck's volume *Evangelisches Andachts-Opffer* (Weimar, 1715), containing a one-year cycle, is featured prominently in Bach's extant Weimar cantatas, with their combination of recitative, aria, and chorale verse (BWV 31, 80a, 155, 161, 162, 163, 165, and 185). In two other cases there is no chorale text (BWV 132, 152). We cannot say yet whether three texts dating from the first half of 1714, containing a biblical text, arias, and a chorale verse (BWV 182, 12, and 172), are connected with Franck. The classification of the large-scale cantata BWV 21, performed in June 1714 and demonstrably originating from heterogeneous material, is simularly uncertain. This is the only one dating back to Bach's pre-Leipzig days that shows all four imaginable components of the "mixed textual form," except for the two Neumeister examples, BWV 18 and 61, and the

Title page of Salomon Franck's Evangelische Sonn- und Fest-Tages-
Andachten *(Protestant devotions for Sundays and feast days).*

cantata BWV 143, which is surrounded in controversy concerning its authenticity and chronological order.

Unlike what he had done in his 1715 volume, Franck abandoned both recitative and biblical quotation in his *Evangelische Sonn- und Fest-Tages-Andachten* (Protestant devotions for Sundays and feast days, printed in 1717 but possibly ready by the end of 1716), stringing together only aria verses and a closing chorale. Cantatas BWV 70a, 186a, and 147a, which have survived in only a more extensive version from Bach's time in Leipzig (BWV 70, 186, 147), belong to this volume of texts.

The text of the Christmas cantata BWV 63 points to an origin in Halle (Saale). Its considerable resemblance to a cantata for the Reformation cele-brations in 1717, with words by the local chief pastor Johann Michael Heineccius (1674–1722) and music by Gottfried Kirchhoff (1685–1746), musical director of the Marktkirche, suggests a close but by no means inter-dependent connection. Perhaps both surviving versions are based on a lost original model. Neither the version composed by Bach nor the one attrib-uted to Kirchhoff contains a biblical quotation or chorale verse, so this tex-tual example follows entirely the model introduced in 1700 by Erdmann Neumeister.

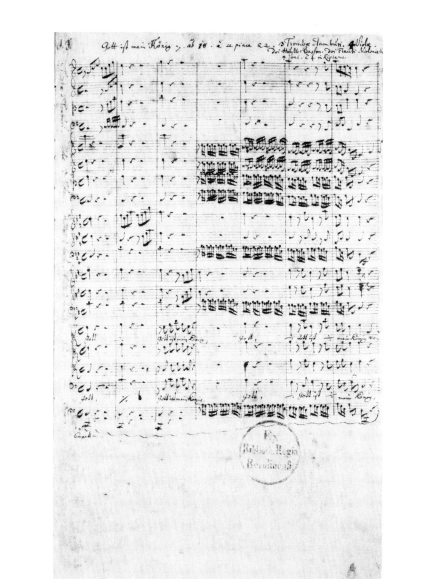

Cantata "Gott ist mein König," BWV 71, opening chorus. (Bach's autograph)

8

LITURGICAL AND THEOLOGICAL ASPECTS

Martin Petzoldt

Of Bach's output in Arnstadt and Mühlhausen, we know the cantatas BWV 4, 71, 106, 131, 150, 196, and the fragment BWV 223. Their texts have one characteristic feature in common: they consist essentially of biblical quotations and hymn verses or similar material. Bach's special treatment of the text shows in the way his compositions follow an individual structuring of the text that does not simply correspond with the text's own structure. Often, the result is a new symmetry in the libretto (and also in the music), which, at the same time, makes it easier to discover the theological approach to the texts. What these cantatas also have in common is that, except for BWV 4 and 71, the purpose for which they were written is not recorded. This lack of information tended to limit regular subsequent performances. Moreover, there are pieces of madrigal text in BWV 71 and 150. Besides, BWV 71 is a sacred work for a political municipal occasion, yet at the time it was written, BWV 71 also received a *de tempore* (one-time) designation.[1]

From a theological point of view, it is important to look at the structure of the libretto throughout the composition, since that will show to which phrases Bach gave special emphasis. Contemporary theology confirms the stress on certain meanings, even if there are often other unmistakable emphases, very likely by the composer himself. We cannot demonstrate this piece by piece, but it is important to examine in some detail the structure of these early cantatas, since they signal preliminary decisions that may shed further light on Bach's handling of his cantata texts.

BWV 4, "Christ lag in Todesbanden" (Christ lay in the bonds of death), which was written as a cantata "per omnes versus," uses Martin Luther's Easter hymn of 1524 in full. Bach arranges the seven stanzas, by means of compositional techniques and musical genres, symmetrically around verse 4. This seems unavoidable, considering the number of verses, but might be questionable because of the short introductory sinfonia.

verse 4 (chorus)

verse 3 (aria)   verse 5 (aria)

verse 2 (duet)   verse 6 (duet)

verse 1 (chorus)   verse 7 (chorus)

sinfonia

The zenith of the composition is undoubtedly reached in verse 4 ("Es war ein wunderlicher Krieg" [There was a wondrous war]), a movement extremely frugal in tone and economically set to music, without instruments, supported only by the accompanying continuo. This increases the impact of the text in an unusual way and gives it a special emphasis: Christ reveals himself as the risen one not only to the world of the living, but also to the world of the dead. This revelation is particularly significant, since Christ's resurrection begins with the defeat of death itself (which, for that matter, also formed part of contemporary Lutheran dogma). This central movement is framed by verses 3 and 5 (movements 4 and 6) with references to the Old and New Testaments that identify Christ as the Easter Lamb. Verses 1 and 2 (movements 2 and 3), within such a structure of crucial testimony, lead to the notion that Christ is the life, whereas verses 6 and 7 glorify the preservation of life with light (the sun) and food (bread, word).

The same can be said of those cantatas in which the text is based only on biblical quotations (BWV 196) or on both biblical quotations and hymn stanzas (BWV 106[2] and 131), although each of them has its own special structure. BWV 106 is built quite differently but can be compared structurally with the cantata BWV 4, for its libretto also relies on a relationship between biblical passages.[3] The second movement ("Es ist der alte Bund"/"Ja, komm, Herr Jesu" [It is the decree of old/O come, Lord Jesus]) produces the high point of its textual development, a movement that brings two different elements into an interesting dialogue (Apocrypha, Sirach 14:17 for the chorus, Rev. 22: 20 for the soprano solo), yet adds a third element with the chorale "Ich hab mein Sach Gott heimgestellt" (I have put my things in God's hands), heralded by instruments, where the actual text is not specifically given but will be associated in the listener's mind. Bach continues this practice, especially in his Weimar cantatas. The hymn used here had eighteen verses in hymn books of the time and enjoyed an immense popularity. The textual context created thereby helps particularly in moving along the special character of movement 2. The added instrumental line (and its text!) not only replaces Olearius's quotation from Phil. 1: 23: "Ich habe Lust abzuscheiden und bei Christus zu sein" (My desire is to depart and be with Christ)—a declaration that helps the dying person concentrate on Christ—but also furthers the dialogue between the other two texts. It is important

Martin Luther; after a portrait by
Lucas Cranach, 1521.

that in the musical treatment of the three text layers, the chorale verse and the Sirach quotation come together explicitly in only one place, i.e., in the last part of the chorale (mm. 173ff.). Otherwise, the text from Revelation 22: 20 corresponds totally (except for a few small changes) with the chorale verse. If one looks at all verses of this hymn, it seems that only verse 17 is suitable as a comparable aid for Christological concentration.[4] The emerging textual combination produces the following interpretive text correspondences (the text of the presumed strophe 17 is given in square brackets):

Measure	Text Correspondences
131/2	Es ist der alte Bund, Mensch, du mußt sterben,
	It is the decree of old: man, you must die,
145/4	Ja, komm, Herr Jesu,
	O come, Lord Jesus,
150/4	[O Jesu Christe Gottes Sohn,]
	[*O Jesus Christ, son of God,*]
	Ja, ja, Herr Jesu, komm, ja, ja,
153/2	[Der du für uns,]
	Ja, komm, Herr Jesu, komm, Herr Jesu, komm,
154/4	[Der du für uns hast gnug getan.]
	[*You who have done enough for us.*]
	Es ist der alte Bund,
	Mensch, du mußt
	sterben,
161/3	Mensch, du mußt sterben,
	Ja komm, Herr Jesu, komm, komm, Herr Jesu, ja komm,
165/4	[Ach schleuß . . . . mich in die Wunden dein]
	[*O pull me into your wounds*]
	Herr Jesu, komm, ja komm, Herr Jesu,
167/3	Mensch, du mußt sterben,
	Ja, ja, Herr Jesu, komm,
170/4	[Du bist allein]
	[*You alone are*]
	Herr Jesu, komm, ja, ja komm, Herr Jesu,
173/4	[Der einge Trost und helfer mein.]
	[*my only comfort and helper.*]
	Es ist der alte Bund, Mensch, du mußt sterben,
180/1	Mensch, du mußt ster - - - - - - - - - - ben.
	Ja, komm, Herr Jesu, Herr Jesu!

We find a completely different arrangement in BWV 131. Two stanzas, numbers 2 and 5, from Bartholomäus Ringwald's eight-stanza hymn "Herr Jesu

Christ, du höchstes Gut" (1588)—based on Psalm 51—are added, in a dialogue manner, as tropes, to the unabridged Psalm 130, which forms the basis of the work. This allows the structure of the cantata text to maintain a clearly defined, symmetrical outline. The text also reveals the extent of its theological depth if one considers this model of inner biblical interpretation as a metatext. It is identical to Psalms 51 and 130 and to the Gospel lessons for the 11th Sunday after Trinity, the Parable of the Pharisee and the Publican (Luke 18: 9–14). Johann Olearius transmits this model: referring to Luke 18: 13, man should "repeat daily these five words 1. God 2. show 3. me 4. a sinner 5. mercy/ . . . according to the instructions of the five main chapters of the catechism. . . and remember thus not only sin/but also the righteousness of Christ."[5] Each of these five words stands for one of the chapters of Luther's catechism, so that the musical composition of Bach's cantatas more or less follows the order of this catechism. The postscript to this cantata in Bach's own hand, "composed at the request of Dr. Georg Christian Eilmar," would hardly have related only to the text, in itself rather lacking in originiality, but, much more likely, to the metatext referred to above, the instruction for confession and repentance in accordance with the chapters of the catechism.

Verses from Psalm 74 used in stanzas 1, 4, and 6 form the essential backbone for the overall text of BWV 71, moving along at three levels:
- God rules from ages past (movement 1: chorus);
- the old (both in age and in terms of office) mayor has the limits of his power laid down for him (movement 4: bass);
- the protection of the people is in God's hand alone (movement 6: chorus).

These three levels are presented with a sense of doubt and consolidation (movements 2 and 3), acknowledgment of God's power (movement 5), and good wishes (movement 7), which must have stirred the old—and at the same time new—mayor in connection with his renewed assumption of office.[6]

This still leaves us with the cantatas BWV 150 and 223. In BWV 150, the sequence of six text sections presents nothing other than a succession of selected verses from Psalm 25 (movements 2, 4, and 6). In accordance with the method of interpreting the Bible through concordances,[7] the verses are explained by means of other material (movements 3 and 5) and lead up to a large-scale chaconne (movement 7). Movements 3 and 5 form a framework around movement 4,[8] which thus becomes the zenith of the work's development. The chaconne text unmistakably serves the same purpose as the

Fragment from the cantata "Aus der Tiefen rufe ich, Herr, zu dir," BWV 131. (Bach's autograph.)

closing chorale of a cantata, namely to tie together the cantata's overall message by using a specific formulation. BWV 223, of which only a fragment survives, is notable for textual reasons: here passages from the Bible are combined that are especially similar to a sermon prepared by Georg Christian Eilmar in 1706 for the Sunday of the Visitation of the Virgin Mary.[9] In his "Praeloquium" (introduction to the sermon) Eilmar quotes from Psalm 103: 1, "Bless the Lord, O my soul," and preaches on the theme "Christians praising God," with special reference to the beginning of the Magnificat in Luke 1: 46: "My soul magnifies the Lord, and my spirit rejoices in God my Savior." Eilmar concludes his homily with a reference to Psalm 150. After an unknown choral movement, the text that Bach set to music begins with the words "My soul should praise God, for that is very good," a combination of Psalm 103: 1 and Luke 1: 46, and ends with a closing movement to the text "Let everything that breathes praise the Lord!" (Psalm 150: 6). Unfortunately, it is impossible to say anything specific about the textual structure of the whole work. However, the fragment of the BWV 223 text seems to point to a theme that can be identified in theological terms and hints at the purpose of the cantata, which, alas, is no longer complete.

An overview of Bach's sacred cantatas from his pre-Weimar period yields the following specific characteristics:

- an orientation of the text overall toward a pre-existent textual structure that has its origins in the Bible or in hymns;
- a structuring (or restructuring) of the libretto by means of a musical treatment that clearly stresses certain connected meanings, perhaps against the background of a metatext (BWV 131);[10]
- the beginning of the custom of introducing hymn melodies or hymn verses for the purpose of dialogue (applicable both to the way special hymn verses were adapted and to the way textless chorale quotations were introduced);
- cantata endings that are not yet defined, musically or textually, by the "closing chorale" that was so typical for Bach in later years with its function of summing up the homily—in fact, the ending is shaped more like Handel's texts, with the close as either a concluding text formula or a fugue);
- a tendency to build up the cantatas symmetrically.

These features give the earliest cantatas a characteristic that sets them apart from the works written at Weimar and Leipzig. But a theological look at Bach's early librettos and the way they were set to music already establishes the essential traits of his relation to this important foundation of his art and his connection with it.

The Texts of the Weimar Cantatas

The order that Bach received on March 2, 1714, in Weimar "to perform new works monthly" (*Dok* II, 66) is our first real opportunity to speak of Bach's Weimar cantatas. During the period from 1708 and March 1714, the only works we can name are the motet "Ich lasse dich nicht, du segnest mich denn" (BWV Anh. 159) and Reinhard Keiser's *St. Mark Passion*. One can add, with some reservations, three cantata compositions that can be dated to the year 1713, at the earliest, and an unknown cantata that Bach performed at Halle on the second Sunday of Advent in connection with his application for the post of organist at the Marktkirche:

Cantata	Title	Sunday	Date	Librettist
BWV 18	Gleichwie der Regen und Schnee vom Himmel fällt	Sexagesima	Feb. 19, 1713	Neumeister
BWV 199	Mein Herze schwimmt im Blut	11th after Trinity	Aug. 27, 1713	Lehms
BWV 21	Ich hatte viel Bekümmernis	Incidental	Oct. 8, 1713	Unknown[11]

None of the text models of these three is in keeping with the so-called Neumeister type of cantata text,[12] since they do not have a regular alternation of two kinds of madrigal texts. The libretto for BWV 18 was first published by Neumeister in 1711 (in Gotha) in an annual volume that Georg Philipp Telemann set to music under the title *Geistliches Singen und Spielen*. The structure of this text differs from any normal form Bach would have been aware of.[13] The beginning, a recitative to a biblical extract (Isaiah 55: 10–11), is followed by a madrigal recitative punctuated by passages from the Litany (four madrigal sections, each followed by four inserted passages from the Litany). Then comes an aria and in closing a verse from a church hymn. Bach adds an opening sinfonia, so that the result is a work in five parts. Theologically the text provides a short discourse, leaning heavily on contemporary religious dogma, on the theme of God's word preached in church from the didactic play *De Ecclesia*, as we would expect on the basis of the Sunday Gospel of the Parable of the Sower. The quotation and dogmatic use of the text in the second movement (Isaiah 55: 10–11) belongs to the usual repertory of this didactic play.[14]

The Liebfrauenkirche (also called Marktkirche) in Halle.

The text for cantata BWV 199, for the 11th Sunday after Trinity, is taken from a volume by Georg Christian Lehms, *Gottgefälliges Kirchen=Opffer* (Darmstadt, 1711). Theologically it offers a clear counter-example to the text by Neumeister mentioned above. Within a context of the characteristic biblical language, we see here affective emphases on certain notions as well as a one-sided, passive view of God (movement 2, recitative; movement 3) that contradicts God's active deeds of reconciliation that are so dominant in the New Testament. While he was in Weimar, Bach set to music only one more text by Lehms (BWV 54) in addition to this one. However, when he went to Leipzig, he turned once more to Lehms's volume (for 1726) and wrote eight additional cantatas but completed each of their texts with a hymn verse.

Movements 2 to 6 and 9 of BWV 21 suggest that this cantata might have had its origins in the funeral music for Aemilie Marie Harress (1665–1713), daughter of the former chancellor Ahasverus Fritsch (1629–1701) in Rudolstadt and widow of a Weimar commission councilor.[15] It would have been performed on October 8, 1713, in the Stadtkirche for the funeral address by Johann Georg Lairitz on the theme of the first part of Psalm 94: 19 (BWV 21, movement 2). Bach also makes liberal use of the other Bible verses that he set to music, Psalm 41: 12 (BWV 21, movement 6; "voritzo dieser Wort in Erwegung der Nahmens-Ehnlichkeit": Harress)[16] and Psalm 116: 7 (BWV 21, movement 9). Regarding Psalm 42: 12, the writer of the funeral address, M. Hebenstreit, reports that this Psalm verse had also been quoted when the dying person was asked the customary questions in connection with her confession.

Until February 1714 Bach had only the occasional opportunity in Weimar to write vocal music, but this situation changed when he was charged with performing new works every four weeks for the services at the court church. The opening is striking in three cantatas that show an impressive uniformity in their structure:

BWV 182	BWV 12	BWV 172
1. Sonata	1. Sinfonia	(instrumental introduction)
2. Chorus Himmelskönig, sei willkommen	2. Chorus Weinen, Klagen, Sorgen, Zagen	1. Chorus Erschallet, ihr Lieder, erklinget ihr Saiten

BWV 182	BWV 12	BWV 172
3. Recitative (bass) Psalm 40: 8–9	3. Recitative (alto) Acts 14: 22	2. Recitative (bass) John 14: 23
4. Aria (bass) Starkes Lieben	4. Aria (alto) Kreuz und Krone	3. Aria (bass) Heiligste Dreifaltigkeit
5. Aria (alto) Leget euch dem Heiland unter	5. Aria (bass) Ich folge Christo nach	4. Aria (tenor) O Seelenparadies
6. Aria (tenor) Jesu, lass durch Wohl und Weh	6. Aria (tenor with instru- mental chorale) Sei getreu, alle Pein	5. Duet (soprano and alto with instrumental chorale) Komm, lass mich nicht länger warten
7. Chorale Jesu, deine Passion	7. Chorale Was Gott tut, das ist wohlgetan	6. Chorale Von Gott kommt mir ein Freudenschein
8. Chorus So lasset uns gehen	-	7. Chorus (repeat movement 1) Erschallet, ihr Lieder

Each instrumental introduction is followed by a large-scale chorus that, taking into account the overall text, meditates in words and music on a theological metaphor: "Arrival of the King of Heaven" (BWV 182), "Lament of the Christians" (BWV 12), and "Dwelling of the spirit" (BWV 172). Supported by a quotation from the Bible, this meditation gets its biblical confirmation in a recitative, which in BWV 182 and 172 is the voice of the risen Christ (therefore the bass) and in BWV 12 the voice of the Church or of Christianity (therefore the alto). The arias that follow unfold a theologically-dogmatic and ethical panorama of the theme, each time in three steps, prompted by the Gospel for the particular Sunday: in BWV 182 (Luke 1: 26–38; Matthew 21: 1–9[17]), the incarnation and the message of the throne of grace (movement 4), belief in man's dedication to Jesus (movement 5), and the imitation of Christ (movement 6); in BWV 12 (John 16: 16–23) the eschatological appearance of the life of Christ (movement 4), imitation of Christ (movement 5), and transience of the cross (movement 6); in BWV 172 (John 14: 23–31), the dwelling of the triune God in the hearts of the believers (movement 3), the spirit of creation as the comforter (movement 4), and responsory love (movement 5). Furthermore, in BWV 12/6 and 172/5, the practice of an introductory chorale melody is taken up, a form of playing spiritually with associations and mystery that forces the listener to reflect and identify. All three cantatas end with a closing chorale—the first time (except for BWV 18) that we see Bach adopting this practice consciously. Still, the use of the undisputed closing chorale of later days does not yet seem to have been established. In BWV 182 the closing chorale is followed by a closing chorus, the text of which refers to the opening movement. In BWV 172 the opening chorus is repeated.

In this way Bach provides an altogether convincing and totally unrestricted prelude to his regular production of cantatas, an artistic, formal, and theological gateway to a great work. It looks as if Bach depended considerably for his texts on the secretary of the council in Weimar, Salomon Franck, who was also employed as court poet. Meanwhile, the fact that Bach also reached for texts written by other poets in his first year seems to have been explained by Franck's tardiness.[18] It is noteworthy that in contrast to the situation in Leipzig, we know all of the poets whose texts were set to music in Weimar, including the texts assigned to Franck.[19] The typical features of Lehms's texts have already been discussed in connection with BWV 199. Neumeister's texts[20] present a decidedly different picture. Characteristically, they frequently incorporate an unchanged verse from the Bible, often interpreted as a message from the Lord (BWV 18, 28, 61), as well as a textual composition in line with a traditional "mental pattern." This is all the more understandable since, in his first edition of texts (1704), Neumeister already draws attention to the origin and provenance of his poetry, i.e., from his preaching activities on Sunday linked to his "devotion." That brings us close to the "metatext" that we mentioned above in connection with Bach's early cantatas in Mühlhausen. Neumeister's poetry is also distinguished by the homiletic method of that time, combining a "simple style" for preaching the faith with an exalted and artistic one, which until then had been used predominantly in wordly matters. Finally, Neumeister introduces a hymn verse in at least one place—not necessarily at the end— a characteristic feature that plays an essential part on the path to developing the basic form of Bach's cantatas in Leipzig.

By contrast, Salomon Franck's cantata poetry, in the 1715 volume of his *Evangelisches Andachts-Opffer*, shows a perfectly regular pattern of alternating arias and recitatives, to which a closing chorale is added. Bach takes the liberty of changing the poet's intended arrangement from time to time by

Title page of Salomon Franck's
"Evangelisches Andachtsopfer".

using an aria text as the basis for a choral movement. In the second annual volume of *Evangelische Sonn- und Fest-Tages-Andachten*, issued in 1717, Franck usually has four arias follow an opening text intended for the chorus and closes with a chorale. In each case, however, Franck's text is also based on a "metatext" that is accessible, although with him this could be seen as more homiletic than dogmatic. BWV 155 can serve as an example. Its format consists of two recitative-and-aria pairs with a completing closing chorale. Franck does not indicate voices for the madrigal parts of the text. This can clearly be traced back to Bach and so includes a theological question decided on by the composer. He assigns movements 1 and 4 to the soprano, movement 2 as a duet to the alto and tenor, and movement 3 to the bass. This decision originated from the text. First of all, Franck provides a libretto filled with biblical references that produce the traditional train of thought for interpreting John 2: 1–11. In a traditional, theological sense Mary is considered the prototype of faith. However, this prototypical example comprises not only the power of faith, but also its weakness or darkness. Against this background a confrontation took place, during the Reformation, with Roman-Catholic Mariology, which saw the Virgin Mary purely as a Queen of Heaven and therefore removed from any worldliness and sin. Luther, on the other hand, emphasized that he would gladly honor

Mary as the mother of Jesus Christ, with the reservation that she should not claim the glory that was due only to Christ. In connection with John 2, Johann Olearius quotes a "Christian poet" in his large, five-volume *Biblische Auslegung* (of which Bach had a copy), who makes a play on words with the idea of "vinum" (wine): "O Mater Christi, num vi deposcere vinum intendis? Christus tempora iusta tenet" (O mother of Christ, you do not aspire to obtain power through wine? Christ determines the appropriate times).[21] Franck's text is influenced throughout by the critical attitude that was therefore taken up against Mary. The train of thought unfolds "when the wine failed." What Mary said (John 2: 3, see the conclusion of movement 1) is explained as a statement of disbelief, for the power of Christ is: "Anything you may be wanting you will find with Me." For to have Christ means to have everything. This defines the mystical composure of movement 2. Franck expresses Mary's disbelief, that is, man's disbelief in general, with a number of *verba defectiva*: concealment, withdrawal, fear, injury, want, falling. The way Bach allocated the voices shows a thorough understanding of Franck's intentions: movements 1 and 4 correspond, on the one hand, in portraying the anxiety and lament of the believing soul (movement 1), and on the other, in recognizing the believing soul (movement 4). Thus the path from movement 1 to movement 4 marks the path of knowledge for the faithful. The believing soul needs encouragement and comfort from a congregation of fellow believers (movement 2), and the word of God (movement 3, written more or less as a message from the Lord, for the bass voice). The closing chorale realizes what is achieved regularly and clearly in the Leipzig cantata texts, i.e., step-by-step identification by the listening congregation of the train of thought from anxiety to recognition, which constitutes the catechistic mission of any declaration of the Christian faith.

The path covered by Bach from his earliest compositions to his works in Weimar in using texts shows a coming to terms with various forms of "meta-textuality" in cantata texts. Bach does not leave the theological intention and interpretation exclusively to the writer. In the Leipzig librettos, whose models we know, this attitude amounted to corrections; it will have to remain a mystery whether textual and theological corrections were made by Bach himself or by an author commissioned by him.

Notes

1. In accordance with an old tradition, the so-called "Ratsstückchen," i.e., the cantata for the council elections, was performed on the Sunday after the election, as religious service music in the Marienkirche (St. Mary's Church). In 1708 this service took place, as usual, on February 4, which was a Saturday. The following day, on February 5, Septuagesima Sunday, the cantata was performed in the Blasiuskirche (St. Blasius's Church).

2. The text of the chorus 2a is a compilation of different passages from the Bible (Psalm 21: 5; Acts 17: 28; James 4: 15; Rev. 14 and 13b, and Prov. 3: 2), whose anticipatory comtemplation creates the interesting title "Gottes Zeit ist die allerbeste Zeit" (God's time is the very best time).

3. Renate Steiger, "J.S. Bachs Gebetbuch? Ein Fund am Rande einer Ausstellung," in: *Musik und Kirche* 55 (1985): 231–34.

4. Alfred Dürr, in *Die Kantaten von Johann Sebastian Bach*, 5th ed. (Munich-Kassel, 1985), p. 837, notes a striking parallel between the cantata text and the overall hymn text.

5. Johann Gottfried Olearius, *Biblische Erklärung*, vol. 5 (Leipzig, 1681), col. 532b.

6. Adolf Strecker, born June 15, 1624, became councilor in Mühlhausen in 1669; in 1695 he became mayor for the first time and in 1708, at the age of 83, for the fifth time. He died in the same year, on September 13. He probably wondered aloud if he should make himself available again at his age, which may have been a subject of public discussion.

7. Preliminary critical methods of interpreting the Bible, whereby the formal principle of self-explanation of the Scriptures (passages traceable through concordances are called upon primarily for a certain theme) and the material priciple of everything being related to Christ prevails in all statements.

8. The rhyming structure of stanzas 3 and 5 correspond with each other in reverse.

9. *Neuer Kirchen-Redner/wie derselbe auf der Cantzel sich gebührend zu erweisen/. . . aufgestellet Durch D. Georg Christian Eilmar, Past.B.M.V. und App. Assessor in Mühlhausen. Franckfurt und Leipzig/Verlegts Joh. Gabriel Ehrt/Bibl. Arnstad, 1706*, pp. 276–77.

10. This should also be considered for BWV 106 to the effect whether the biblical quotations from Johann Olearius's prayerbook do not represent a sort of metatext that may have prompted the cantata.

11. This is perhaps an early version of BWV 21; see note 15.

12. Characterization of a textual form with madrigal features that has in the meantime been used incorrectly (cf. chapter 7).

13. This can be taken as the customary basic form in six parts that Bach set to music later in Leipzig, in which an opening chorus is followed by two recitative-and-aria pairs and a closing chorale.

14. L. Hutter, *Compendium Locorum Theologicorum ex Scripturis Sacris et Libro Concordiae . . . collectum, Lipsiae & Francofurti 1712, Locus XVII. De Ecclesia*, pp. 408–11.

15. Concerning this possible early version of BWV 21, see Martin Petzold, " 'Die kräfftige Erquickung unter der schweren Angst-Last': Möglicherweise Neues zur Entstehung der Kantate BWV 21," *BJ* 79 (1993): 31–46.

16. This could be translated roughly as: "particularly this word, considering the similarity of the name: Harress." The specific analogy refers to the family name Harress and the original German text in the Psalm: "Harre auf Gott, . . ."

17. In 1714, Palm Sunday coincided with the feast of the Annunciation of the Virgin Mary, on March 25, so that the text of BWV 182 clearly creates a link between both occasions.

18. Klaus Hofmann, "Neue Überlegungen zu Bachs Weimarer Kantaten-Kalender," *BJ* 79 (1993): 18.

19. BWV 12, 21, 172, and 182.

20. Elke Axmacher, "Erdmann Neumeister—ein Kantatendichter J.S. Bachs," *Musik und Kirche* 60 (1990): 294–302.

21. Olearius, *Biblische Erklärung*, vol. 5, col. 610a.

J. N. J.

Die Heilige Bibel

nach S. Herrn D. MARTINI LUTHERI

Deutscher Dolmetschung/ und Erklärung/
vermöge des Heil. Geistes/
im Grund-Text/

Richtiger Anleitung der Cohærentz,
Und der gantzen Handlung eines jeglichen Texts/
Auch Vergleichung der gleichlautenden Sprüche/ enthaltenen
eigenen Sinn und Meinung/
Nechst ordentlicher Eintheilung eines jeden Buches und Capitels/
und Erwegung der nachdrücklichen Wort/und Redens-Art
in der Heil. Sprache/
sonderlich aber
Der Evangelischen allein seligmachenden Warheit/
gründ- und deutlich erörtert/
und mit Anführung
Herrn LUTHERI deutschen/und verdeutschten Schrifften/
also abgefasset/
daß der eigentliche Buchstabliche Verstand/
und gutes Theils auch
der heilsame Gebrauch der Heil. Schrifft
fürgestellet ist/
Mit grossem Fleiß/und Kosten ausgearbeitet/
und verfasset/
von
D. ABRAHAM CALOVIO,

Im Jahr Christi cIɔ Iɔc XXCL
welches ist das 1681
5681ste Jahr/ von Erschaffung der Welt.
Zu Wittenberg/
Nicht uns HERR/ nicht uns/ sondern deinem Namen gib Ehre/
umb deiner Gnade und Warheit!

Gedruckt in Wittenberg/ bey Christian Schrödtern/ der Univ. Buchdr.

27911

Bach.
1700.

Title page of Bach's Calov Bible, signed below right.

9

BIBLE, HYMNBOOK, AND WORSHIP SERVICE

Martin Petzoldt

The Liturgical-Historical Context of Bach's Early Cantatas

On the basis of the observation that Bach's church cantatas—including those from his earliest days—were composed as music for the Gospel, for worship on Sundays and holidays, it is perfectly evident why they were written. Neither Weimar nor Mühlhausen provides any clues as to whether Epistle cantatas were customary in addition to music for the Gospel, as we know they were in Rudolstadt, Gotha, and Zerbst. In any case, the texts themselves, set to music, make due reference thereto, by virtue of both their content and their structure. This recourse of falling back on a formative function of the Gospels, as already handed down by the old church for all Sundays and feast days in the ecclesiastical year, could have stemmed partly from the composer's decision, but might also have been a response to what the church authorities expected. As long as there are no sources available to provide actual information to the contrary, we must assume that Bach—like many of his colleagues—had to produce, first and foremost, vocal music for the main devotional services on Sundays and on feast days. Until the nineteenth century this type of music conformed in all respects to the relevant reading of the Gospel, independent of any other Epistle that might also be read. Apart from the "main" (i.e., vocal) music for the Gospel, this applied above all to the choice of hymns that had to be made by the cantor. Other parts of the service were determined throughout the church year for the appropriate Sundays or feast days and therefore needed no special selection (the so-called collect prayer, which set the keynote of the day in the form of a prayer, and the prefaces for holy days, which served as a liturgical introduction to the Lord's Supper and led to a vocal rendering of the Sanctus).

While he was in Arnstadt Bach does not seem to have been in charge of the preparations and organization of vocal music for church services, yet he was obliged to "help out in all music-making."[1] This does not imply in any way, however, that he was required to compose vocal music regularly. Nevertheless, we must assume that Bach's time in Arnstadt gave a considerable stimulus to his way of thinking and subsequent practice, since it was here that he met Johann Christoph Olearius, son of the officiating superintendent, Johann Gottfried Olearius, who had made a name for himself with his *Historia Arnstadiensis, Historie der alt-berühmten Schwarzburgischen Residentz Arnstadt, Jena 1701* and, above all, with his publications on hymnology.[2] The possible influence exercised by Olearius on Bach is an important area for research that must still be taken up. For instance, the peculiar form of the Agnus Dei in Bach's Mass in B minor, BWV 232, could be explained plausibly by Olearius's reflections on the hymn "O Lamm Gottes unschuldig" in his *Hymnologia passionalis* (1709).[3] Moreover, Olearius also published the standard hymn book in the days when Bach worked in Arnstadt.

An astonishing number of Bach's surviving early sacred cantatas were written for incidental services, i.e., occasions of a personal or family nature that were celebrated in church. Some special features of cantatas BWV 106 (written for a funeral) and 196 (assumed to be a wedding cantata) hint at that. In a wider sense, BWV 71 (for the council election in 1708) also belongs to this genre. The somewhat mysterious handwritten postscript on the score of cantata BWV 131 may point equally in that direction. Bach's remark when he requested his discharge from Mühlhausen on June 25, 1708, that he had "acquired, not without cost, a good store of the choicest church compositions"[4] speaks for itself in this connection and should not be disregarded. It raises the question of which compositions of his personal choosing these may have been and gives reason to believe that Bach added contributions of his own to this collection. Even if it seems that, practically, this question cannot be answered, some indications definitely justify the assumption that he contributed personally to that "store." His appointment, dated June 15, 1707, does not mention any specific obligation regarding vocal music but states in general terms that he should "show himself willing in the execution of the duties required of him and be available at all times, particularly to attend to his service faithfully and industriously on Sundays, feast days, and other holy days".[5] However, the application procedures as we know them from a letter by Johann Gottfried Walther[6] and the practice of—at least—Bach's two immediate predecessors[7] explicitly include vocal music for the Gospels throughout the ecclesiastical year. If one looks, therefore, at the pieces that have been handed down in accordance with their appropriate liturgical occasion, then we have before us in BWV 4 an Easter cantata, in BWV 223 a fragment of music for the Visitation of the Virgin Mary (July 2), in BWV 131 a piece for the 11th Sunday after Trinity, and in BWV 150 a cantata for Jubilate Sunday.[8] A similar inquiry and more precise assessment remains to be done for the other city organists and cantor colleagues in Mühlhausen, especially those at the Blasiuskirche (St. Blasius's) and Marienkirche (St. Mary's).

As to Bach's duties in Weimar, we stand on rather firmer ground beginning no later than his appointment in March 1714, even if our complete knowledge of all his cantata performances in the castle church while he worked there and their dates are still far from clear. As far as I know, no thorough investigation of sources has been undertaken regarding the possibility of unofficial cantata performances by Bach in the Stadtkirche in Weimar, where his children were baptized, nor of his friendly relations with his cousin and colleague Johann Gottfried Walther, town organist, or with the town cantor Georg Theodor Reineccius.

With the exception of two fixed dates per year that were ordered by the court—the prince's birthday on December 10 and New Year's Day—Bach's likely worship-service activities in Cöthen were, where possible, in the environment his own faith, that is, that they took place during services in the Lutheran Agnuskirche. There is no evidence as yet for that, apart from references to repeat performances of Weimar church cantatas that may be culled from available performance parts from Cöthen.[9] This applies to single movements from the wedding cantata "Herr Gott, Beherrscher aller Dinge," (BWV 120a), to the cantatas "Bereitet die Wege, bereitet die Bahn" (4th Sunday in Advent, BWV 132), "Erschallet, ihr Lieder" (Whitsun, BWV 172), "Ich hatte viel Bekümmernis" (3rd Sunday after Trinity, BWV 21) and "Mein Herze schwimmt in Blut" (11th Sunday after Trinity, BWV 199), as well as to Francesco Conti's motet for soprano "Languet anima mea," which Bach copied in score at Weimar, then preparing a set of parts in Cöthen, and probably also to "Wer mich liebet, der wird mein Wort halten" (Whitsun, BWV 59) and "Ich habe genug" (the Purification of the Blessed Virgin Mary, BWV 82). Still to be investigated in detail are Bach's relations with the organist at the Agnuskirche, Christian Ernst Rolle, who served there 1714–28, with the cantor of that church, Johann Caspar Schultze (1688–1751), at the church from 1717, with the organist of the Jakobikirche (St. Jacobi's) Johann Jacob Müller (around 1731), with the cantor of the same church, Johann Jeremias Göbel, and with the court organist Johann Christian Kreyser.

On the subject of liturgical matters, we certainly should also consider Bach's official and personal contacts with clergy serving at that time. For Arnstadt we have already alluded to Johann Christoph Olearius (1668–1747). Of Mühlhausen we know that Georg Christian Eilmar (1665–1715), cited in literature as a friend of Bach, showed great interest in designing the order of divine services and supplied the kind of outlines—sometimes unsolicited—that put him into unfortunate confrontations, especially with superintendent Johann Adolph Frohne (1652–1713). The search for information on the newly emerging liturgical cohesiveness also falls into this category; for instance, questions about the confirmation ceremony[10] and the annual and bicentenary celebrations of the Reformation[11] remain largely unanswered. In Cöthen the tense atmosphere cleared up a little after the death of the uncompromising Calvinist superintendent Nathanael Gottlieb Splithusen (1654–1719) and his succession by Johann Conrad Lobethan (1688–1735). Later, the two denominations would work together much better under the Pietist influence (Bach, of course, was not able to witness this). At first, any effort at getting together was made more difficult by the headstrong Lutheran court pastor Paulus Berger (ca. 1670–1732), with whom even Princess Gisela Agnes got into a dispute. The situation finally returned to normal under Georg Friedrich Zeideler (1684–1745), Lutheran deacon for many years, and Johann Ludwig Konrad Allendorf (1693–1773), who was in Cöthen from 1724 and was later pastor at the court.

LITURGICAL ORDERS OF SERVICE ACCORDING TO SERVICE BOOKS AND HYMNBOOKS

In order to make it easier to follow the liturgical questions, we will now give an overview of the service books, prayerbooks, and hymnbooks, and the way they were used when Bach worked. In many cases, it remains unclear which particulars that were customary at a given place may also have played a part, because mere knowledge of the service books used at the time hardly ever tells us more about the actual practice. It may be assumed that the order of service then in use provided a fundamental basis for the celebration of the divine service and sacramental rites. Someone today looking at service books found in libraries and archives will at least get a vivid picture of how occasional handwritten alterations and supplementary entries made divine celebrations variable and changeable. However, it is often difficult to draw any conclusions from these insertions, since their dating raises problems that can be solved only by chance. We rarely come across a datable list of alterations in the liturgy for the year as we find in Leipzig.[12] References to the distribution among the local churches of daily and Sunday services and prayer hours help in sketching a more detailed outline of Bach's duties.

Arnstadt

In 1675, a new edition of the 1650 church order of service was published under the aegis of the Arnstadt printer Heinrich Meurer. On the whole, its instructions were based on the Wittenberg service book of 1536, although the results of the examinations of 1533, 1553, 1575, and 1587 were also taken into account. The people of Sondershausen had their own manual in 1605, which was recommended for use again in 1618. The service book that evolved from that of 1650 must also have been the basis of Bach's religious duties, since the foreword to the *Agende Schwartzburgica das ist Verzeichniß der Ceremonien*, which the new edition of 1675 was called, restricts the "Christian freedom" of the divine service specifically to the preacher's

> solemn obligation, pledged at his ordination, and his public undertaking promised thereafter at his investiture, to be well instructed at all times and therefore not to make the slightest alteration for himself of the Church ceremonies but to keep the same unchanged, in accordance with these service books.[13]

For comparison, the order of the main service for Sunday mornings and for the entire mornings of the feast days is as follows:

On Sundays	On Feast Days	
Komm Heiliger Geist, erfüll	Veni Sancte Spiritus, (or) Komm Heiliger Geist	
Versicle	Latin versicle	German versicle
Collect prayer	Latin collect	German collect
Kyrie, *de tempore*	Kyrie	

Gloria with Latin or German intonation	Gloria with Latin intonation
Allein Gott in der Höh, *or*	Et in terra pax
Sein Zorn auf Erden hat kein End	
Collect *de tempore*	Collect *de tempore*
Lesson	Lesson
Hymn, chosen by the preacher	"Fest-Gesang" chosen by the preacher
Gospel reading	Gospel reading
Credo intonation [*]	
Polyphonic piece	Polyphonic piece
Canticle	Canticle
Sermon: *de tempore* hymn [**]	Sermon: *de tempore* hymn [**]
Lord's Prayer	Lord's Prayer
[Bible text for sermon]	[Bible text for sermon]
[Sermon]	[Sermon]
General confession	General confession
Prayers and intercessions [***]	Prayers and intercessions [***]
Communion [****]	Communion [****]
German preface	German preface
Sanctus, sung by the chorus	Sanctus, sung by the chorus
Luther's Communion exhortation	Luther's Communion exhortation
Lord's Prayer	Lord's Prayer
Prayer of consecration	Prayer of consecration
Administration of the Sacrament	Administration of the Sacrament
Versicle	Versicle
Collect of thanks	Collect of thanks
Blessing	Blessing

With regard to the Credo [*], the formulation "follows the gospel, and when appropriate the Credo [with details of Credo intonation], after which a piece of music will be played and, when seasonally appropriate, the Creed sung"[14] does not make it clear whether only the Credo intonation followed, without the continuing "Patrem omnipotentem," that is, the polyphonic music was performed immediately instead of the "Patrem," as Bach witnessed at certain times in Leipzig. The hymn to be sung at the beginning of the sermon part of the service [**] can be found listed in a special index, which gives rules for all Sundays and other feast days.[15] As in Leipzig, prayers and intercessions [***] also included notices and announcements of a personal and institutional nature that were relevant to the municipal community. The prefatory prayer and Sanctus indicate the choir as the responding partner. The order of service does not tell whether the scheduled Introit, particularly in its Latin form, as well as the Kyrie and Gloria—at least in part— were performed as polyphonic music. Surprisingly, the Vesper Service[16] on feast days could be provided with much more polyphonic music:

On Sundays	On Feast Days
De tempore hymn	*De tempore* hymn
Reading of a Psalm or the Gospel	Reading of a Psalm, the Gospel, *or* a chapter from the Bible
Polyphonic piece or hymn	Polyphonic piece or hymn
Sermon, preceded by	Sermon, preceded by
De tempore hymn	*De tempore* hymn
Prayers	Prayers
Information about catechism	Polyphonic piece or "choral piece"
"Singing"	
Versicle, collect, blessing	Versicle, collect, blessing

The local hymnbook would obviously have been of great importance to Bach while in Arnstadt, although those attending the divine service may well, as elsewhere, have used a considerable variety of hymnbooks. At any rate, the parish possessed hymnbooks from Rudolstadt, Gotha, Eisenach, Erfurt, Weimar, and Jena. The Arnstadt hymnbook, however, is particularly important, since its compilation and organization had been delegated by the local council to the aforementioned Johann Christoph Olearius, son of the super-intendent. The same Olearius had published important hymnological research under the title *Neu-Verbessertes Arnstädtisches Gesangbuch* (Arnstadt, 1700; corrected ed., 1702). The edition of 1700 was provided with a three-part frontispiece, which illustrates, with a certain intensification, (1) a strengthening of faith in the face of sin by looking upon Christ elevated on the cross, (2) a strengthening of faith in the face of inner doubt through participation in the Lord's Supper, and (3) the resounding praise of God for His help.[17] This is unmistakable proof of an attempt at musical theology as advocated probably by Johann Christoph Olearius and as it was character-istic of Bach, as shown by his annotations in his Calov Bible.

MÜHLHAUSEN

If the present collection of church archives in Mühlhausen has any critical value, then the existence of a Schwarzburg service book (see above) not only shows signs of having been used but also contains remarks and correc-tions, leading us to the conclusion that it was the foundation for services and religious rites. This makes it quite difficult, of course, to decide if and when the Schwarzburg service book or the Saxon-electoral *Agende, Das ist, Kirchen-Ordnung* in the Leipzig edition of 1691 (which was also available and utilized) were being employed in Mühlhausen. We must assume, then, that in fulfilling his duties in Mühlhausen, Bach could turn to both forms.

In contrast with the Schwarzburg service book, the Saxon-electoral service book sets the order of service as follows:

On Feast Days   On Sundays

    Polyphonic Introitus for Sunday or the Feast
    Kyrie, in Latin [= Greek]
    Gloria, in Latin
Collect, in Latin   Collect, in German
    Epistle, read in German[18]
    Sequence, Psalm, or hymn, de tempore,
       by the congregation
    Gospel, read in German[19]
    Creed intonation[20]
       Continuation "Patrem omnipotentem"
         by the choir
    Wir glauben all an einem Gott,
       by the congregation
    Sermon, based on the Gospel
Preface, sung in Latin[21]   Paraphrase of the Lord's
                                                              Prayer
Sanctus, sung in Latin (polyphonic)   Communion exhortation
Our Father, sung in German by celebrant
    Verba testamenti, sung in German
       by the celebrant
    Jesus Christus unser Heiland,[22] *or*
       Gott sei gelobet und gebenedeiet,
         by the congregation
       Agnus Dei, in Latin, "during communion"
       I will give thanks unto the Lord with
         my whole heart, Psalm 111
    Verse
    Collect prayer
    Blessing

The service book differentiates the order of service "in the towns where there are schools" from that "in the villages." As a beginning it stresses that, after the bells have been rung, the students should sing the Introit, Kyrie, and Gloria. This direction explains why everywhere in seventeenth-century Saxony and Thuringia—thus including Mühlhausen—a rich output of motets and Kyrie-Gloria Masses can be traced. So the Schwarzburg service book (discussed above under "Arnstadt") had already undergone a development that does not appear even in later editions of the Saxon-electoral service book, i.e., replacement of the "Patrem omnipotentem" by *de tempore* polyphonic music, which later became the cantata or principal music. By virtue of Luther's theologically refined idea about sacrifice (confession as an offering of praise), this peculiar tradition of a double Credo (the Nicene creed and Luther's Credo hymn) developed on the basis of bringing together polyphonic music and the congregational Credo. As music by one Johann Rudolph Ahle, clearly written *de tempore*, shows, Mühlhausen also conformed to the Schwarzburg service book, which was already in an advanced state of development and which in turn became the general practice in accordance with the Saxon-electoral service book, as the example in Leipzig shows. What this meant for Bach's work in Mühlhausen is not at all clear.[23]

The hymnbook tradition in Mühlhausen that pertained to Bach goes back to the 1686 edition, published by the father of Johann Bernhard Frohne, the officiating superintendent at the time of Bach. This hymnbook was reprinted in 1697 and 1703. In 1712 Johann Adolph Frohne published the hymnbook once more, with some added hymns, as *Vermehrtes Gesangbuch* (Mühlhausen, 1712). In addition to a detailed *de tempore* index this hymnbook contains an "Order of the Psalms of David as they are sung in the churches in Mühlhausen for Matins and Vespers."

WEIMAR

In 1707 a revision of the church service book of 1658 was printed in Weimar under the title *Agende, oder kurtzer Auszug aus der Kirchen-Ordnung*. The order of service can be gathered from only two out of a total of twenty sections: the "Order of confirmation for those instructed in the catechism or for children/Will thus be admitted for the first time to Confession and the Lord's Supper" and the "Order and form of singing at Holy Communion."

The first section outlines the normal order of service (including some suggestions for hymns that relate to the occasion) and after the sermon adds the celebration for confirmation (this can be disregarded at present). In the first part, up to the sermon, the service contains specific indications for polyphonic music. In general terms, the order looks as follows:

> Introit
> Kyrie, set to music
> Gloria intonation by the pastor in front of the altar
> "Allein Gott in der Höh sei Ehr" (congregation)
> Versicle, collect prayer
> Epistle reading
> Hymn (relating to the Gospel or appropriate to the text of the sermon)
> Reading of the Gospel
> A piece of music performed
> "Wir glauben all an einen Gott" (congregation) and
> "Liebster Jesus wir sind hier" (congregation)

Sermon

[Sermon hymn]

Intercession

⎯⎯> Lord's Prayer, hymn verse, versicle,
closing collect, blessing

The second section in question, the order for communion, continues after the intercession as follows:

Versicle

Lord's Prayer sung by the celebrant

Paraphrase of the Lord's Prayer and communion exhortation (spoken)

Verba testamenti (according to Luther's "German Mass," sung by the celebrant)

[Administration of bread and wine]

Versicle

Closing collect

Blessing

The basic order corresponds to the outline of the electoral service book that was generally in use in Saxony. From a musical point of view, it is interesting that there was evidently neither a Gloria set to music nor a Preface with a musical rendering of the Sanctus, as in Leipzig. The Gloria was sung as a hymn by the congregation; the Preface and Sanctus were replaced by a versicle.[24] The cantata, however, appears unaffected, in its usual place after the reading of the Gospel. All the same, the provision of a Kyrie set to music follows the practice of towns in Saxony, which had Latin schools that were capable of training a "chorus symphoniacus."

The Weimar hymnbooks in Bach's time were *Auserlesenes Weinmarisches Gesangbuch* (1681) and *Schuldiges Lob Gottes oder Geistreiches Gesang-Buch* (1713). The editor of the 1681 edition, Conrad von der Lage (1643–1694), was general superintendent from 1673 to 1694. The 1713 edition was supplied by his second successor, Johann Georg Lairitz (1647–1716), who held office from 1697 to 1716. Bach had to work together with him for services in the court church.

The *de tempore* index in this hymnbook is of special significance with regard to the layout of Bach's Weimar *Orgel-Büchlein*; this includes the curious placement of the hymn "Herr Christ der einig Gottes Sohn" among the tunes for Advent and the sequence of the hymns in the *Orgel-Büchlein*, which is nearly identical to the order in the *de tempore* index.

Cöthen had become Lutheran following the introduction of the Reformation in 1527. This changed when, as a result of Johann Georg von Anhalt's conversion in 1596, the ruling dynasty and the people were forced to adopt the Calvinist creed. Only the landed gentry remained Lutheran. A schism between the denominations was characteristic at the time Bach worked in Cöthen, yet under the reign of the prince's mother, Gisela Agnes (1669–1740), née von Rath of Klein-Wülknitz, her diplomatic attitude toward denominational matters started a development that benefited the small Lutheran municipalities.[25] In 1692 she married Prince Emanuel Lebrecht of Anhalt-Cöthen, against the wishes of his family. She must have been an extraordinarily determined and capable person, but one who was also kind and charming. After the wedding she gradually expanded the authority of Lutherans in the area. In 1693 the order was given to build a Lutheran church in Cöthen, and in 1694 her husband had her raised to the rank of imperial countess by a decree from the emperor. Henceforth, she was Imperial Countess von Nienburg. In the same year the foundation stone was laid for the Agnuskirche, and in 1696 her brother Wilhelm von Rath was appointed privy councilor, director of the chamber, and head of the province. In 1698 Lutherans were granted the right to hold ministerial office conditional on the double payment of the fees. The same year saw the completion of the Agnuskirche. Its consecration took place on May 7, 1699, conducted by the first Lutheran pastor, Johannes Tobias Sechting of Halberstadt (d. 1712), with a sermon on Isaiah 38:22. Both this text and the inscription of the medal[26] struck in honor of the laying of the foundation stone are characteristic of the defiant yet self-conscious attitude of the Lutheran minority in Cöthen at the time. Even if much was lost again because of the more restrictive conditions after her son ascended the throne in 1715, Gisela Agnes had nevertheless achieved considerable status for Lutherans in Cöthen.

As far as we know, services in the Agnuskirche were celebrated in accordance with the Saxon-electoral service book (see the section on Mühlhausen, above). We have not yet discovered which hymnbook may have been the main one. Was it the one from Zerbst, derived from the Braunschweig hymnbook? Since the first Lutheran pastor of the Agnuskirche, Johann Tobias Sechting, came from Halberstadt, there is much to be said for the Halberstadt-Wernigerode hymnbook, which had just appeared in a new edition in 1716 as the *Halberstädtisches Gesang-Buch* and was also used in Aschersleben.

It is not very likely that, during Bach's tenure in Leipzig, it was the Freyling-hausen hymnbook from Halle, which appeared in many editions beginning in 1704 and was known in Cöthen during the early 1720s. Pietism, which was practiced in Halle, made its first appearance in Cöthen only when Gisela Agnes began to show interest in it. That may have been around 1720. However, such interest is not reflected immediately in ecclesiastical decisions, as, for instance, in the use of a hymnbook. The development of Cöthen's own Pietism finds its expression just under a decade later with the publication of the *Gantz neue und auserlesene Lieder* (Halle and Cöthen, [1733]) and its subsequent enlarged reprints of 1736, 1738, and 1744, produced by the future court preacher Allendorf. But that goes far beyond Bach's activities in Cöthen and is a matter to be discussed separately.

Division of Church Services at Arnstadt and Mühlhausen

The order of service in the four churches at Arnstadt shows that Bach had to carry out four weekly assignments as organist at the Neue Kirche (New Church):

	BK[27]	LK	NK	HK
Sunday		6–7 Deacon* + A		
	9–10 Superin-tendent + A 1–2 Deacon*		9–10 Sermon	9 o'clock (mostly on feast days and Sundays
Monday	7–8 Hour of prayer		7–8 Hour of prayer	7–8 Hour of prayer
Tuesday	7–8 Deacon* (same as Sunday 1–2/BK)			
Wednesday			2 o'clock Vespers and confession	
Thursday			7–8 sermon by deacon* + A (same as Sunday 6–7/LK)	
Friday	7–8 superintendent, + litany			7–8 Sermon
Saturday	1 o'clock Vespers and confession	12 noon Vespers and confession		

Undoubtedly Bach would also have substituted for others. But the list also shows that the New Church stood just below the Barfüsserkirche in the number of services.

The "order of weekly homilies"[28] in Mühlhausen followed a somewhat complicated system of interchange between the Blasiuskirche (St. Blasius's) and the Marienkirche (St. Mary's), and the clergy officiating at any given time. Both main churches each employed two clergymen; St. Blasius's had a deacon, in support of the superintendent,[29] and St. Mary's also had a deacon in support of the archdeacon. The superintendent and the archdeacon preached from each other's pulpit every other Sunday. Sermons during the week, however, were subject to a four-week rotation, which made it necessary for those attending the services to know exactly what the sequence for the week in question would be. An overview, linked to the Sunday services, gives the picture of a rich religious life in the course of one week:

	Sunday		Monday		Tuesday		Wednesday	Thursday		Friday		Saturday
Week	DB[30]	BMV	DB	BMV	DB	BMV		DB	BMV	DB	BMV	
1 f.	Archid.	Sup.	-	-	-	Archid.	-	-	Diac.	Diac.	-	-
n.	Diac.	Diac.	Sup.	-	-	-	-	-	-	-	-	-
2 f.	Sup.	Archid.	-	-	Sup.	-	-	-	Diac.	Diac.	-	-
n.	Diac.	Diac.	-	Archid.	-	-	-	-	-	-	-	-
3 f.	Archid.	Sup.	-	-	Sup.	-	-	-	Archid.	Diac.	-	-
n.	Diac.	Diac.	-	Diac.	-	-	-	-	-	-	-	-
4 f.	Sup.	Archid.	-	-	Sup.	-	-	-	Archid.	-	Diac.	-
n.	Diac.	Diac.	Diac.	-	-	-	-	-	-	-	-	-

This schedule does not take into account Bach's activity as organist during services at the Brückenhofkirche, where he alternated with the organists of St. Mary's, Johann Gottfried Hetzhenn, and the Nicolai-Kirche (St. Nicolas's), Franciscus Anthon Neuforst. They should be added to the four listed services at St. Blasius's.[31] At present, we do not yet know how many extra services were involved as a result of Bach's duty at the Brücken-hofkirche, which could be reached quickly from St. Blasius's.

ORDER OF THE GOSPELS AND DE TEMPORE

It must be emphasized that there is hardly another musician among Bach's contemporaries who made such unrestricted reference to the Gospels in his cantatas or showed the same commitment to them as did Johann Sebastian Bach. This observation is founded on the hermeneutic faith and accuracy with which Bach also interprets and handles his texts elsewhere. It becomes a vivid reality especially in the cantatas that Bach revised with the objective of altering their designation. This happened to the Weimar cantatas that he could no longer use for their original purpose because of the *tempora clausa* in Leipzig (Invocavit Sunday until Palm Sunday, the 2nd to the 4th Sunday of Advent). When such cantatas were made serviceable for another date, the text was changed throughout by means of subtle theological adaptations. Contemporary understanding of the Bible and its interpretation was not at its peak, by today's standards of formulating and displaying the range of a limited section of text with the aid of all the historical and critical methods available for analysis. Rather, it restricted itself to finding certain connections within specific and explicit texts in a biblical, theological, or dogmatic sense and to interpreting them. The dogma at that time did not pretend to be much more than a systematic compilation of biblical passages arranged by thematic context. As far as we know, Bach never performed any random cantata for any random occasion, not even when the content of one Gospel text might come close to that of another one. In fact, the indication *per ogni tempo* for Cantata BWV 21 really signifies nothing more than that this cantata has not been strictly defined in a *de tempore* sense; it does not mean that the cantata could be used at just any time. The indication is there instead of a *de tempore* designation and denotes that it might be suitable for different—but not specifically determined—occasions. It does not allude to any use that is unconnected with the ecclesiastical year. Obviously, Bach generally believed in looking at things in this way. This also enables us to assign a designation to cantatas whose purpose is unknown or doubtful by means of a meticulous analysis of the text on the basis of a contemporary understanding of the Bible.

Notes

1. *Dok* II,14, for August 19, 1705; as well as *Doks* 16 and 17 (summary: *BR*, 51).
2. *Kurtzer Entwurff einer nützlichen Lieder-Bibliotheck . . .* (Jena, 1702); *Erbauliche Betrachtungen des Passionsliedes "Jesu, meines Lebens Leben etc."* (Jena, 1704); *Evangelischer Liederschatz . . .* (Jena, 1705–06); *Mart. Crusii homiliae hymnodicae . . .* (Arnstadt, 1705); and *Hymnologia passionalis, i.e. Homiletische Lieder-Remarquen . . .* (Arnstadt, 1709).
3. See Martin Petzoldt, *Bachstätten aufsuchen* (Leipzig, 1992), p. 17.
4. *BR*, 60.
5. *Dok* II, No. 21 prints only the draft of the appointment. The original can be found in the records of St. Blasius's Church in Mühlhausen, see Petzoldt, *Bachstätten aufsuchen*, pp. 128–29 and 131–32.
6. Letter to Johann Mattheson dated December 28, 1739, in Johann Gottfried Walther, *Briefe*, ed. Klaus Beckmann and Hans-Joachim Schulze (Leipzig, 1987), pp. 218–22.
7. In particular Johann Rudolf Ahle (1625–1673), whose arias (dating from 1660 on) and meditations (dating from 1662 on) were composed in series, including all Sundays and feast days of the ecclesiastical year and based strictly on *de tempore* readings of the Gospel.
8. See *Bachstätten aufsuchen*, pp. 135–37.
9. See Andreas Glöckner, "Anmerkungen zu Johann Sebastian Bachs Köthener Kantatenschaffen," in: *Cöthener Bach-Hefte* 4, pp. 89–95.
10. Although there is nothing like this known from Arnstadt and Cöthen, there is a confirming service-book note that exists for Mühlhausen dating from 1696 and for Weimar from 1707 or earlier. The Schwarzburg service book has a "Formula to be used as directed for the confirmation of those children who shall be admitted for the first time to Holy Communion" (see note 16), pp. 167–72.
11. What might Bach have contributed to this 1717 celebration in Weimar? Franck wrote a poem of praise and thanks; see Petzoldt, *Bachstätten aufsuchen*, p. 176.
12. Johann Christoph Rost, *Nachricht, Wie es, in der Kirchen zu St: Thom: alhier, mit dem Gottes-Dienst, Jährlichen sowohl an Hohen Festen, als anderen Tagen, gepfleget gehalten zu werden* (Leipzig, 1716).
13. Service book (title as indicated in text), front cover.
14. Ibid, p. 3.
15. Ibid, pp. 37–39. It is notable that in the Weimar *Orgelbüchlein* a prelude is available or at least provided to be inserted into all hymns that are listed in this index, with the exception of two little-known ones and two hymns mentioned as alternatives:

Advent:	Gott durch deine Güte	BWV 600
or:	Herr Christ der einig Gotts Sohn	BWV 601
Christmas:	Ein Kindelein so löbelich	BWV 605
New Year's:	Ein Kindelein so löbelich	BWV 605
or:	Jesu, nun sei gepreiset	without prelude
Purification of the		
Blessed Virgin:	Herr, nun lässest du	without prelude
or:	Magnificat (German)	prelude planned
Annunciation		
of the Blessed Virgin:	Herr Christ der einig Gotts Sohn	BWV 601
or:	Magnificat (German)	prelude planned
Lent:	O Lamm Gottes unschuldig	BWV 618
or:	Ehre sei dir Christe	prelude planned
Easter:	Christ ist erstanden	BWV 627
or:	Also heilig ist der Tag	without prelude
Ascension:	Christ fuhr gen Himmel	[BWV 627]

Whitsun:	O h. Geist du Göttlichs Feur	prelude planned
or:	Nun bitten wir den h. Geist	prelude planned
Trinity:	[Gott der Vater] wohn uns bey	prelude planned
or:	Nun bitten wir den h. Geist	prelude planned
Other Sundays:	Herr Jesu Christ dich zu uns wend	BWV 632
St. John and Visitation		
of the Blessed Virgin:	Herr Christ der einig Gotts Sohn	BWV 601
or:	Der Lobgesang Zachariae	prelude planned
or:	Magnificat (German)	prelude planned
St. Michael:	Gelobet sei der ewige Gott	without prelude
or:	Es stehn vor Gottes Throne	prelude planned

16. "For Sunday afternoons," order of service, p. 3; "For the entire afternoons on feast days," ibid., p. 5.

17. On the reverse side, a four-stanza poem appears, under the heading "Explanation of the frontispiece."

18. Sung on the Epistle intonation.

19. Sung on the Gospel intonation.

20. The indication "After the Gospel one sings the Latin Patrem until the end/to the customary tune; the same with the German/We believe" (service book, p. 114) leads to a double Creed—like other similar ones—which could be used in different ways in the order of service when Bach was in Leipzig: during Sundays in Lent, Credo intonations by the celebrant and afterwards the "Patrem omnipotentem" sung by the choir (no polyphonic music); during a period of Sundays without special occasions the Credo intonation, and instead of the "Patrem omnipotentem" polyphonic music was performed; on feast days the intonation was also left out; in any event Luther's Credo hymn was sung.

21. Different Latin prefaces were available for feast days; the Sanctus was not allotted expressly to the choir, although it may be assumed that all Latin pieces that were not sung by the celebrant were given to the choir.

22. "During the singing the congregation will be informed sub utraque specie" (service book, p. 80).

23. Compare what has been said on this subject under "Mühlhausen."

24. A fixed feature was 1 Corinthians 11:26, which one still finds today written on many altars in Thuringia: Vers.[ikel] So offt ihr von diesem Brot esset/und von dem Kelch des HErrn trincket/Halleluja! (Verse: As often as you eat this bread/and drink the cup/Alleluia!) Resp.[onsorium] Solt ihr des HErrn Tod verkündigen/biß daß er kommt/Halleluja! [Response: you would proclaim the Lord's death/until he comes/Alleluia!]

25. Samuel Lenz, *Becmannus enucleatus, suppletus et continuatus* (Dessau and Cöthen, 1757), p. 865, gives special credit to Gisela Agnes for the way she led the province in political, diplomatic, legal, and economic matters, and concludes: "She has become a legend for having established an evangelical Lutheran church and school in Cöthen, together with her husband, and with her help the population of the town is increasing. Along with her husband she has happily suppressed all difficulties that occurred and helped to settle matters in a peaceful way."

26. Isaiah 38:22: "Hezekiah also had said: 'What is the sign that I shall go up to the house of the Lord?'" The medal was struck on the occasion of the princess's twenty-fifth birthday, on October 9, 1694, the same day on which the foundation stone was laid. On the front one sees the likeness of Prince Emanuel Lebrecht, on the reverse a horse leaping against a rock with the legend "Virtus repulsae nescia sordidae!" (Virtue, beware of humiliating resistance!).

27. Abbreviations: BK = Barfüsserkirche or Oberkirche; LK = Liebfrauenkirche, Unterkirche, or Frühkirche; NK = Neue Kirche, Bonifatius, or Sophienkirche, also Kirche zur Heiligen Dreifältigkeit, today the Bachkirche; HK = Hofkirche; Deacon* = one of the three dea-

cons/subordinate pastors alternating; + A = divine service including communion celebration.

28. Printed in *Mühlhäusisches Gesang-Buch*, published by Johann Jacob Lungershausen (Mühlhausen, 1717), at the end of the hymnbook, unpaginated.

29. The history of the introduction of the Reformation to Mühlhausen is very complicated, see the general account in Petzoldt, *Bachstätten aufsuchen*, p. 127. That the position of superintendent existed at St. Blasius's Church for several centuries is explained by the fact that St. Mary's as council church remained rooted in Roman Catholicism much longer than St. Blasius's.

30. Abbreviations: DB = Divi Blasii (St. Blasius's); BMV = Beatae Mariae Virginis (St. Mary's Church); Sup. = superintendent; Archid. = archdeacon; Diac. = deacon; f. = early or main service; n. = afternoon service or Vespers, celebrated as an hour of prayer during the week; The "Ordnung der Wochen-Predigt" from the Mühlhausen hymnbook of 1717, discusses in note 28, remarks on the once-a-month Apostle days at the end: "If an Apostle day falls on a Monday then it will be celebrated on the Tuesday in order to maintain the hour of prayer, which is canceled only in the event of a feast falling on a Monday or Tuesday."

31. See H. Peter Ernst, "Joh. Seb. Bachs Wirken am ehemaligen Mühlhäuser Augustinerinnenkloster und das Schicksal seiner Wender-Orgel," in *BJ* 73 (1987): pp. 75–83.

Musical performance; from an engraving in the "Musikalisches Lexicon"
by Johann Gotfried Walther, 1732.

10

CHOIR AND INSTRUMENTS

Christoph Wolff

Bach's cantatas are indebted to older traditions in many ways—as are the cantatas by Telemann, Graupner, Stölzel, and other contemporaries. This is particularly true in respect to two crucial aspects of the cantata genre that complement each other, form and scoring. Toward the end of the seventeenth century, the different and previously isolated genres of vocal polyphony (including, especially, concerto, aria, and chorale) joined together into the unified structure of the cantata comprising several movements. The end result produced a greatly differentiated picture of score and sound, since the originally separate form elements exhibited totally different kinds of vocal and instrumental ensemble playing. Pure vocal music, i.e., *a capella* music unaccompanied, or supported only by the organ or basso continuo, had long ago lost its traditional importance. And now that court chapels and larger town churches, in particular, often commanded eminently capable ensembles, the cantata composers were presented with a multitude of new possibilities for developing vocal-instrumental music.

In his *Syntagma Musicum,* vol. 3 (Wolfenbüttel, 1619), Michael Praetorius offered an organizational system for musical ensembles that, in retrospect, did not lose any of its relevance for understanding the cantata practice in the late seventeenth and early eighteenth century. According to this system, a vocal-instrumental ensemble consisted of two groups: the "choro pleno" combining all of the available performing forces ("capella vocalis et instrumentalis"), and the "voces concertatae," i.e., singers and players used as soloists. Furthermore, the complete vocal ensemble consisted of four voices: soprano, alto, tenor, and bass, and as such formed a more or less standardized and homogeneous body of sound. In contrast, the instrumental ensemble was rather heterogeneous and often changed according to local and other conditions. An essential stable factor remained, however, in that each instrumental ensemble consisted of "Fundament-" and "Ornament Instrumenta." "Fundament" instruments included organ, harpsichord, or lute, which "support the whole corpus and achieve complete harmony." The "Ornament" instruments comprised all wind instruments and the strings, which "can produce only one single part" and preferably serve to "support and embellish the singing."

The possibilities thus created for the development of diversified sounds were practically unlimited. On the one hand, the working together of voices and instruments could be achieved by means of alternating and combining "capella vocalis & instrumentalis," both with the full ensembles ("omnes," "tutti," or "ripieni") or, in succession, with the "voces concertatae." On the other, the division of the instrumental ensemble allowed for varieties that went still further. Nuances of sound are obtained not only by bringing together or alternating fundamental and ornamental instruments, but also by calling upon wind and string instruments "pro variatione," in distinct groups ("capella tibicinia & fidicinia") or individually.

For singers and players the differentiation of tutti and solo, ripienists and soloists, is not purely a matter of functional principle and performance practice. As much as it provides an opportunity for contrasts between musical pieces, sections, or parts reflecting different compositional intentions, there is also the important factor that usually within an ensemble some musicians are more accomplished performers than others. For instance, court ensembles normally recruited their soloists from full-time personnel, whereas the ripienists carried out their musical duties mostly on the side.

An art that was aimed at tonal versatility was directly favored by the multi-movement cantata form as it had developed toward the end of the seventeenth century, from a combination of different types of musical settings, text categories (Bible, hymn, free poetry) and text forms (prose, metrical and rhymed poetry). Composers were given latitude for setting and interpreting those texts with musical sounds in a way that greatly exceeded the possibilities suggested by Praetorius at the time. Other advances could now be included, especially those from opera and the new instrumental genres, sonata and concerto. Finally, the progress of Andreas Werckmeister and others in the field of musical tuning and temperament, which eventually freed composers from the limitations of meantone temperament, greatly influenced the technical and compositional effects on the harmonic and tonal design of multimovement works. Bach's earliest cantatas already stand out because of their enormously wide range of keys and, indeed, in both their choice of remote keys (BWV 106: E-flat–c–f–b–A-flat–E-flat) and their juxtaposition of sharp and flat keys (BWV 71: C–e–a–F–C–c–C).

Overall, the cantatas from around 1700 show an unusual Janus-faced stylistic tendency. The customary way of dealing with the old traditions of the seventeenth century and the attempt to break away from them are clearly at loggerheads with each other. This is also the case, to a considerable extent, with Bach's cantata work in his pre-Leipzig period. It shows the kind of broad range of form and spectrum of sounds that the Leipzig repertory clearly lacks, despite its wider scope. The inclination toward consolidation and even standardization of the form of the cantata texts, which was ever more noticeable toward the end of the Weimar period, became the norm for the Leipzig texts and had inevitable consequences for the musical design as well. The way Bach handled his cantata texts shows great sensitivity toward their structure. Whereas he creates a homogeneous musical casing around a poetic and uniform cantata text, he generally strives for a heterogeneous solution when using texts compiled from the Bible and hymnal, interspersed with free poetry. This applies above all to the structure and sound of Bach's oldest cantatas, which reveal no attempt to impose conventions, either in the choice of instruments or in their compositional handling. While Bach observes the norm of having four voices in the vocal score in his pre-Leipzig cantatas, he is more flexible, as a matter of principle, in his treatment of the instrumental scoring, partly in keeping with seventeenth-century traditions, partly with the intention of dealing with a still new genre of composition whose parameters were barely established.

VOCAL-INSTRUMENTAL ENSEMBLES

We lack information on the makeup of ensembles for church music in Arnstadt and Mühlhausen during Bach's time. The Neukirche (New

Church) in Arnstadt had a choir of students with a choir prefect but without a competent *director musices*, a situation that Bach criticized. We cannot tell to what extent Bach was connected with the Count of Schwarzburg's court orchestra in Arnstadt and whether this ensemble was available for church services. At any rate, the conditions for regular, ambitious concerted music were not particularly good at the New Church. The situation in the free imperial town of Mühlhausen was different, judging, at least, by the extravagant demands of the cantata BWV 71, written to celebrate the council election. Bach would hardly have aimed for "a well-regulated church music" if there had been inadequate performance conditions in the town. Thus, the extremely varied scorings of the pre-Weimar cantatas reflected the typically erratic conditions under which "Organisten-Musik" (organist's music), which was restricted to special occasions, used to be produced.

There is better information available about the conditions in Weimar. Church music at the court consisted of a Capelle (professional ensemble) and a *Cantorei* (school choir). A list of members of the court ensemble in 1714–16 shows a roster of 22 (full-time) musicians (*BR*, 69–70). There were 7 singers (soloists), including 2 sopranos, 1 alto, 2 tenors, and 2 basses. The tenor Döbernitz was court cantor at the same time and led the *Cantorei* at the Latin school. As many as 7 trumpets and a kettledrum appear among the instrumentalists, but only 3 violins are listed. Another list of musicians dated 1714 (*Dok* II, No. 69), however, explicitly mentions 4 violins. Regarding the size and balance of the instrumental ensemble, we must take into account that most court musicians usually carried out other duties as well. For instance, one of the trumpeters also worked as a "Cammerfourier" (chamber servant), one of the violinists as secretary, and one of the bass singers as master of the pages. Obviously, many musicians were not included in the ensemble list at all, if their primary duties were elsewhere. Even Bach, when he first worked briefly at the Weimar court in 1703—before his appointment as organist in Arnstadt—was then listed only as a lackey. In any case, there is no doubt that at the Weimar court each of the duke's households in both castles (the Red and the Yellow Castle) had an ensemble with a fairly large supply of full- and part-time musicians; this is borne out, not least of all, by the fact that the list was headed by a Kapellmeister, vice-Kapellmeister, and concertmaster.

Overall, it is impossible to determine more precisely how many musicians Bach had at his disposal at any of the places where he worked, nor how they were assigned to the various vocal-instrumental sections. Considering this, we must also include Bach's personal pupils, who in return for instruction

Interior of the Neue Kirche in Arnstadt, before the restauration.

(and sometimes accommodation) were available for copying and all kinds of other odd jobs and were at hand, at any rate, as assistants during performances.

Among Bach's earliest traceable pupils (with particulars of the place and period when they studied) are Johann Martin Schubert (1690–1721), beginning in Mühlhausen or earlier, until 1717; Johann Caspar Vogler (1696–1763), from 1710 (probably already as a ten-year old in Arnstadt); Johann Sebastian Koch (1689–1757), in Mühlhausen; Johann Tobias Krebs (1690–1762), ca. 1710–17; Johann Philipp Kräuter (1690–1741), 1712–13; Johann Lorenz Bach (1695–1773), 1713–17; Johann Bernhard Bach (1700–1773), in Weimar and Cöthen; Johann Gotthilf Ziegler (1688–1747), around 1715; Johann Georg Voigt (ca. 1689–1766); Prince Johann Ernst of Weimar (1697–1715); Samuel Gmelin (1695–1752) in Weimar; Johann Christoph Baumgarten (1687–1770), beginning in 1708; and Cornelius Heinrich Dretzel (1698–1775), around 1716–17. If such a roster of names can be representative only very approximately, and even if the specifics of the pupils' vocal-instrumental participation remain largely unknown, it still becomes evident how important the role of Bach's professional assistants must have been in those days.

The demands that Bach's scores made on the court musicians suggest the capability of the Weimar ensemble in particular. By comparison, the *Cantorei* was given a modest role as a ripieno ensemble. However, the Easter cantata BWV 31 illustrates that, if necessary, Bach could expect a five-voice ripieno (with divided soprano) from this choir. In principle we must take for granted that the vocal soloists took part in the choral movements. There is no evidence of solo-tutti differentiation (i.e., alternation of soloists and ripienists in large-scale choruses) during the Weimar period, but there is some for the performance of cantata BWV 71 on the occasion of the council election in Mühlhausen, and later for the performance of the two cantatas BWV 22 and 23 for Bach's audition as cantor in Leipzig. Reference to the appearance of an "unfamiliar maiden" in Arnstadt (*BR*, 53) emphasizes the apparent rarity of a female soloist. The Weimar solo cantatas BWV 54 and 199, however, were clearly reserved for male sopranos of the court choir. But it is by no means impossible that the solo part of BWV 199 was assigned to the royal court singer Anna Magdalena Wilke, Bach's second wife, when this cantata had its repeat performance in Cöthen.

In Arnstadt and Mühlhausen the changes in instrumentation had to do with the different occasions. However, the numerous variations in the scor-

Performing at court; detail of an eighteenth-century engraving.

ing of the Weimar cantatas point above all to the interest of Bach the virtuoso in concertante instrumental music in general, and later to the composer's intention to experiment with the orchestra's wide range of sound and
to use all available resources to their fullest extent. Also indicative of the
special conditions in Weimar is that in 1714, in conjunction with Bach's
appointment as concertmaster, a special decree was issued that in the
future, "rehearsing of the musical pieces" should no longer take place in the
Kapellmeister's own lodgings, as before, but "should always take place in
the church chapel" (*BR*, 70). This shows how much importance Bach apparently attributed to rehearsing his works meticulously in the location of the
actual performance.

INSTRUMENTAL MOVEMENTS AND SCORING

Johann Sebastian Bach, son of Johann Ambrosius Bach, who was the
director of town music in Eisenach, had since childhood been accustomed
to dealing with the most varied instruments and instrumental music of all
kinds. Even though the young Johann Sebastian's virtuoso ambitions were

concentrated primarily on the clavier and organ, this did not imply that his talents as an instrumental musician were in any way restricted. Not only had he played the violin and probably several other instruments, such as the violoncello piccolo/viola pomposa all his life, but he had a lively interest in instrument making, gave advice about it, and therefore possessed an exceptional knowledge of the special features and technical requirements of all major instruments. Furthermore, there is no doubt that from early on, instrumental ensemble music formed part of Bach's field of activity and even, in fact, his professional sphere of responsibility. His first brief employment at the Weimar court, in 1703, concerned chamber music, and even his later position as court organist in Weimar carried the obligation to be involved in chamber music. Unfortunately, there are scarcely any traces of this early period in Bach's oeuvre as a composer for instrumental ensemble. The only exception, the violin fugue in G minor, BWV 1026, from around 1712, could hardly be considered as representative. So, in the end, we are left with only the cantata repertory as a pale reflection of a more extensive instrumental output. Nonetheless, the cantatas offer impressive testimony to the intensity and originality of Bach's efforts in the domain of instrumental ensemble music.

Most of Bach's earlier cantatas begin with an independent instrumental prelude that in general introduces the full orchestral ensemble of the work: a sinfonia (BWV 4, 12, 18, 21, 131, 150, and 196), a sonata (BWV 31 and 182), a sonatina (BWV 106), and a concerto (BWV 152). The abundance of different sonorities in these pieces could hardly be greater and ranges from homogeneous string settings (BWV 4, 150, 196) and several combinations of strings and wind instruments (BWV 12, 21, 106, 131, 152, 182) to the most astonishing large-scale scoring imaginable (BWV 31), not without the occasional presentation of special instrumental effects (as, for instance, in BWV 18/1, with its unison parts for four violas). This interest in unusual sound effects can also be found in the kind of instrumental accompaniment for several vocal movements, especially in the obbligato treatment of the violoncello (BWV 71/6) or the bassoon (BWV 150/2 and 5). The latter reminds one of Bach's suggestions for the renovation of his organ in Mühlhausen, in which he writes that the installation of a 16-foot *fagotto* (bassoon stop) "is useful for all kinds of new inventions" (*BR*, 59).

Calling a movement "sinfonia" often signifies the close links between the introduction and the subsequent content of the work. In this way, for instance, the chorale melody "Christ lag in Todesbanden" is introduced in BWV 4/1, while in BWV 131/1 the instrumental movement and the choir are tightly interwoven with each other. The latter work serves as a model for the way instrumental and choral parts permeate each other in later cantatas and for the increasing influence gained by the instrumental forms where even the choral element prevails. Examples of this are the introductory chorus of BWV 61, in the style of a French overture, and the passacaglia in BWV 12/2.

The following systematic summary illustrates the extraordinary diversity in Bach's choice of instruments, regardless of whether the scoring is for strings, for mixed instruments, or for a large-scale ensemble. BWV 106, 71, 18, 152, and 31 depart from the norm more than any other cantatas. What the list does not show is the further differentiations in sound that can be heard within these works through all possible combinations of vocal and instrumental solo parts in the individual movements.

The older layer of cantatas (up to Easter 1715) tends not to repeat similar types of scoring, but for the later ones that is no longer a matter of principle. This tendency is particularly striking in, for example, cantatas scored for

Oboist and viola player; eighteenth century-engraving by C. Weigel.

string instruments only. Here, pre-Weimar cantatas show quite a variety of solutions (BWV 4, 150, 196); the Weimar cantatas dated after Easter 1715, however, show a uniform arrangement (BWV 155, 162, 163, 165). Even in the category of large-scale scoring there are variations between the retro-spective polychoral features in BWV 71, on the one hand, and, on the other, the different designs for an orchestral tutti in the cantatas BWV 21, 31, 63, and 172.

The older cantata scores (again, up to Easter 1715) are predominantly based on the French model of a five-voice string score with two violas, whereas the later ones are, without exception, rooted in the Italian type of a four-voice string setting. In the older group of works the three solo cantatas occupy a rather special position, with BWV 54 being the only one that represents the normal five-voice string scoring, while BWV 152 and 199 include wind instruments and thereby reduce the scoring at the same time.

SUMMARY: INSTRUMENTAL SCORING*

Category	Work	Instruments
1. Pre-Weimar cantatas		
without wind instruments	BWV 196:	2 v, va, bc
	BWV 4:	2 v, 2 va, bc
with wind instruments	BWV 131:	ob, v, 2 va, bc
	BWV 106:	2 rec, 2 va da gamba, bc
	BWV 150:	2 v, bc
large-scale orchestra	BWV 71:	(chorus I) 3 tr, timp;
		(chorus II) 2 rec, vc;
		(chorus III) 2 ob, bsn;
		(chorus IV) 2 v, va;
		(chorus V) bc
2. Weimar cantatas up to Easter 1715		
without wind instruments	BWV 18:	4 va, bc
	BWV 54, 61:	2 v, 2 va, bc
with wind instruments	BWV 152:	rec, ob, va d'amore, va da gamba, bc
	BWV 199:	ob, 2 v, va, bc
	BWV 182:	rec 2 v, 2 va, bc
	BWV 12:	ob, tr, 2 v, 2 va, bc

large-scale orchestra	BWV 21:	3 tr, timp, ob, 2 v, 2 va, bc
	BWV 172:	3 tr, timp, fl, ob, 2 v, 2 va, bc
	BWV 31:	3 tr, timp 3 ob, taille, 2 v, 2 va, bc (5-voice chorus: SSATB)

3. Weimar cantatas after Easter 1715

without wind instruments	BWV 155, 162, 163, 165	2 v, va, bc
with wind instruments	BWV 132, 185:	ob, 2 v, va, bc
	BWV 161:	2 rec, 2 v, va, bc
large-scale orchestra	BWV 63:	4 tr, timp, 3 ob, 2 v, va, bc

4. Leipzig audition pieces, 1723

with wind instruments	BWV 22:	ob, 2 v, va, bc
	BWV 23:	2 ob, 2v, va, bc; additionally cornet, 3 tbn

Abbreviations:

bc	= basso continuo
bsn	= bassoon**
ob	= oboe
org	= organ
rec	= recorder
tbn	= trombone
timp	= timpani
tr	= trumpet
v	= violin
va	= viola
vc	= violoncello
vne	= violone

* NB. Scoring changes for repeat performances in Leipzig are not taken into account.

** Shown only if used in obbligato fashion.

Bassoonist; eighteenth-century engraving by C. Weigel.

Present-day interior of the Blasiuskirche (St. Blasius's) in Mühlhausen.

11

CANTATA CHORUSES AND CHORALES

Daniel R. Melamed

CHORUSES

The chorus is an element strongly associated with Bach's cantatas, but as a movement type, "chorus" is elusive and relatively difficult to define, compared to other kinds of pieces in the cantatas. Recitatives and arias are textual types (irregular and regular poetry, respectively) in the modern so-called Neumeister-type librettos, strongly associated with certain kinds of musical settings for solo singers. In earlier cantatas, arias are less distinctive textually, often being settings of biblical texts, but they are still recognizable by musical features such as melodic character and solo scoring. Chorales, despite the tremendous variety in their settings, have in common the use of hymn texts and tunes, and form a clear if musically varied category.

Defining a "chorus" in a cantata, however, is a little more difficult. There are certain musical styles that are appropriate only to choruses, but choruses can draw on almost any type of text (poetry, biblical prose, chorales), they can be in almost any style, and they can vary widely in musical characteristics. Rather than being a style or a text type, "chorus" is primarily a matter of scoring: a movement that calls for the entire vocal ensemble, with or without instruments. This is not an issue of performance practice; it makes no difference how many singers are on a part. Even a collection of all the soloists in a dramatic cantata is a chorus (for example, several movements in "Was mir behagt, is nur die muntre Jagd," BWV 208).

The importance, function, and musical construction of choruses vary with the type of cantata. (A cantata need not contain any choruses, as demonstrated by three of Bach's works for vocal soloists only: "Widerstehe doch der Sünde," BWV 54, "Mein Herze schwimmt in Blut," BWV 199, and "Tritt auf die Glaubensbahn," BWV 152.) Most of Bach's pre-Weimar cantatas revolve around their choral movements, which not only represent a substantial fraction of the music but also serve as the framing and organizing pieces. Choruses largely define these earlier cantatas, and most of their texts consist of the biblical prose and chorales that dominate these librettos overall. The musical style and organization of these choruses are a direct legacy of the seventeenth-century vocal concerto. In contrast, the Neumeister-type cantatas Bach composed later are dominated by their free poetic texts, set mostly as solo recitatives and arias. Choruses play an important role in these works, but the influence of "madrigalian" free poetry makes itself felt in them: most of the choral movements in Bach's Weimar cantatas are settings of free texts (the remainder are chorale settings), and their musical style reflects this very different kind of text, compared to earlier works.

Choral movements give structure to all of Bach's pre-Weimar cantatas, which are built, for the most part, around biblical texts, often Psalms. "Aus der Tiefen," BWV 131, for example, has opening, central, and concluding choruses with intermediate arias; "Gottes Zeit ist die allerbeste Zeit," BWV 106, has the same structure, as does the oldest layer of "Ich hatte viel Bekümmernis," BWV 21 (movements 2–3–6–8?–9); "Gott ist mein König," BWV 71, and "Nach dir, Herr, verlanget mich," BWV 150, each adds a final chorus on a free poetic text to this model; "Christ lag in Todes Banden," BWV 4, uses the same structure for its chorale texts; and "Der Herr denket an uns," BWV 196, is similarly constructed, lacking a central chorus but retaining the outer framing movements. (Some of these works begin with an instrumental movement, but the first vocal movement is always a chorus). In length, musical weight, and position, these choruses dominate their cantatas.

The musical construction of these movements is strongly influenced by the characteristics of the biblical prose texts. Following the model of the late

Final chorus of the cantata "Aus der Tiefen rufe ich, Herr, zu dir,"
BWV 131. (Bach's autograph)

seventeenth-century vocal concerto, many of these choruses are sectional, changing meter, tempo, texture, and affect with each textual phrase. For example, BWV 106/2a begins with the voices declaiming the first phrase of the text (actually a biblically-derived prayer, "Gottes Zeit ist die allerbeste Zeit" [God's time is the very best time]) more or less simultaneously, changes to a faster dance-like meter with imitation among the voices for the second phrase ("in ihm leben, weben und sind wir, so lange er will" [in him we live, move, and have our being]), and then slows down once again for the final phrase ("In ihm sterben wir zu rechter Zeit" [In him we die at the appointed time]), illustrated with expressive harmonies. BWV 131/5 begins with three slow block statements of an exhortation ("Israel, Israel, Israel . . . "), presents the continuation of the phrase (". . . hoffe auf den Herrn" [Let (Israel) hope in the Lord]) in a much more animated setting, returns to slow declamation for the next phrase ("denn bei dem Herrn ist die Gnade" [for with the Lord there is mercy]), and then erupts into fast vocal and instrumental motion for the phrases that finish this portion of the text and for the concluding section ("und viel Erlösung bei ihm. Und er wird Israel erlösen von allen seinen Sünden" [and with him is plenteous redemption. And he shall redeem Israel from all its iniquities]). A particularly telling example is BWV 21/2, whose slow opening section ("Ich hatte viel Bekümmernis in meinem Herzen" [I had much affliction in my heart]) turns, after a stop and a block statement of the crucial word "aber" (but), to a fast, exuberant setting of the concluding phrase (". . . deine Tröstungen erquick-en meine Seele" [. . . your comforts delight my soul]). Although the tendency toward sectionalization has disadvantages—it threatens musical continuity—its strength is the ability to change affect almost instantly, and Bach takes particular advantage of this feature to illustrate the strong expressive contrasts in these texts.

Many of these sectional choral movements in the early cantatas turn to fugal (imitative) writing for large portions of the text, especially concluding phrases of multisection choruses. Two tendencies are noteworthy in these fugal pieces. First, Bach tends to work out his material at relatively great length, presenting many statements of the text phrase and its musical subject in each of the voices and in many combinations (for example, BWV 131/5, "Und er wird Israel erlösen"). Second, many of these movements employ a particular technique (the so-called permutation fugue) in which Bach sets each of four text phrases to four different musical ideas, and then builds a fugal movement out of them by deploying them in the four voices in ever-changing permutations. A good example is BWV 71/3; the four text segments, each set to two measures of music, are (a) "Dein Alter sei wie deine

Jugend"; (b) "und Gott ist mit dir in Allem, das du tust"; (c) "und Gott ist mit dir in Allem, in Allem"; and (d) "das du tust, das du tust." Bach has a new voice enter every two measures, each singing phrases a, b, c, and d in order, resulting in many different combinations of the four phrases in the four voices. In this movement Bach calls only for soloists, without the larger group of singers (the ripienists), reminding us that the movement's use of ensemble voices, not the size of the forces, makes the designation "chorus" appropriate.

In BWV 71/3, too, there is no role for instruments other than the supporting basso continuo, but most of the choruses from Bach's early cantatas use both voices and instruments. Their relationship varies from movement to movement, but one characteristic feature is that Bach often treats voices and instruments equally. Voices will sometimes imitate phrases first presented by instruments, and instruments will often add extra parts to imitative vocal textures. One also gets the sense in many of the early choruses that material first presented by instruments was conceived with text and singers in mind, in contrast to the situation in many of Bach's later vocal movements. There, the essential musical substance seems to have been designed with instruments in mind, and the vocal parts overlaid afterwards.

In addition to the predominant biblical texts, a few of Bach's pre-Weimar choral movements use other kinds of texts. BWV 4/2, 4/5, and 106/4 are chorale settings (see below). BWV 21/9 combines a biblical text and a chorale in the manner of the contemporary genre of the motet. Two movements use free poetic texts. BWV 71/7, which sets two stanzas of poetry, is constructed much like a setting of a biblical text: it has frequent changes of meter and tempo, contrasts of instruments with solo voices and chorus, and a substantial permutation fugue. BWV 150/7 presents a variety of vocal textures (including block writing for all four parts, solo turns for individual voice parts, and imitations among the voices) above a short melodic pattern that repeats over and over in the instrumental bass. This movement, derived from the dance type known as a chaconne, is the one from which Johannes Brahms borrowed the repeating bass for the finale of his Fourth Symphony. In Bach's cantata movement, the repetition of the bass line and the metrical regularity of the poetic text contribute to a musical character that is very different from that in his choruses on biblical texts, which dominate the early cantatas.

Just as biblical texts are prevalent in Bach's pre-Weimar cantatas overall and their choral movements in particular, the most characteristic textual element of Bach's Neumeister-type Weimar cantatas—free "madrigalian" poetry—dominates the choral movements in those works. The turn to free poetry set mostly as solo recitatives and arias brought several important changes to the choruses in Bach's cantatas. Choruses are restricted to opening vocal and closing movements, the interior movements of these works being almost exclusively paired solo recitatives and arias. The one exception—and the only intermediate chorus—is the fifth movement of "Komm, du süße Todesstunde," BWV 161, clearly a substitute for the solo aria that the librettist presumably had intended. That Bach could choose to set it for chorus should remind us that the "aria" textual type was appropriate to choral setting as well as to solo pieces, and that the free poetic texts of Bach's Weimar cantata choruses are largely indistinguishable from those of solo arias.

Another feature of the Weimar works is that arias and choruses become more closely related musically as well. A substantial number (the first and seventh movements of "Christen, ätzet diesen Tag," BWV 63, the first vocal movement and eighth movement of "Himmelskönig, sei willkommen," BWV 182, the first movement of "Erschallet, ihr Lieder," BWV 172, which is also the last movement, and the first vocal movement of "Weinen, Klagen, Sorgen, Zagen," BWV 12) are in da capo form, like so many of Bach's cantata arias. Many choruses—or large sections of them—are, in effect, four-part arias, with animated but largely chordal presentation of text (for example, BWV 63/1, 172/1 [first section]). Most begin and end with idiomatic instrumental passages, essentially the equivalent of the ritornellos in the parallel places in solo arias.

Like the choruses from Bach's early cantatas, though, these movements also show a tendency to imitative and fugal writing (for example, the first movement of "Herz und Mund und Tat und Leben," BWV 147a, the first vocal movement of "Der Himmel lacht," BWV 31/2, BWV 182/2, and BWV 172/1 [second section]). These Weimar-era choruses tend to be unified in their affects, but a few show the tendency to sectionalization so characteristic of earlier cantata choruses (for example, "Der Himmel lacht, die Erde jubiliret," BWV 31/2, with its slower intermediate section "Der sich das Grab zur Ruh erlesen"). One movement, BWV 12/2 (later reused in the "Crucifixus" of the Mass in B minor), is a chaconne. Despite its modern free poetic text, this movement, with its spare instrumental writing and stereotyped lamenting bass line, is old-fashioned—a striking combination of the old and the new.

"Nun komm, der Heiden Heiland," BWV 61, opens with a chorale movement, a striking adaptation of the French-overture style. This movement is the exception, though; all of the other opening choruses in Bach's Weimar cantatas are free poems, an indication of how thorough the influence of the new taste in cantata librettos was. The remaining choruses (mostly last movements) in Bach's Weimar cantatas are chorale settings, discussed below. One large group consists of four-part chorale harmonizations that conclude a number of cantatas. BWV 61/6, a more elaborate setting, also rounds off its cantata, and BWV 182/8 may originally have been the final movement of that work.

After a long hiatus in Bach's composition of church cantatas during his employment as a court musician in Cöthen, he composed two cantatas ("Jesus nahm zu sich die Zwölfe," BWV 22, and "Du wahrer Gott und Davids Sohn," BWV 23) containing a small compendium of choral movement types for his test for the Leipzig cantorate in 1723. There are two chorale settings (BWV 22/5, an elaborated four-part setting, and BWV 23/4, itself demon-

Fragment of the cantata "Weinen, Klagen, Sorgen, Zagen," BWV 12. (Bach's autograph)

strating several different treatments of a hymn); a setting of a biblical text, BWV 22/1, which begins with the words of an Evangelist and of Jesus, set in aria style, and then concludes with a fugal motet-like chorus; and finally, a setting of a free poetic text, BWV 23/3, which alternates a tenor/bass duet with recurring statements of the opening music and text by the chorus. Bach thus demonstrated nearly the full range of choruses in this kind of cantata, set to three different kinds of texts in a variety of musical styles.

CHORALES

Chorales play a significant role in Bach's church cantatas, and in these works he gave them a great variety of musical settings. To understand both the importance of these hymns in Bach's cantatas and the ways in which he treated them, we need to look back to the place of hymns in Lutheran practice and to the strong traditions of musical settings that grew around them. The importance of chorales—and their very presence—in eighteenth-century church cantatas results from the influence of Martin Luther himself, and the musical styles of chorale settings in cantatas from this time trace their roots to the earliest years of the Reformed church.

Sacred songs were part of the earliest stages of Lutheran reform. This is especially true of the liturgical material Luther prepared in the vernacular; one need only look at the Deutsche Messe (1526), which is taken up largely with musical settings of liturgical items for the celebration of the Mass in German. Further, among the earliest publications by Luther and his contemporaries were small collections of hymns, some by Luther himself. The direct connection of these pieces to him and to members of his close circle must have had immediate significance to his contemporaries as well as strong historical associations for later musicians, even apart from the emphasis Luther placed on music and singing in his writings.

Chorale poetry served several essential functions, among them inspirational, devotional, and catechistic. But chorales were most important for two other functions, and their integration into the cantata was really just a continuation of these. The first concerned the close relation of chorales to Scripture, which they often paraphrased, reflected on, and explained. Church cantatas were closely tied to scriptural readings, and together with the preacher's sermon, often helped interpret the biblical text of the day. To this extent, the chorales in a cantata text, usually chosen to complement or comment on Scripture, still served an exegetical role. The carefully

Advent songs in the Eisenach Hymnal, 1673.

designed juxtapositions of biblical and chorale texts found in so many cantatas were a link to the chorales' original purposes.

This function of chorales depends on their identity as texts—as poetry—for chorales are texts as much as they are music. The person assembling a cantata libretto turned to chorale stanzas primarily for their texts and the relation of those texts to others in the libretto. The tunes associated with these chorale poems were the composer's concern, part of the musical realization of the libretto. The importance of the chorale text is made even clearer in movements that use an instrumental chorale without text. In such a movement the composer almost always implies a particular stanza of the chorale poetry; the melody may end up as an important part of the musical substance of the piece, but it is used primarily to evoke the text.

The second important function of chorales lay in their role as a vehicle for direct congregational participation in worship—everybody sang. The participatory associations of chorales were indirect, because it is almost certain that the congregation did not sing along in a cantata. But one common kind of chorale setting in the cantatas Bach composed in Weimar and later (simple four-part settings—see below) may represent congregational hymns symbolically. In addition, the hymns that were sung by the congregation during the liturgy must often have coincided with those in the day's cantata, strengthening the connection between them.

One of the hallmarks of Bach's cantata output is the dazzling variety of different musical treatments of chorales, but the overwhelming majority of his chorale settings, both in pre-Neumeister and Neumeister-type librettos, use one of only two basic techniques, both of which had been important in Lutheran music for generations. The first type is a simple, four-voice chordal harmonization with the melody in the highest part. This type, sometimes known as a "Kantionalsatz" (cantional setting), is just like that found in certain modern hymnals. This kind of setting traces its roots to collections of such pieces published in the late fifteenth and early sixteenth centuries, the most famous of these by Johann Hermann Schein (1627).

These four-part settings, closest to congregational singing, are a feature of Bach's Weimar cantatas and later, after his adoption of Neumeister-type librettos with mixed text. These settings almost always appear as the last movement of their cantata ("Gleichwie der Regen und Schnee," BWV 18, "Alles nur nach Gottes Willen," BWV 72, "O heilges Geist- und Wasserbad," BWV 165, "Barmherziges Herze der ewigen Liebe," BWV 185, "Ach! ich sehe, itzt, da ich zur Hochzeit gehe," BWV 162, and "Mein Gott, wie lang, ach lange?," BWV 155). We do not have the music for the closing chorales of two contemporary works ("Bereitet die Wege, bereitet die Bahn," BWV 132, and "Alles, was von Gott geboren," BWV 80a), but it is most likely that they were also of this type. "Nur jedem das Seine!," BWV 163, presumably also ended this way; in his score Bach wrote out only an instrumental bass line and the indication "Choral. Simplice stylo," representing, with the melody line, the skeleton of a four-voice harmonization.

In all these pieces the role of instruments is limited to doubling the vocal lines; we know from surviving performing parts that Bach typically distributed all the available instruments among the vocal lines according to range. A number of other chorale settings—especially concluding movements of cantatas—elaborate on the simple four-voice model by slightly expanding the role of the instruments. BWV 12/7, 172/6 (but not the last movement), and 31/9 each add an independent instrumental line above the hymn tune in the vocal soprano, resulting in a five-voice texture. The last movement of "Wachet! betet! betet! wachet!," BWV 70a, adds three independent string lines, yielding a seven-voice texture. In BWV 161/6 Bach adds a fast-moving obbligato line, played by two recorders, to the basic four-part texture. The closest similar setting in Bach's pre-Weimar cantatas is BWV 106/4, the closing section of the cantata. In this piece an ornamented four-part setting is introduced by brief instrumental material that reappears between chorale phrases. The last phrase of the chorale is presented in fast, active imitation among the voices, leading up to the presentation of the last phrase in long notes.

This final section of BWV 106/4 points to the other principal kind of chorale setting found in Bach's cantatas. This type presents the chorale melody in long note-values in a voice or an instrument, embedded in or floating atop faster-moving material. The nature of this supporting material can vary widely and may be vocal, instrumental, or vocal-instrumental. The oldest type is purely vocal, with chorale phrases in long notes (the "cantus firmus") supported by the other voices singing musical ideas taken from the chorale tune itself, in imitation of each other. Settings of this type go back to the earliest musical publications of Martin Luther's immediate circle, for example, the many settings in Johann Walter's *Geystliches Gesangk Buchleyn* (Wittenberg, 1524). Cantus firmus chorale settings had their roots in German secular song (where, as in the earliest chorale settings, the cantus firmus is typically in an inner part rather than the top one), but the technique soon became strongly associated with chorales.

A page of Johann Walter's "Geystliches Gesangk Buchleyn," 1504.

The closest of Bach's settings to such sixteenth-century ancestors are those that use voices only, without independent instrumental parts (motets, in essence). The structure of these pieces centers on imitative entrances of three voice parts that anticipate and then support the "true" entrance of the chorale melody in long notes in the fourth voice. The purest example is BWV 4/5, in which the cantus firmus is in the alto part. BWV 182/7 is similar in construction but uses more active parts supporting a soprano cantus firmus. BWV 21/9 adds another element characteristic of the contemporary motet: the supporting voices in this movement present a biblical text to support the chorale cantus firmus, presented first in the tenor and then in the soprano. BWV 4/2 adds yet another element. Here, the soprano cantus firmus setting is framed and articulated by instrumental passages. Bach integrates the technique of the chorale cantus firmus into the texture of the vocal concerto.

In Bach's Weimar cantatas cantus firmus technique appears most often in connection with the most characteristic feature of these later works, the aria. In a large number of pieces, Bach writes an aria with a chorale tune presented phrase by phrase in an instrument. Among the many settings of this type, Bach provides great variety. There are arias for each voice part;

both solo arias (BWV 12/6, 31/8, 80a/1, 161/1) and closely related duets (BWV 163/5, 172/5, 185/1); pieces with a plain cantus firmus, those with a slightly ornamented one, and those with the chorale tune elaborately decorated; presentations of the cantus firmus in woodwinds, strings, brass, and solo organ; and arias with basso continuo only and those with both continuo and an obbligato solo instrumental line. In all these pieces, whatever the details of scoring, the governing musical forces are those of the aria and not the chorale. For example, the pieces reach their final cadence when the voice or voices and (typically) the concluding instrumental ritornello have finished, well after the last chorale phrase has ended. These movements are arias first, with an added cantus firmus.

Closely related to these arias with instrumental chorales are arias with a sung cantus firmus. Such pieces are largely characteristic of Bach's pre-Weimar cantatas (BWV 131/2, 131/4, 106/3b, 71/2). All are continuo arias, with no obbligato instrument, and all are settings of biblical texts paired with chorales in contrast to the free poetry used in the Weimar-era pieces just discussed. Two other pieces, one from Weimar and one probably written earlier, combine the aria with a chorale in a different way: in BWV 199/6 and 4/4, Bach offers an active instrumental obbligato line (with continuo, of course) and a simple chorale cantus firmus presented by a solo voice. These pieces might be described as being like an aria-with-chorale but without the aria.

Bach's Weimar cantata for the beginning of liturgical year, the first Sunday in Advent, contains two singular chorale treatments. The last movement of this cantata (BWV 61/6) sets the second part of a chorale tune for chorus, with the chorale melody in the soprano against active lower voice parts and a violin obbligato line. The first movement (BWV 61/1) is among Bach's most striking creations. Its vocal parts aside, this piece is an example of the so-called French overture, typically a purely instrumental genre found in opera overtures, dance suites, and the like. It has a slow, stately opening with a characteristic long-short rhythmic pattern, and a second half usually cast as a fast dance, beginning with parts imitating each other. In BWV 61/1 Bach lays a sung chorale melody over the instrumental overture. In the slow first part voices from the choir each sing cantus-firmus-like statements of the first line of the chorale; in the second part the remainder of the chorale melody forms the basis for the fast part of the overture, complete with imitation and dance-like meter. There is also a brief return to the opening slow tempo, typical of overtures, for the presentation of the last line of the chorale. This movement is perhaps the best example of Bach's imaginative treatment of chorales and his fusing of musical types.

Another extraordinary combination of musical types is found in BWV 106/2d. This section (strictly, one cannot speak of movements in a work like this) combines three elements: a motet-like imitative treatment of an Apocrypha text, an arioso setting of a New Testament text, and an instrumental chorale. Each of the three texts (the chorale text is implied) comments on and interacts with the others. This interaction of texts is matched by Bach's combination of musical types.

A special case among Bach's early cantatas is BWV 4. This cantata is a setting of all the verses of the Easter hymn "Christ lag in Todes Banden." The cantata opens with a short sinfonia drawing on melodic ideas from the chorale tune, followed by settings of each verse of the chorale in different musical styles. Movements 2 and 5 are cantus firmus settings (see above). Movements 3 and 7 are vocal duets in which the chorale melody itself is never fully presented, but in which each phrase of the tune is given in paraphrase by the two solo voices. There are two aria treatments: movement 4 (discussed above), which has a violin obbligato with a solo tenor cantus firmus; and movement 6, a bass solo, which presents a vocal paraphrase of the chorale tune beginning in the style of a lament, with an instrumental cantus firmus woven into the first violin line. The original last movement of BWV 4 does not survive; Bach wrote a simple four-voice setting when he reused the piece later in his career, adding one more kind of treatment to this compendium of chorale settings from his earlier years.

Bach returned to vocal chorale settings in his two test pieces for the cantorate in Leipzig in early 1723. BWV 22/5 ends its cantata with an expanded four-voice setting, but one different from that seen in Bach's Weimar chorales. Here, the harmonization of the chorale melody is embedded in an instrumental texture (a continuous fast-moving line in the violin and oboe, and slower, steady continuo) that is capable of standing on its own musically.

In BWV 23 Bach used the same chorale melody twice in the version he ultimately performed in Leipzig. In BWV 23/4 the chorus sings three repetitions of the melody "Christe, du Lamm Gottes" (the German Agnus Dei of the Mass Ordinary), drawing both on four-voice style and cantus-firmus technique. The chorale phrases appear with framing orchestral material, and in the middle repetition Bach shows that the chorale melody in the soprano can be imitated in canon both above and below by the oboe and violin. Here, Bach explores the possibilities of a simple and repetitive melody by enriching it with an instrumental accompaniment, with two kinds of chorale treatment, and with canonic technique. In BWV 23/2, an orchestrally accompanied recitative for solo tenor, Bach works in the same chorale in long notes in the violin and oboe—a kind of cantus firmus in a recitative, surely a remarkable accomplishment. In both the recitative and the chorus, Bach treated the chorale melody as material to be explored and deployed in elaborate, unexpected, and striking ways. He moved beyond traditional chorale settings to create new combinations of genre and movement type. The movement categories of chorale and chorus in cantatas, so little bound to particular musical styles, were the perfect place for Bach to exercise his imagination in this way.

Fragment of the cantata "Du wahrer Gott
und Davids Sohn," BWV 23.
(Bach's autograph)

Musicalisches
LEXICON
Oder
Musicalische Bibliothec,

Darinnen nicht allein

Die Musici, welche so wol in alten als
neuern Zeiten, ingleichen bey verschiedenen Natio-
nen, durch Theorie und Praxin sich hervor gethan, und was
von jedem bekannt worden, oder er in Schrifften hinter-
lassen, mit allem Fleisse und nach den vornehmsten
Umständen angeführet,

Sondern auch

Die in Griechischer, Lateinischer, Italiänischer und
Frantzösischer Sprache gebräuchliche Musicalische Kunst-
oder sonst dahin gehörige Wörter,

nach Alphabetischer Ordnung
vorgetragen und erkläret,

Und zugleich

die meisten vorkommende Signaturen
erläutert werden

von

Johann Gottfried Walthern,
Fürstl. Sächs. Hof-Musico und Organisten an der Haupt-Pfarr-Kirche
zu St. Petri und-Pauli in Weimar.

Leipzig,
verlegts Wolffgang Deer, 1732.

Title page of Johann Gotfried Walther's "Musikalisches Lexicon,"
Leipzig, 1732.

12

CANTATA ARIAS AND RECITATIVES

Peter Wollny

The introduction around 1700 of recitatives and arias marked the codification of the sacred cantata genre and determined the course of its further development as no other innovation had done before. The term "aria" had been used in relation to sacred vocal music, but at this time it acquired a totally new meaning. Arias of the seventeenth century were set mostly to strophic poetry that was tinged with subjective Pietism. Composers often troped a biblical verse that formed the basis for the cantata text or replaced it with a rhyming paraphrase. From then on arias were understood to be madrigal-like settings of non-strophic poetry, derived from the Italian chamber cantata and the opera, and more often than not requiring a da capo structure in their musical realization. By the same token, the concept of a "recitative" was not really new either (although the term was hardly ever used in the seventeenth century), because the monodic recitation of biblical prose had been practiced in Germany at least as early as Heinrich Schütz's *Weihnachts-Historie* (1664). This older style of recitative, however, with its expanded melismatic passages, was vastly different from the new and strongly declamatory type. Looking back in 1739, Johann Mattheson was right in suggesting that "in time and rhythm" the older recitative would have been "like our arioso."[1] Only gradually did the original connotation of the terms "aria" and "recitative" give way to the new. Even as late as 1732, in Johann Gottfried Walther's *Musicalisches Lexicon*, the terms were still being used in the original sense.

The decision to insert recitatives and arias into cantatas or to construct cantatas entirely out of these two elements was made initially at a textual level and was caused by a basic change in perception of the genre's theological purpose. If the older cantatas and their often colorful assortment of biblical quotations provided direct access to the Bible, then the new recitatives, with their iambic verses of variable length, effectively illustrated and reflected the Gospel text designated for a certain Sunday. The arias, in their epigrammatic compactness, were deliberately subjective because of the requirement to "always contain an affection, or a *Morale* [lesson], or something else special,"[2] and in this way create a direct emotional link with the listener. Contrary to the old strophic aria, the da capo aria, with its cyclic form, is especially suitable for dialectic subject matter.

Arias in the modern sense are rare in Bach's cantatas dating from his Mühlhausen period, and there are no recitatives at all. The backbone of each of these compositions is a text from the Bible, supplemented with chorale stanzas. Only the Easter cantata "Christ lag in Todes Banden," BWV 4, is characteristic of a pure chorale cantata *per omnes versus*, making use of all chorale stanzas and symmetrically alternating the performing forces employed in each movement. Bach's noticeable reservation about employing modern forms ought not be seen necessarily as a conservative attitude toward church music. It was customary for members of the church council to require composers to submit pieces of music for approval, as indicated in Bach's official appointment as organist of the Halle Liebfrauenkirche, dated December 1713. The document contains a special note that Bach was "obliged to communicate in good time to the Chief Pastor of our Church, the council member, Dr. Heinecke, for his approval, the *textus* [texts] and *cantiones* [music] chosen" (*Dok* II, No. 63). Often the choice or drafting of the text was directly in the hands of the pastor of the church, who then handed it to the composer to set to music. Such was the case, presumably, with the cantata "Aus der Tiefen rufe ich, Herr, zu dir," BWV 131: the handwritten score is marked, "Set to music at the request of Mr. Georg Christian Eilmar." The attitude of an ecclesiastical superior could therefore determine in large part the style of the music. The free imperial town of Mühlhausen and the small court seat at Arnstadt were both rather conservative in matters of church music, and it must be noted that the reforms instigated by Erdmann Neumeister were slow in reaching the two localities.

Organ in the Liebfrauenkirche in Halle.

In the case of the young Bach, his reluctance to set modern cantata texts may simply reflect his inexperience with setting such texts. It is quite like- ly that in those days Bach did not know or could not procure the earliest settings of Neumeister texts by such composers as the Weissenfels Kapellmeister Johann Philipp Krieger (cantata cycle of 1700) or the Rudolstadt Kapellmeister Philipp Heinrich Erlebach (cantata cycle of 1708). Bach's early da capo arias reveal that he had had little contact with this genre, lacked fully developed examples, and had barely begun to explore their inherent possibilities and subtleties. Only with the Weimar series of cantatas, begun in 1714, did he start to devote much time to this new form, preferring at first texts by the Weimar court poet Salomon Franck. Franck's texts, while containing fully realized da capo arias, usually dispensed with recitatives and thus created a link between the old form of the cantata and the new. We do not know whether Bach composed any arias and recitatives during the five years between the Mühlhausen cantatas (around 1707–08) and his first ones in Weimar (from approximately 1714). No sacred cantatas and only one secular one—the Hunting Cantata, BWV 208, written around 1712–13—survive from that period.

From the beginning Bach's handling of the modern aria avoids any formalism. It is hard to judge to what extent the experimental nature of his early arias was extraordinary, considering the lack of detailed information about cantatas produced by his contemporaries. In any event, the composition of da capo arias alternating with recitatives was a new exercise for all composers. Yet Bach's works consistently display a higher level of musical-technical perfection and spiritual perception than those of his contemporaries.

According to recent scholarship, the earliest sacred vocal work by Bach is the cantata "Nach dir, Herr, verlanget mich," BWV 150, the authenticity of which had long been questioned. In this composition Bach inserted three stanzas in free rhyme between selected verses of Psalm 25, the first two of which he wrote as arias and the last one as a chaconne with an ostinato bass. The proportions of the two arias are quite small-scale, and they lack any textual or musical da capo structure. Nonetheless, Bach unifies the two movements by taking up the ritornello at the end of the third movement and by using a steady, quasi-ostinato bass formula in the fifth.

The Mühlhausen cantatas BWV 4, BWV 106, and BWV 131 do not contain any arias and do not make use of free poetry. Both BWV 106 and BWV 131, however, have expanded *ariosi,* which display aria-like features such as the appearance of ritornellos and a homogeneous, coherent development. We can therefore conclude that Bach had begun experimenting with a new style, even if the presentation of the texts did not yet permit any real arias. For instance, the tenor solo "Ach Herr, lehre uns bedenken" and the subsequent bass solo "Bestelle dein Haus" from the *Actus Tragicus,* BWV 106, recall the motto aria of the Italian opera around 1700 in the treatment and presentation of the text and its use in a ritornello.

Bach had the opportunity to try out da capo forms within a vocal composition when he wrote the large-scale cantata "Gott ist mein König," BWV 71, for the town council elections in early February 1708. The occasion for which the work was composed came close to a secular event; it was therefore acceptable, even in conservative Mühlhausen, to include modern elements in a church composition. Bach shapes the composition of movements 4 and 5—the former based on the verse of a Psalm, the latter on free poetry—along the principles of the da capo aria, although, according to Alfred Dürr, he still adheres to "the structure of a sacred concerto." Bach intended, with this ambitious work, to write the most modern music possible at the time. This is borne out by his decision not to compose the two identically constructed stanzas of the final movement as a strophic aria alternating with ritornellos but rather to create a single, through-composed movement.

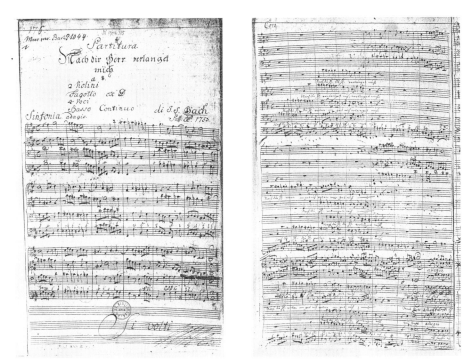

The first two pages of the cantata "Nach dir, Herr, verlanget mich," BWV 150.
(Copyist's score, second half of the eighteenth century)

Bach took a further step forward in the wedding cantata "Der Herr denket an uns," BWV 196. Although the purely biblical text—a selection from Psalm 115—did not invite experimentation, Bach took the liberty, in the third movement, to write a short but fully developed da capo aria to the line "Er segnet, die den Herrn fürchten" (He will bless them that fear the lord). Voice (soprano) and continuo are joined by an obbligato instrumental part played by the tutti violins, as in the soprano aria "Doch bin und bleibe ich vergnügt," BWV 150, which develops its own ritornello theme. The arrangement of the vocal part may be indebted to the motto aria, but the aria contains early examples of elements found in Bach's mature vocal works, including a simultaneous combination of the voice part with the ritornello.

As stated above, at the end of Bach's Mühlhausen period we temporarily lose sight of him as a composer of sacred vocal music. When he re-emerged as a cantata composer in Weimar in 1713, the genre had changed radically. Bach worked through the entire range of stylistic possibilities that the aria genre permitted, occasionally coming up with highly unconventional solutions. Whereas the arias of his first Weimar cantatas (BWV 21 and BWV 18) are still reminiscent in their brevity and many other details of those of the Mühlhausen period, the works Bach created from March 1714 on show the composer forging new paths. Bach's early cantatas are composed primarily with regard to the biblical text and occasionally the chorale, thus putting great emphasis on tutti movements. Arias and arioso sections are considered interpolations (not an insignificant reason for these works being more popular than the later cantatas during the Bach revival of the nineteenth century). The new type of cantata, on the other hand, is composed along the lines of free poetry, and the compositional choices are aimed predominantly at the presentation of arias and their relation to each other, as well as their alternation with recitatives. With regard to the overall architecture of a work, the choruses often yield to the arias, and chorales tend to appear only as concluding, simple four-part settings, without an obbligato instrumental part. Not until the large-scale biblical text choruses of his first Leipzig cantata cycle (1723–24) and the chorale-based choruses of the second (1724–25) did Bach manage to create tutti movements that were equally imposing, artistically elaborate, and musically flexible.

This change of priorities affects everything concerned with composition and technique. On the one hand, the arias portray an affection that is clearly developed and remains consistent throughout an entire movement, whereas formerly the musical realization of biblical prose allowed for merely stringing together segments of various length. On the other hand, the arias, being large-scale, self-contained creations, often have imaginative and original orchestrations that lead to the even stronger individualization of the separate movements of a cantata. The first work of a series written between 1714 and 1716, the cantata for Palm Sunday "Himmelskönig, sei willkommen," BWV 182 (composed for March 25, 1714), contains one aria for each of the three soloists (alto, tenor, bass). The arias achieve their individual character through the following instrumental variations:

BWV	182/4	Bass + strings
	182/5	Alto + recorder
	182/6	Tenor + continuo

The third part of the cantata "Der Herr denket an uns," BWV 196, for soprano and tutti violins (Copy, second half of the eighteenth century).

In his large-scale Easter cantata "Erschallet, ihr Lieder," BWV 172 (written for May 20, 1714), Bach proceeds in the same systematic way following the introductory tutti (which is repeated at the end):

BWV	172/3	Bass + trumpets
	172/4	Tenor + strings (unison)
	172/5	Soprano, alto + oboe

As a result of this musical treatment, the arias stand out more strongly in contrast with each other, each displaying a different affection, and they receive more individual emphasis than had been possible in older cantatas.

A special feature of the arias in Bach's Weimar church cantatas is a tendency to avoid the strict da capo form, with its systematically applied key scheme, or to use it in a modified manner. This trait can be traced through to his Leipzig compositions and clearly distinguishes him from his contemporaries. The strict da capo aria was still associated with its secular origins in the Italian solo cantata, and Bach's modifications may reflect his desire to achieve a sacred style disassociated from the secular style, as prescribed by eighteenth-century theorists. Bach did write some strict da capo arias, however, including "Widerstehe doch der Sünde," BWV 54, and "Mein Herze schwimmt im Blut," BWV 199. The arias are settings of texts, written by the Darmstadt court poet Georg Christian Lehms, that Bach specifically labeled "cantata." These pieces seem to be modeled more closely on the conventions of Italian secular solo cantatas than many of Bach's other church cantatas, both in scoring (solo voice and orchestra) and in the designation "cantata," a term usually avoided in sacred music at the time.

Bach's arias from his Weimar period often stand out not only for their employment of new forms, but also for their technical innovations. Particularly attractive are those arias in which a chorale tune has been introduced as a vocal or instrumental cantus firmus. The chorale text, which is either sung or implied by instruments, creates almost a second semantic level. On the one hand, the chorale stanza comments on the free poetry; on the other, the text of the aria is reflected in the chorale. This combinatorial technique was not new with Bach; it belongs to the repertory of older sacred vocal music and is very often found among such Northern German masters as Dietrich Buxtehude, Nikolaus Bruhns, and Johann Valentin Meder, who—and this is certainly no coincidence—were of great significance for Bach's stylistic development in other aspects of his craft as well. It is a testament to Bach's talent that he was able to transfer this technique to the realm of the church cantata and thus to have recaptured it as a means of expressing sacred music in his day. There is usually no reference to these added chorale stanzas in the cantata librettos that Bach set to music. We may therefore take them to be Bach's personal contribution, which, to a certain extent, reflects his own interpretation of the text.

Bach was very fond of writing such combined passages or movements, which presented a chorale simultaneously with other texts. Even as early as his Mühlhausen cantata "Aus der Tiefen rufe ich, Herr, zu dir," BWV 131, he combines the two aria-like movements with two different stanzas from the hymn "Herr Jesu Christ, du höchstes Gut." And there are instrumental cantus firmi contained in individual solo movements of the cantatas "Gott ist mein König," BWV 71, and "Gottes Zeit ist die allerbeste Zeit," BWV 106. Within the context of the more intricate Weimar arias, however, combining the aria form based on the da capo principle (whether used strictly or freely) with the bar form (AAB) of the chorale raises problems that require mature compositional craftsmanship. It looks almost as if Bach set himself this task in order to make his own composing more difficult and hence more interesting. The arias exude the most perfect form, harmony, and rhetoric despite the independence of the cantus firmu. Bach later developed these techniques still further, as in the introductory choruses of many cantatas, in the opening chorus of the St. Matthew Passion, and finally (the *opus summum* in this respect), in the colossal opening movement "Ein feste Burg ist unser Gott," BWV 80/1, which refashioned the Weimar cantata for the third Sunday in Lent (Oculi Introïtus), "Alles, was von Gott geboren," BWV 80a, into a monumental Reformation work.

In the series of cantatas composed in Weimar following his appointment as concertmaster (March 2, 1714), Bach began using a combination of aria and chorale in his second work, the cantata "Weinen, Klagen, Sorgen, Zagen," written for a performance on April 22, 1714. In this work the form of the aria, which is accompanied only by the continuo, closely matches the chorale tune played by a trumpet. In the Pentecost cantata "Erschallet, ihr Lieder," BWV 172, written four weeks later, Bach goes one step further: in the fifth movement he turns the text, consisting of three stanzas, into a through-composed duet for soprano and alto, accompanied by a continuo and set within a unifying ritornello. To this, the chorale melody "Komm, heiliger Geist, Herre Gott" is added as a cantus firmus, played by the oboe (at a subsequent performance the part was taken over by the organ) and embellished almost beyond recognition. The two voices are linked in a dialogue, the bass line adding an ostinato—with the beginning of the chorale

The castle of Weimar; eighteenth-century engraving.

tune emerging from its highest notes—and the complex contrapuntal texture is expanded by the oboe into a quartet. The compositional problem of this aria, to which Bach found a masterly solution, lay mainly in its contrapuntal structure. The formal design did not present any particular difficulties because of the strophic organization of the text and the fact that the chorale melody does not contain any repeats.

Bach once more turned to the problems of form in the aria "Letzte Stunde, brich herein" from the Easter cantata "Der Himmel lacht, die Erde jubilieret," BWV 31 (1715), a work of comparable structural complexity, with its four obbligato parts. The text by Franck is presented in a free but unmistakable da capo construction, whereas the chorale melody "Wenn mein Stündlein vorhanden ist" unfolds in the characteristic AAB bar form, played by the strings in unison. On the one hand, this calls for distinct embedding and harmonization of the repeated first lines of the chorale melody, while on the other, the A part of the aria must also be combined twice, in different ways.

Inserting vocal or instrumental chorale melodies within the context of an aria not only creates new links on the textual level, but often—and perhaps above all—also contributes to the work's musical homogeneity. In as many as four of the Weimar cantatas, the instrumental chorale melody contained in one of the arias is the same as the one in the closing chorale. In three of them (BWV 80a, 161, and 185) the chorale melody is introduced in the opening aria, thereby establishing a musical link with the closing movement and creating a neat framework for the entire work that the text did not provide. In the fourth (BWV 31), the chorale cantus firmus appears in the penultimate movement and thus foreshadows the closing chorale.

Another structural experiment evident in Bach's Weimar cantatas is his attempt to combine aria form and fugal techniques. The problem was once again to bring diverging principles into line. Bach had already successfully employed fugal techniques in chorale movements, even in polyphonic chorale settings. With respect to the formal model of the aria, however, this became a great deal more difficult, since the structure of the aria is diametrically opposed to polyphonic treatment. Considering Bach's systematic experiments with contemporary musical genres and styles, it is only consistent and logical that a few years later he achieved a synthesis of a fugue and a concerto movement in the final movement of the Brandenburg Concerto No. 4.

Bach's first fugal aria is found in the concluding movement of the cantata "Widerstehe doch der Sünde," BWV 54, apparently composed for the third Sunday in Lent (March 23) in 1715. The two instrumental parts (violins and violas) are joined by the solo alto as a third partner in the treatment of the chromatic fugal subject. The bass line moves in continuous eighth notes that are identified only as the obbligato countersubject, sung by the alto on the words "denn dieser hat sie aufgebracht." The ritornellos and the solo sections, constructed according to the principle of a free da capo, have been composed as fugal expositions, which constantly gain in contrapuntal (stretto from the 35th bar) and harmonic density (modulations to C minor, G minor, F minor, and A-flat major) up to the end of the B section. Bach follows this with a varied recapitulation of the A section and concludes with a new version of the ritornello, in which the continuo plays the theme for the first time, in its entirety. This device does equal justice to the symmetrically rounded da capo form of the aria and the linear, constantly intensified structure of the fugue.

Bach found a different way of integrating fugal techniques within the aria framework in the opening movement of the cantata "O heilges Geist- und Wasserbad," BWV 165, written for Trinity Sunday in 1715 or 1716. The ritornellos are conceived here as fugal expositions for four voices, whereas in the solo sections the texture is reduced to three parts (first violin, soprano, continuo). Nevertheless, the motivic development remains strongly related to the theme. Both the subject and the obbligato countersubject, which occasionally appears separately, are presented in their original and inverted forms.

During the Weimar period the recitatives of Bach's sacred cantatas were perfected in the same way as his arias. A great many librettos by Franck that Bach set to music provided few or no recitatives, but whenever Bach had the opportunity to use texts written by other authors, he devoted a great deal of attention to the composition of recitatives. Compared with his contemporaries, Bach cultivated a decidedly personal recitative style, in which the melody is by no means subordinate to the speech rhythm, as in the Italian opera or chamber cantata. Accordingly, his recitatives are musically more independent, more expressive, and in the end more dramatic. In his Weimar cantatas, Bach adhered to the type of recitative cultivated in the seventeenth century, which very closely followed the style of the arioso. This style is apparent in the frequent melismas on words carrying strong affections and the long arioso insertions and closing sections of his Weimar recitatives; these characteristics disappear gradually in his Leipzig cantatas.

Recitatives play a central role in the cantata "Gleichwie der Regen und Schnee vom Himmel fällt," BWV 18. Apart from an introductory instrumental movement, a short aria, and the concluding chorale, the work is one large sequence of recitatives, interrupted only by litany-like interpolations sung by the choir. In the cantatas "Ich hatte viel Bekümmernis," BWV 21, "Christen, ätzet diesen Tag," BWV 63, and "Mein Herze schwimmt im Blut," BWV 199, extended accompanied recitatives laden with affections and expansive harmonies serve as preparation for expressive and solemn arias.

During his Weimar days Bach explored in a most individual manner the musical potential offered by the recitative and aria forms that had been introduced into Protestant church music through Erdmann Neumeister's efforts at reform. Bach's multifaceted compositional concept enabled him to expand established genres and styles by blending together instrumental and vocal principles, as well as aspects of the traditional and the modern. In his own assessment of his church music, Bach described the result of this complex process as "intricate" (*BR,* 141). Bach's pupil Lorenz Christoph Mizler attested in 1739 that in his sacred vocal music Bach had taken as his model "the music of twenty or twenty-five years ago" (*BR* , 249), suggesting that Bach's stylistic ideals concerning the composition of cantatas found their decisive artistic expression during his time in Weimar.

Notes

1. Johann Mattheson, *Der Vollkommene Capellmeister* (Hamburg, 1739), p. 78.
2. Erdmann Neumeister in the preface of his collected texts, *Geistliche Cantaten statt einer Kirchen-Music* (Weissenfels, 1700).

Performing in the Thomaskirche (St. Thomas's) in Leipzig, presumably conducted by Bach's predecessor Johann Kuhnau; engraving, 1710.

13

AFFECTIONS, RHETORIC, AND MUSICAL EXPRESSION

Ulrich Leisinger

Opera as a Model for Church Music around 1700

For centuries music has had its proper place in the system of liberal arts. Together with arithmetic, geometry, and astronomy it formed the quadrivium of educational disciplines in Latin schools, as opposed to the trivium, which consisted of grammar, rhetoric, and logic. By 1600, however, theories that interpreted music as a mathematical science had moved a very long way from practical musical performance. It is difficult to imagine a more glaring contrast than the one between the speculative structure of the harmony of the spheres, expounded by Johannes Kepler in 1619, and Italian opera of the same period. On the one hand, there was the strong belief in a well-regulated cosmos whose order was reflected in musical proportions; on the other was the exciting, and alarming, notion that the composer of an opera was able, almost at will, to arouse, transform, and satisfy the passions of both the actors and the audience.

Vocal music seemed particularly suitable for stirring those who listened to it since, according to a commonly held view, instrumental music lacked emphasis and therefore the power of persuasion. Heinrich Bokemeyer, cantor in Wolfenbüttel from 1717, expressed this opinion in his treatise

Der melodische Vorhof:

> The aim of music is to educate the listener in a charming and pleasant way. Therefore, understanding must be constructed, directed at the listener's desires, and not just tickling of the ear. Indeed, a mere instrumental melody, without any text, may have great power over the human mind, if it is so inclined. Alone, no matter how affecting a melody may be, it will scarcely be understood if there is no text to go with it to spur on the mind simultaneously, and therefore make the impact that much stronger, in order to achieve its true purpose.[1]

Around 1700 at the latest, Protestant church music came under the spell of opera. Until then the repertory of church music had been based predominantly on biblical texts of a didactic nature. From that time on an effort was made to incorporate elements from the opera stage into the church. Johann Mattheson of Hamburg, who composed operas and wrote about music, argued that music for the church and music for the theater had different aims only if one looked at them superficially:

> Furthermore, in church . . . I have precisely the same idea about music as in the opera, that is to say: I want to stir the listener's mind and get it moving in a certain way, whether toward a feeling of love, compassion, joy or sadness, etc. . . . Especially here, during worship, intense, serious, long-lasting, and extremely profound emotions are needed.[2]

The influence of opera first became obvious in the choice of text and continued at the level of the music. Mattheson gave the following purpose of music: "Direct praise of God should be the principal aim of church music, and indirectly also the purpose of all music. After that, not just to teach the listeners, but, above all, to move them."[3]

Mattheson no longer set his sights on instructing listeners, but on touching their emotions. Using as examples good speakers and preachers, Mattheson asserted that a lasting impression is more easily attained by stirring up emotions than by using rational arguments.

This fundamental change in the appreciation of church music becomes clear when we compare two early cantatas by Bach. The so-called "Actus tragicus," BWV 106, written during Bach's Mühlhausen period, represents the older type. Its text is based on biblical and chorale verses. Each individual part of the text stands on its own, but as a whole the texts are arranged in such a way as to form a theological unity: our life, like our

Opening of the "Actus tragicus," BWV 106 (copyist's score, late eighteenth century).

death, is in God's hands. The old covenant that God made with Moses states that every human being is mortal. But the covenant renewed by Christ through the sacrifice of His death fulfills the promise of eternal life.

In contrast, the cantata "Mein Herze schwimmt im Blut," BWV 199, dating from Bach's Weimar period, is much less straightforward in its construction and contains a complex psychological interchange. The theological message results from a succession of emotional steps that develop logically one after another: The Christian is aware of his sins that make him "into a monster in God's sacred eyes." Grief brought about by this thought is followed by repentance and a confession of sins. Trust in God, which the repentant sinner derives from the comforting verse of a hymn, brings new confidence and joy.

The declarations in the *Actus tragicus* that "God's time is the very best time" and that "in Him do we live, move, and are" contrast with the dramatically depicted personal bewilderment of "My heart swims in blood." How sober and didactic are the words "Oh, Lord, teach us to remember that we must die," in comparison with the aria "Lowly bent and full of repentance, I lie, dearest God, before Thee." In the *Actus tragicus* the individual movements of the work are almost equal in weight; in the cantata "Mein Herze schwimmt im Blut" they are arranged in subtle succession. The carefully constructed arias, which try to make full use of the text by repeating it in different ways and presenting it from various perspectives, are preceded by recitatives that prepare for and explain the change of mood. Conveying a theological meaning is a secondary purpose of the arias; the first is the portrayal of an emotional state of mind. For Mattheson, a good aria text suggests both the portrayal of an affection and the interpretation of a general theological declaration:

> Strictly speaking, an aria should be nothing else but a clear, thought-provoking scriptural text and axiom with a certain affection, which ought to be used and applied continuously to the subject with which it deals.[4]

If, therefore, an aria is an emphatic presentation of an affection, then the recitative serves as a foundation for the affection. The separate functions of the recitative and aria had already been established in opera. Derived from this model, the newer sacred cantata is made up of recitatives and arias whose contents are related to each other but call for different musical treatment. One of the principal postulates of the time, the demand for unity through diversity, was easily met in this way. This new type of cantata, with its succession of recitatives and arias often enhanced by opening and closing choruses based on a biblical text, proved to be highly effective. Within a few decades it almost completely supplanted the older forms, such as cantatas with verses from the Bible or hymns taken over almost unchanged.

The Doctrine of the Affections

The success of the new form of cantata is best explained if we go back to contemporary theories on the emotions. The greatest minds of the seventeenth century, including René Descartes and Baruch Spinoza, devoted themselves to this subject. Their attempts at interpretation spread quickly and were adapted by writers on music in order to make the fascinating impact of music intelligible. The ideas formed around 1650 remained alive for many decades and subsequently informed the views of music during Bach's youth.

The starting point for every doctrine of the affections is the relation between body and mind. It was believed that affections, being passions of the mind, had physical origins, and theorists hoped that the progress in natural science might shed light on this emotional phenomenon. Descartes viewed the spirit as a mediator between body and soul, and he defined passion as an experience or emotion of the soul that must be prompted, supported, and strengthened by an agitation of the spirit. Contrary to appearances, emotions are not brought on by a conscious act of the soul. It is much more a case of the soul being touched, thereby creating an affection over which the soul has no conscious control. This meaning can be traced back to the Latin expression *affectus* (from *afficere* = do something to someone) and to the French synonym "passion" and the German term "Leidenschaft." Along these lines Spinoza defined affections as those influences upon the body that increase or reduce, cultivate, or check its efficacy.

Based on the ancient doctrine of temperaments, philosophers such as Descartes and music theorists such as the Jesuit Father Athanasius Kircher tried to explain the origin of affections and were convinced that emotions were the result of a physical state of agitation. According to Kircher, when something raises our ire, it acts on our bile, whose fiery vapors produce such affections as anger, fury, and frenzy. An attempt was made to explain the impact of music in a similar way. Sound affected the body and could arouse it both within and without. If the resulting physical emotions corresponded with those normally produced by external stimuli, one could easily conclude that music, like external stimuli, provoked an emotional response. Kircher argues:

> As it is, music and the affections have something in common, i.e., when the harmonic *numerus* (i.e., the musical proportions and the vibrations emanating therefrom) first stirs up the spiritual breath, and when these *vapores* [vapors] are mixed with the inner breath or mind, then they move a human being in the direction they are going; and in this way harmony moves passions and affections.[5]

From a present-day point of view, this explanation appears complicated, almost muddled. One should not forget, however, that modern attempts to answer the question of how something from the external world manages to move us are no less abstract and hardly less speculative. In any case, the model outlined above satisfied the demands of the time and made possible a rational explanation of music's strong impact. Furthermore, if one embraced the proposition that musical stimulation is a physical one, rules could be borrowed from the doctrine of the affections and used as an effective means of musical expression.

For instance, in accordance with Descartes' general definition, grief is an unpleasant inconvenience to the soul caused by some misfortune or mistake. This assumption leads easily to musical analogies: weariness requires a slow tempo, a "weiche Tonart" (minor key), and small intervals; failure shows itself through "übellautende" (bad-sounding) tones and chords—that is, dissonances. Chromaticisms, especially a descending pattern referred to as *passus duriusculus* (a somewhat hard step), could represent the "inconvenience to the soul."

The doctrine of the affections answers the question of how the composer can ensure that a singer's excitement may be transmitted to the audience. If the performing musician and the listener are in the same mood, then understanding will develop between the two, as Kircher explains:

> If two instruments are tuned to the same pitch and only one of them is struck with harmonic *modulus* [=in a harmonious way], it will bring out the same harmony from the other instrument, without its having been struck.[6]

Spinoza adds a further element of explanation: the soul remembers earlier experiences. After it has been exposed to a certain affection, it will always remember the affection in case it enters the same circumstances as before or is moved by similar events. This explains why composers reused techniques, hoping that those means would produce the same response. Along those lines, a piece that had once been regarded as sad would always have that effect. Since we have seen above that affections are not the work of the individual but are brought on from the outside, the description of affections could be generalized. What seemed at first to be an immense number of affections could be reduced to a few basic ones: love, hate, joy, sadness, compassion, and fear, as Mattheson termed them in the passage quoted above.

The cover illustration of a treatise by the Jesuit priest Franz Lang illustrates the standardization of the affections. The title of the work, *Theatrum affectuum humanorum*, reflects the Baroque-era conviction that all the world is a stage, and life is a play determined and directed by the will of the Highest. Following scholastic tradition, the top ranking in Lang's description is given to virtue, which other authors did not always count among the affections. The reason for its position can be found in the philosophy of Spinoza, who defined virtue as blissful happiness and love for God. The more the soul can enjoy divine love, the greater its power over the affections and the less it is at their mercy. Thus virtue can be seen as a state of independence from the affections and subsequently as the highest aim in life. Lang arranges personified, paired affections around virtue, placing each positive affection on the right and its negative counterpart on the left. Love (*amor*) stands opposite hate (*odium*), courage (*audacia*) opposite fear (*timor*), and desire (*desiderium*) opposite aversion (*fuga*). In the forefront we see hope (*spes*) and despair (*desperatio*), and in immediate proximity to virtue are joy (*gaudium*) and sadness (*tristitia*). Finally, anger (*ira*) appears in the background without a corresponding positive affection, so the opposite niche remains empty.

Each affection can be given essential attributes, as in Lang's allegorical illustration. It is likewise possible to form purely musical analogies. The character of the arias in the cantata "Mein Herze schwimmt im Blut" has been defined by such specific musical attributes that words are not needed to indicate the affection of sadness in the first aria and joy in the last. But the central aria of this cantata shows the limitations of a musical portrayal of the affections and suggests that music is the servant of the text, not its master. Although the ritornello radiates optimistic peace, only the text can depict humility, composure, or repentance.

The beliefs we just touched upon are impressively summarized by Johann Kuhnau in the preface to his *Musicalische Vorstellung einiger biblischer*

Johann Kuhnau, pen drawing.

Johann Mattheson, engraving, circa 1746.

Historien in 6. Sonaten auff dem Claviere zu spielen. Even if Kuhnau, who served as Thomaskantor from 1701 to 1722 and was therefore Bach's immediate predecessor in Leipzig, attempted to translate biblical verses into wordless instrumental pieces, he valued vocal music most highly:

> Vocal music has been widely used when one wanted to touch the mind with something special, because words contribute much, if not the most, to stirring it. Speech already makes that sort of impact to a large extent, but its penetrating power is achieved completely only through music. Many pieces of church music bear witness to this . . . particularly those by composers who understand the proper meaning of *musica pathetica* [i.e., a way of composing that is aimed at portraying an affection]. The example of theatrical style and of opera, which could have either a sacred and a profane story for a subject, has shown us sufficiently how happy the masters were in their expression of affections and other things.[7]

It seems plausible to translate "Expression der Affekte" (expression of affections) as "musikalischer Ausdruck" (musical expression). We ought to realize, however, that the word "expression" now has a connotation that was unknown in the early part of the eighteenth century. Since we are familiar with music from the Classical and Romantic eras, we commonly understand musical expression as an attempt by the composer to transmit his experience and feeling to others by means of his music. In the Baroque era this way of thinking was unheard of, since at that time affections were not considered the condition of an individual but rather an outside influence. Saying that a subject "wanted to express itself" is therefore not applicable to the early part of the eighteenth century. In a letter dated September 1687 to the mathematician and philosopher Antoine Arnauld, Gottfried Wilhelm Leibniz speaks to this issue:

> In my way of speaking something "expresses something else" if there is a constant and well-regulated relation between what is said by the one and by the other.[8]

Thus a successful "expression of the affections" assumes a well-regulated relation between the affection to be portrayed and the music representing it. From this viewpoint, one could conclude that during the Baroque era the portrayal of an affection was highly standardized and typified, since that is the only way to imagine "geregelte Beziehungen" (well-regulated relations) between music and affection. In current parlance, "expression of the affections" could best be translated as "representation" or "portrayal" thereof.

It is not surprising that Kuhnau referred to opera as the perfect model for portrayal of the affections. A wide circle of Protestant clergy, however, looked at opera with suspicion, and inflamed discussions ensued about whether opera was more harmful than useful. For that reason many—but by no means all—members of the Protestant clergy were skeptical about church music drawing nearer to theatrical music, as was especially apparent when emotional recitatives and arias with a strong emphasis on the affections were introduced into church cantatas. Georg Motz, the cantor and musical director at the Latin school in Tilsit, skillfully incorporated operatic elements into his church music without provoking attacks from the more conservative members of the clergy. In a written defense against charges leveled by Pastor Christian Gerber of Lockwitz, Motz made use of his knowledge that many cantors were also schoolmasters. He declared rhetoric, which formed a solid and undisputed part of the schools' curriculum, to be a standard for church music. Motz pointed out that an appropriate portrayal of the affections included in the text would be the primary criterion for a musical composition. Suggesting that in church the mind should be directed toward discovering what is good, he draws a comparison with a preacher's task:

> Joyous texts must be sung joyfully, and sad ones sadly. Hymns of praise and thanks cannot be set to sad music, nor hymns of penitence to brisk and cheerful tunes. A sad melody does not evoke joy, nor a cheerful one a sense of sadness. In every possible way people's minds must be directed toward what is good. But in rhetoric no rebuke is heard when priests preach the word of God to their congregations joyfully on high holy days and sadly on days of repentance. Their intention for doing so is to move the congregation's mood even more toward devotion. What is not sinful or irritating in rhetoric is not wrong in singing either.[9]

Gerber's reproach, that composers of his day aimed only at entertaining their audience without due regard to spiritual matters, is termed absurd:

> The opposite can be demonstrated and proved with many thousands of pieces of church music. You only have to look at an honorable composition to detect exactly what you find in a good preacher. For he takes as much care to guide his listeners toward what is good as a musician stimulates his audience toward the same goal through different variations and motions.[10]

Music should actually be preferred to a sermon:

> What is more, when such a composition is performed, it can indeed be called a wonderful musical oration; in addition, you can also hear a charming and beautiful harmony, in which the great God grants His people on earth a foretaste of heavenly joy and the marvelous and sweet sound of the "englische Kapelle" (choir of angels), so that they can be reminded even better of the divine being, which is impossible during a mere oration that consists only of the melodious sound of rhetoric.[11]

Consequently, church music possesses the same merits as a sermon; a competent composer is the equal of a good preacher:

> Thus, righteous composers, using all their qualities for expressing every word of a text artistically in a religious composition, show sufficiently that they are not concerned only about sweetness, but also about religious matters as true Christians. And therefore a well-worded piece of church music consists not only of a melodious exterior, but even more of true holy devotion and meditation.

This argument ought not be dismissed as the shrewd construct of someone defending "modern" church music against its conservative critics. It is the consequence of music's changed position within the liberal arts. Johann Adolf Scheibe addresses this issue in the description of music in his *Compendium Musices* (c. 1730):

> Music is a scholarly science. In its search for sound and tone it shows that while the affections of man can be expressed and aroused by means of a good melody and harmony, the various movements of nature can only be imitated.[12]

This definition recognizes the connection with tradition and the change in the conception of music, which is still defined as a science but no longer as a mathematical discipline. Music effectively broke away from mathematics in the early part of the seventeenth century; around 1700 theorists discovered far-reaching concurrences with rhetoric.

The vocal composer paid close attention to punctuation and word stress when setting the text. One might then apply musical grammar to these aspects, which was just as indispensable a foundation for serious musical performance as was the technical correctness of a sentence. The adoption of musical analogies is only one step away. At that time a composer would hardly fail to portray musically such words as "hoch" (high), "tief" (low), "steigen" (rising), "fallen" (falling), "eilen" (hastening), or "ruhen" (resting).

A composer's objective went further and resembled the task of an orator, as Motz pointed out. What mattered was the transmission of a certain meaning to the audience. Proceeding from this basic approach, composers often used rhetoric when composing music. The art of speaking suggested structural elements, and composers relied on rhetorical figures with musical parallels. It would be wrong to imagine that composers had copies of Quintilian's *Institutio oratoria* or the textbook of one of his contemporaries lying on their desks. Nor would a pastor have picked up a book on rhetoric when writing his sermon. The composer, rather, had to familiarize himself with the principles of public speaking and apply them in a suitable way to music. A composer worthy of his reputation was expected to have more to offer than just practical knowledge. The aim of composing was to express and arouse human affections. Further, it was not enough to translate word for word into music, as Mattheson maintained:

> For an affection is not simply this or that specific word, but the entire sense and context of an oration. So first we have here the doctrine of the affections, which one should look for in rhetoric, ethics, physics, etc., and not in grammar, and then wisely *ad melodicam* [in the art of melodic invention].[13]

So the wheel comes full circle. Mattheson did not mean to imply that the composer should first study natural science, ethics, and rhetoric. Rather, reference to these disciplines reveals the belief during the late seventeenth and early eighteenth centuries that all spheres of science were closely interwoven. They were all part of one cosmos that God had created in the most perfect way. Consequently, all music was intended, first, to praise the Creator and, second, to teach and move the listeners.

Notes

1. Heinrich Bokemeyer, *Der melodische Vorhof,* in: Johann Mattheson, *Critica Musica,* vol. 2 (Hamburg, 1725), p. 297.
2. Johann Mattheson, *Der musicalische Patriot* (Hamburg, 1728), p. 105.
3. Johann Mattheson, *Critica Musica,* vol. 2 (Hamburg, 1725), p. 297.
4. Ibid., vol. 1 (Hamburg, 1722), p. 104.
5. Athanasius Kircher, *Musurgia universalis* (Rome, 1650); quoted from the German partial translation by Andreas Hirsch (Swäbisch Hall, 1662), p. 139.
6. Ibid.
7. Johann Kuhnau, *Musicalische Vorstellung einiger biblischer Historien in 6. Sonaten auff dem Claviere zu spielen* (Leipzig, 1700), preface.
8. Gottfried Wilhelm Leibniz, *Die philosophischen Schriften,* ed. Carl Immanual Gerhardt, vol. 2 (Berlin, 1878), p.112.
9. Georg Motz, *Die vertheidigte Kirchen-Music* . . . ([Tilsit, East Prussia], 1703), pp. 14–15.
10. Ibid., p. 52.
11. Ibid.
12. Johann Adolf Scheibe, *Compendium Musices,* first printed in: *Peter Benary, Die deutsche Kompositionslehre des 18. Jahrhunderts* (Leipzig, ca. 1960), part 1, section 1, § 21.
13. Johann Mattheson, *Critica Musica,* vol. 2 (Hamburg, 1725), p. 360.

Sources (see also notes, above)

Heinrich Bokemeyer, *Der melodische Vorhof,* in: Johann Mattheson, *Critica Musica,* vol. 2 (Hamburg, 1725).
René Descartes, *Les Passions de l'âme* (Paris, 1649).
Athanasius Kircher, *Musurgia universalis* (see note 5).
Johann Kuhnau, *Musicalische Vorstellung* . . . (see note 7).
Franz Lang, *Theatrum affectuum humanorum* (Munich, 1717).
Gottfried Wilhelm Leibniz, *Die philosophischen Schriften,* ed. Carl Immanuel Gerhardt (Berlin, 1875–90).
Johann Mattheson, *Critica musica* (see note 3).
———, *Der musicalische Patriot* (see note 2).
Georg Motz, *Die vertheidigte Kirchen-Music* . . . (see note 9).
Erdmann Neumeister, *Fünffache Kirchen-Andachten, bestehend in theils eintzeln, theils niemals gedruckten Arien, Cantaten und Oden auf alle Sonn- und Fest-Tage des ganzen Jahres,* pub. Gottfried Tilgner (Leipzig, 1717).
Johann Adolf Scheibe, *Compendium Musices* (see note 12).
Baruch Spinoza, *Ethica ordine geometrico demonstrata,* in: his *Opera posthum, qorum series post praefationem exhibetur* ([Amsterdam], 1677); numerous reprints and translations.

Mühlhausen in the seventeenth century, engraving.

14

ASPECTS OF PERFORMANCE PRACTICE

Ton Koopman

Ever since Bach's first cantatas were heard in Arnstadt and Mühlhausen, many performances of his music have been given, and very many different ones, too. The recordings that we are in the process of making have a special character of their own. That is so, of course, because over the years I have developed my own way of performing works by Bach. This interpretation continues to develop further through research conducted in cooperation with musicologists and through the actual performance of the music. Naturally, we are often faced with questions and problems. They may vary from "Which tuning do we use?" "At what tempo do we play?" and "Which instruments do we use?" to "How large should the choir be?" I am pleased to take you behind the scenes and give you an inside view of performance practice with regard to Bach's music.

PITCH AND KEYS

Making recordings is a marvelous opportunity to perform Bach's enormous cantata output according to what we know at present. Playing day-to-day concerts is a little more complicated. Some very specific problems cannot always be solved quite so easily.

A clear example of such a problem is the question of *Chorton* (choir pitch), or *Kammerton* (chamber pitch). When performing cantatas dating from different periods in Bach's life, it is difficult to use the correct pitch for each cantata. It does become possible, however, if one groups all of the early cantatas into three periods.

Nearly all of the sacred cantatas written by Bach before he became cantor at the Thomaskirche in Leipzig were performed in the higher "choir pitch." This system conformed to the way the organs were tuned, which means that notes sounded a semitone higher than we are used to. In other words, an A on the organ is a B-flat on the modern piano. The organ was tuned to A = ca. 465 Hz, whereas today's piano is tuned to A = ca. 440. Baroque woodwinds were tuned to the lower "chamber pitch," that is, A = ca. 415 or 392. They consequently sounded either a semitone or a full tone lower than the present-day piano.

Woodwind parts (oboe, bassoon, and recorder) were therefore notated by Bach so as to accommodate the two possible tuning systems. Today, this tuning requires some players in the wind section to buy additional instruments. And violin players have to purchase thinner gut strings because normal gut strings cannot manage the high pitch (A = ca. 465) and tend to snap if they are tuned that high.

In performing Bach cantatas, one must find solutions to some specific problems, for instance, the obbligato bassoon part in "Nach dir, Herr, verlanget mich," BWV 150. Nowadays, many people play this part on a contrabassoon, but when Bach wrote this (oldest surviving?) cantata, such an instrument did not yet exist. If one transposes the original notation, the part can be played without any problem on a baroque bassoon. The strings, except for the viola d'amore, play at the high pitch (A = ca. 465), the bassoon at the lower (A = ca. 392). Through transposition, the pitch sounds the same.

This also applies to "Tritt auf die Glaubensbahn," BWV 152. The strings have been notated in E minor but are tuned high (A = ca. 465). The wind instruments have been notated in G minor but are tuned low (A = ca. 392).

If one were to perform the entire cantata in E minor, based on a modern tuning of A = ca. 440, the vocal bass part would sound too low. The opposite would apply to a performance in G minor: the soprano would be too high. In the original tuning, both soloists sing at an agreeable pitch.

Comparing today's editions with original performance material or, even better, autograph scores, provides us with much fascinating information. "Gott ist mein König," BWV 71, was performed in Mühlhausen in a polychoral arrangement. The groups were placed on balconies far away from each other, producing an exciting spatial impression. Today, one would speak of a "stereo effect."

The autograph shows this very clearly: the score calls for one group of strings (without a cello), a second consisting of two recorders and a cello, a third with two oboes and a bassoon, a fourth with trumpets and tympani, and a vocal group consisting of a choir and soloists. Even the organ sometimes plays a solo part.

The end of the cantata "Gott ist mein König," BWV 71. The brackets on the left indicate the different groups of instruments. (Bach's autograph)

Excerpts for soprano and oboe from the cantata "Ich hatte viel Bekümmernis," BWV 21 (Bach's autograph).

In this same cantata, whose orchestral and choral material was printed (a great exception for Bach's cantatas), we find something surprising. When a singer is accompanied by the continuo, the cello, violone, and bassoon parts are marked "tacet," that is to say, organ accompaniment only. We have become used to the fact that the "basso continuo" always includes a cello, but this cantata clearly proves the opposite. The concept of *basso continuo* or *figured bass* originated during the Baroque period, and the bass line served as the foundation of the music. In the cantatas this part was played by the organ, with or without the cello, violone, double bass, and bassoon, and only the bass line was notated. The organist improvised an accompaniment by using the figures under the bass line.

"Ich hatte viel Bekümmernis," BWV 21, is deservedly one of Bach's best known cantatas. Different versions of the oboe part in the sinfonia have been uncovered, and Bach did not give the tenor a real solo part until the Leipzig performance in 1723. Before that time, the soprano was the only soloist. The presence of a bassoon in the recitatives accompanied by strings and organ remains a curious phenomenon. Even more curious is the fact that the chord on the "Lob" (praise) text in the final chorus, as notated in the autograph score, did not appear in any modern version, as far as I know.

The lack of clarity in the extant manuscript score for "Gottes Zeit ist die allerbeste Zeit," BWV 106, can be attributed to its late date. The score, which dates from the latter part of the eighteenth century, indicates that the recorders play in the same key as the strings. If this is so, however, the players would have had to play pitches unavailable on the recorder. It is possible that in later performances these parts were played by flutes. The problem can be solved by having the recorders play a whole tone lower, based on a tuning of A = ca. 415. All others play at a tuning of A = ca. 465, and everything is in tune.

We still have one further problem with the continuo. Did a cello join in or, as seems more reasonable, did one of the viola da gambas play the bass line of "In deine Hände," BWV 106/3a? There were no cellos in BWV 106.

It seems that before 1723 the double bass sounded one octave higher than the current double bass. An instrument that sounds the same octave as the modern piano is called an 8 foot (8'), and one an octave lower is called a 16 foot (16'), designations that stem from organ building. Unless marked *violone grosso*, this 8' violone or double bass would certainly have played the remainder of the continuo. In this way the violone player could pause for a few bars after the aria while the double bass took over the bass line. After that, the gamba player could again concentrate on the solo part.

In his remarkable book *Bach's Continuo Group* (Cambridge, 1987), Lawrence Dreyfus expands on the notorious problem of the double bass 16' versus 8'. The cantatas "Nach dir, Herr, verlanget mich," BWV 150, and "Der Herr denket an uns," BWV 196, as well as Bach's Brandenburg Concerto No. 6, are convincing examples of the use of an 8' violone. Thus, for all of the early cantatas I almost always use a double bass/violone with frets, unless a violone grosso has been notated. Bach started using the 16' double bass only after his arrival in Leipzig. His predecessor, Johann Kuhnau, had bought one of the instruments for the Thomaskirche. A cantata, such as "Christ lag in Todesbanden," BWV 4, that had been performed originally on an 8' fundamental without wind instruments, would have been performed in Leipzig with a 16' instrument, accompanied by cornett, trombones, and additional strings.

Articulation slurs as used by Bach pose tremendous problems for musicologists, with such questions arising as: "Are the indications intended exactly as they appear?" and "Where does the slur start or finish?" When a modern scholarly edition is prepared, all kinds of sources are painstakingly compared, and the new score either is or is not reconciled with the sources. In the original sources the articulation slurs often vary enormously, without any apparent logic or clarity. Was this due to excessive haste, or did each of Bach's good players really know what Bach meant? "Barmherziges Herze der ewigen Liebe," BWV 185, part 1, provides a famous example of this problem. There is no simple, uniform solution for the articulation slurs in the bass part. Some slurs vary incredibly. A single solution may be inconceivable, and perhaps in Bach's time different players solved the problem in different ways according to their appreciation and knowledge of eighteenth-century articulation.

Other questions of notation abound. In the same section of BWV 151, of which, unfortunately, there is no autograph manuscript, a cantus firmus text has been notated for the oboe that is curiously missing in modern editions. Another notation problem that recurs in many cantatas relates to the bass lines for secco recitatives (voice with continuo). The continuo part is often notated in long note-values that must in fact be played short in order to make the text audible. The *Neue Bach-Ausgabe* correctly published the string recitative of BWV 151 without the short bassoon notes, because this bassoon part surely dates from an earlier version of this recitative in which

Violone; engraving by Bonannini.

String instruments; engraving by Praetorius.

only bassoon and organ accompaniment were provided. To reflect these differences, our new recordings of the Bach cantatas for Erato frequently include several versions of the same cantata, as a sort of appendix.

Bach often changed the key of a cantata when he performed it in Leipzig. He did so with "Mein Herze schwimmt im Blut," BWV 199, which he played in D minor in Leipzig, based on a tuning of A = ca. 415. Earlier, the cantata had been performed in C minor, with the tuning A = ca. 465. The result was identical for the singers. In Leipzig the organist transposed, whereas previously the woodwinds did so. Performing cantatas at the higher "choir pitch" presented certain performance problems. The soprano and tenor parts are very high, and Bach obviously trained his singers to be able to perform the works. We are, however, confronted with Baroque violins at a high pitch that will not stay in tune, since the instruments are used to A = ca. 415. Even thinner strings change their pitch by the minute. After a few days they stabilize, and the instruments then sound clearer than ever. Another exciting world of sonorities has thus been created.

CHOIR VOICES

Bach's choir consisted of boys' voices and adult male voices. Church leaders adhered to the command "Mulier taceat in ecclesia," which forbid females from performing in the choir or as soloists. According to a story attributed to Johann Mattheson, choirs sometimes ignored the ruling. Apparently, the choir in Hamburg had been praised for the sound of its boy sopranos. In actuality, women had secretly strengthened the choir for years until finally, overcome by frustration, the female singers let themselves be seen at the end of a service. The ban was imposed again, and the sound of the sopranos must surely have suffered.

A boy's voice changed later in the eighteenth century than it does nowadays, and there are accounts of boys who could still sing soprano or alto at the age of seventeen or eighteen. A ten- or twelve-year-old angelic boy soprano was not the ideal in the eighteenth century. Older boys were used for solo parts, and by virtue of their age they were more developed musically and emotionally than the boy singers who had just turned twelve.

It is interesting to follow the boy soprano Sebastian Hennig on the Leonhardt/Harnoncourt's Teldec recordings from the 1970s and 1980s. He sang for several years until he was nearly sixteen. One can hear enormous development. I assume that this situation is rather similar to what Bach was familiar with: a musical youngster, like Sebastian Hennig, is able to produce a lovely vocal quality shortly before his voice changes. Today it seems easier to use young female voices, provided they sing clearly, have full control over their vibrato, and possess great presence.

Bach was well acquainted with falsetto singers (now referred to as countertenors). Women were not admitted to the university, so it was normal in student circles for men to use head voice, i.e., falsetto, in order to sing alto and soprano parts. This tradition has been preserved in England. Outside of England, countertenor Alfred Deller (1912–1979) revived interest in falsetto singing. His efforts contributed in large measure to the popularity of falsetto singing in the current early-music movement.

ACCOMPANIMENT ON ORGAN AND HARPSICHORD

As in most German churches, wherever Bach worked there was a harpsichord standing in the organ loft. Arnold Schering, who disliked the harpsichord, discusses the use of the instrument in his book *Bachs Leipziger Kirchenmusik*. He suggests that Bach used the instrument during rehearsals in order to save the organ blower, or in an emergency, for instance when the organ had to be repaired. Bach may also have sometimes performed as *maestro a cimbalo*, without a lid on the harpsichord, directing the choir and orchestra as he played. How well could the harpsichord be heard in comparison to the organ? Played simultaneously, the organ could provide volume and the harpsichord could ensure that choir and orchestra maintained the rhythm. But using the organ and the harpsichord at the same time is not conducive to tonal purity. If it gets warmer in the church, the organ's pitch rises, but the harpsichord's goes down.

How much use was made of the organ pedals in the course of playing the basso continuo part? Friedrich Ehrhart Niedt writes that one needed to play with a 16' register and even a 16' reed stop (such as trombone or trumpet) to hear the bass very clearly. These registers therefore sounded an octave lower than the same notes on the present-day piano. Would the 16' stop that Bach proposed for the Mühlhausen organ have been intended as amplification for the bass line when playing the continuo? It seems like a plausible explanation, but the bass part's dynamic flexibility would certainly have suffered.

Organ player; eighteenth-century engraving by C. Weigel.

Harpsichord player; eighteenth-century engraving by C. Weigel.

Is one allowed to claim authenticity if one experiments in this way? I have tried it out and found it delightful and exciting, just as it is fun, as a church organist, to play the complete orchestral part of Mozart's *Krönungsmesse* if there is no orchestra available. But artistically speaking, making such changes ought to be a last resort.

Eighteenth-century musicians were at times confronted with problems of a practical nature. Even Bach was faced with singers and players falling ill. And what were the accoustics like? How much of the sound got lost? Today we often use portable organs. There are advantages and disadvantages to this: the small organs are easy to tune at any pitch, and the overall placing of the choir and the orchestra becomes less complicated. Conversely, the position of the organ loft in a church is problematic, because the organist has difficulty seeing the singers and players and because the full organ's standard pitch is often different from that of the other musicians. The scaling of the pipes of a portable organ differs greatly from that of a church organ. Bach presumably used a normal church organ with registers that were not too loud. Although the portable organ offers many practical advantages, the full organ allows for a more prominent role as a soloist.

INSTRUMENTS FROM THE BAROQUE PERIOD

Ideally, one should perform Bach's cantatas on the instruments of his day. Bach knew the Baroque instruments inside and out, and he was fully aware of what his musicians could and could not do. I am convinced that performances under Bach's direction reached a high degree of perfection. If we examine the technical complexity of Bach's vocal and instrumental parts, we cannot but hold his musicians in the highest esteem. We can only hope that Bach would have accepted us as members of his orchestra or choir.

In the early cantatas, the probability of transposing oboe parts has destroyed a fascinating theory. If the text of a cantata expresses sadness, as in "Ich hatte viel Bekümmernis," BWV 21, and "Weinen, Klagen, Sorgen, Zagen," BWV 12, then Bach—according to this theory—always wrote oboe parts in keys that sounded uncomfortable. In C minor or F minor, fork fingering gives the oboe a tormented sound. But in actuality, Bach wrote them transposed, i.e., in a simple D minor or G minor key, respectively. So it appears that the "Trübsal" (grief) had to be produced much more through the oboist's musical interpretation than through imperfect-sounding keys. Baroque instruments were by no means primitive—that is the erroneous judgment of a later period. The level of performance on such instruments has recently increased in response to the heightened interest in early music.

There is often some uncertainty about the Baroque violin. Is the expensive Stradivarius actually a Baroque instrument, possessing the original Baroque scaling, or has it been adapted over time to conform to modern performing traditions? Almost all string instruments have been altered to increase their volume and to adjust to the heavier steel strings. To accomplish this, the neck was placed at an angle to the body and the instrument was internally strengthened. For a string instrument to produce a Baroque sound accurately, it must be reconstructed. Wind instruments from the eighteenth century, conversely, were not modernized; they were simply replaced by modern ones, which explains why so many original wood instruments survive. Mattheson describes the complete range of Bach's

Opening of the cantata "Weinen, Klagen, Sorgen, Zagen," BWV 12. (Bach's autograph)

instruments in his *Neu-eröffnete Orchestre* (1713), which Johann Christoph Weigel quoted and annotated in his *Musicalisches Theatrum* (Nuremberg, ca. 1722).

Playing Techniques and Style

We can find information on playing technique and style in the small number of published German treatises on playing. In 1738 J. P. Eisel published his *Musicus Autodidaktos*, which presents, among other things, a modern view on what one might expect from a good bassoonist. He recommends that the bassoonist use a proper reed and have at his command agile fingers and an agile tongue for the articulations. Daniel Speer gives excellent instruction to string players in his *Grundrichtiger Unterricht* (Ulm, 1687).

Friedrich Ehrhart Niedt's *Musicalische Handleitung* (Hamburg, 1717, repr. in 1721 by Mattheson) is an absorbing and particularly practical textbook for instruction on the continuo. The most useful treatises for woodwind players are from France, including Freillon Poncein's oboe manual, *La veritable manière d'apprendre à jouer en perfection du hautbois* (Paris, 1700) and Jacques Hotteterre's method for flute (and recorder), *Principes de la flûte traversière* (Paris, 1707).

What Is Authenticity?

The word "authentic" has become synonymous with the playing of old instruments in accordance with the stylistic conventions of the period during which the music was written. Moreover, it has acquired a negative connotation in the sense that its proponents claim a "monopoly on wisdom." It is impossible to perform Bach's music as he himself did. One may try to reconstruct Bach's world of sound and his aesthetics by studying the available information and using historical instruments or copies thereof. One may well succeed, but one also runs the risk of getting entangled in a jumble of historical rules. The same danger exists for those who try to ascertain the exact number of singers and musicians that Bach used. The number does not tell anything about the quality of the players. Did the player produce a loud or soft sound, did he play energetically, did he use a superior instrument? How big was the room in which the music was made? How large was the budget that could be spent on music? It is impossible to recreate every aspect of a Baroque performance.

Looking at the parts that have been preserved, we still cannot make out exactly what instruments were employed. How many duplicates (extra orchestral scores) were around? How many have been lost, because they were not autographs and were therefore less attractive to the nineteenth-century collector? Were there spare scores that were kept simply because they were in good condition?

I am, in fact, convinced that Bach corrected any mistakes in the material as he went along with rehearsals. The original parts for "Der Himmel lacht, die Erde jubilieret," BWV 31, part 2, contain mistakes that were never corrected. One wonders, then, if what we now possess may not have been reserve material.

Thanks to the advent of photocopiers, errors in multiple parts are relatively rare. But anyone who copies by hand knows how easy it is to make mistakes. It does not take much to forget a sharp or a flat, nor to write inadvertently on the incorrect line. Sometimes we are too quick in wielding our red pencil and marking something as wrong simply because it looks strange. A composer has the right to disagree with himself and make changes. The transmission of intact manuscripts from generation to generation is unreliable, and it is often difficult to determine which version of a score is the "original." But we must be careful in making corrections and should preserve all feasible sources.

Composition of the Choir and Orchestra

I should like to add something about the composition of the choir and the orchestra. Sometimes, knowledge of the performing forces available in a certain church or a royal chapel may help in solving performance problems.

Musically speaking, it seems obvious that BWV 4, 150, and 196 should be played with single string instruments, as the manner of composition is soloistic. But what do we make of BWV 196/3? Both violin parts contain typical solo passages. If two violins play this solo part, then accuracy and flexibility suffer. For the early Bach cantatas I generally prefer single strings (except for BWV 21 and 31) and a choir with three or four singers per part. In addition to the extant iconography, the bassoon part in Bach's B-minor Mass ("Hohe Messe") indicates that more than one person could have sung or played the same part: bassoons 1 and 2 have been notated one above the other in the same bassoon part.

Any deficiency of balance can be solved, of course, by our modern microphone technique, but we must not overdo this. In the early to mid-twentieth century it was customary to perform the works of Bach with 200 to 400 performers on stage. Gradually, the size of choirs has decreased to a more acceptable level of some twelve to twenty singers, which sounds sufficiently clear. I would not recommended fewer than twelve singers. A single or almost single arrangement (in which one would arrange the choir in the "Hohe Messe" with only one singer per part) would ignore the amateur status of Bach's singers, however skilled they might have been. They were, after all, pupils and not professional singers.

Finally, mention should be made of the practice of performing Bach's music on modern instruments while taking into account the available information about Baroque performance practice. Nikolaus Harnoncourt has done pioneering work in this field. It is clear that recordings featuring historical instruments have exposed musicians who play modern instruments to the developments in the field. Fortunately, Bach's works as performed by Mengelberg and Richter are a thing of the past. We have no right to be know-it-alls, nor should we play the part of policemen. All we can hope to achieve is a greater understanding of Bach's music and the surroundings in which it was created.

Viola d'amore player; eighteenth-century engraving by C. Weigel.

Literature

Michael Praetorius, *Syntagma musicum*, Musicae Artis Analecta, 3 vols. (Wittenberg, 1614–19), facs. (London, New York, 1958).

Daniel Speer, *Grundrichtiger Unterricht der musikalischen Kunst oder Vierfaches musikologisches Kleeblatt*, Georg Wilhelm Kühnen (1679, repr. Leipzig, 1974).

Johann Christoph Weigel, *Musicalisches Theatrum* (Nuremberg, 1732), facs. (Kassel, 1964).

Johann Mattheson, *Das Neu-Eröffnete Orchestre* (Hamburg, 1713; repr. New York, 1993).

Friedrich Ehrhart Niedt, *Musicalische Handleitung, dritter und letzter Theil* (Hamburg, 1717).

Filippo Bonanni, *Gabinetto armonico* (Rome, 1723), facs. (New York, 1964).

Anonymous [J. P. Eisel], *Musicus αυτοδιδακτοσ oder der sich selbst informirende Musicus* (1738).

Arnold Schering, *Johann Sebastian Bachs Leipziger Kirchenmusik, Studien und Wege zu ihrer Erkenntnis* (Leipzig, 1936, 2nd ed. Leipzig, 1954).

Sources for Bach's cantatas

"Der Himmel lacht, die Erde jubiliret," BWV 31; manuscript, partly autograph: parts and score, Krakow, Biblioteka Jagiellonska, Mus.Ms.Bach.St.14.

"Gottes Zeit ist die allerbeste Zeit," BWV 106 (*Actus Tragicus*); manuscript: score, Berlin, Staatsbibl. Preussischer Kulturbesitz, Mus.Ms.Bach.P.1018.

"Barmherziges Herze der ewigen Liebe," BWV 185; manuscript (partly autograph): parts, Berlin, Staatsbibl. Preussischer Kulturbesitz, Mus.Ms.Bach.St.4.

"Barmherziges Herze der ewigen Liebe," BWV 185; manuscript: parts, Berlin, Staatsbibl. Preussischer Kulturbesitz, Mus.Ms.Bach.P.59.

"Christ lag in Todesbanden," BWV 4; manuscript, partly autograph: parts, Leipzig, Bach-Archiv, Thomasschule.

"Der Herr denket an uns," BWV 196; manuscript: parts, Berlin, Staatsbibl. Preussischer Kulturbesitz, Am.B.102/104.

"Gott ist mein König," BWV 71; Bruckner, Mühlhausen: parts, The Hague, Gemeentemuseum.

"Gott ist mein König," BWV 71; autograph: score, Berlin, Staatsbibl., Preussischer Kulturbesitz, Mus.Ms.Bach.P.45; DVfM, Leipzig.

"Ich hatte viel Bekümmernis," BWV 21; autograph: parts, Berlin, Staatsbibl., Preussischer Kulturbesitz, Ms.Bach St.354.

"Mein Herze schwimmt," BWV 199; autograph/copy: parts, Berlin, Staatsbibl. Preussischer Kulturbesitz, Mus.Ms.Bach.St.459.

"Nach dir, Herr, verlanget mich," BWV 150; manuscript: parts, Berlin, Staatsbibl. Preussischer Kulturbesitz, Mus.Ms.Bach.P.1044.

"Tritt auf die Glaubensbahn," BWV 152; autograph, Berlin, Staatsbibl. Preussischer Kulturbesitz, Mus.Ms.Bach.P.45.

"Weinen, Klagen, Sorgen, Zagen," BWV 12; autograph: parts, Berlin, Staatsbibl. Preussischer Kulturbesitz, Mus.Ms.Bach.P.44.

"Weinen, Klagen, Sorgen, Zagen," BWV 12; autograph/copy: parts, Berlin, Staatsbibl. Preussischer Kulturbesitz, Mus.Ms.Bach.St.109.

BIBLIOGRAPHY

Selected literature, pertaining primarily to the subject area of Bach's sacred cantatas from the pre-Leipzig period.

Reference Works

Wolfgang Schmieder, *Thematisch-systematisches Verzeichnis der musikalischen Werke Johann Sebastian Bachs: Bach-Werke-Verzeichnis* (Leipzig, 1950); 2nd rev. and enl. ed. (Wiesbaden, 1990) [*BWV*].

Hans-Joachim Schulze and Christoph Wolff, *Bach Compendium. Analytisch-bibliographisches Repertorium der Werke Johann Sebastian Bachs*, 1, 4 pts. (Leipzig and Frankfurt, 1985–89); vols. 2–3 in prep. [*BC*].

Christoph Wolff ed., *Bach-Bibliographie. Nachdruck der Verzeichnisse des internationalen Schrifttums zu J. S. Bach* (*BJ* 1905–1984), with a *Supplement* and *Register* (Kassel, 1985).

Rosemary Nestle, "Das Bachschrifttum 1981–1985," *BJ* 75 (1989): 107ff.

———, "Das Bachschrifttum 1986-1990," *BJ* 80 (1994): 75ff.

Werner Neumann and Hans-Joachim Schulze, eds., *Schriftstücke von der Hand Johann Sebastian Bachs, Bach-Dokumente*, I (Leipzig and Kassel, 1963) [*Dok* I].

———, *Fremdschriftliche und gedruckte Dokumente zur Lebensgeschichte Johann Sebastian Bachs 1685–1750, Bach-Dokumente*, II (Leipzig and Kassel, 1969) [*Dok* II].

Hans-Joachim Schulze, ed., *Dokumente zum Nachwirken Johann Sebastian Bachs 1750–1800, Bach-Dokumente*, III (Leipzig and Kassel, 1972) [*Dok* III].

Werner Neumann, ed., *Bilddokumente zur Lebensgeschichte Johann Sebastian Bachs, Bach-Dokumente*, IV (Leipzig, 1978) [*Dok* IV].

Kalendarium zur Lebensgeschichte J. S. Bachs, ed. Bach-Archiv, Leipzig (Leipzig and Kassel, 1970, 2nd rev. ed. 1979).

Werner Neumann, ed., *Sämtliche von J. S. Bach vertonte Texte* (Leipzig, 1974).

Hans T. David and Arthur Mendel, eds., *The Bach Reader: A Life of Johann Sebastian Bach in Letters and Documents* (New York, 1945; 2nd rev. ed. 1966) [*BR*].

Kritische Berichte (critical commentaries) to *J. S. Bach, Neue Ausgabe sämtlicher Werke* (Neue Bach-Ausgabe), ed. Johann-Sebastian-Bach-Institut, Göttingen and Bach-Archiv (Leipzig, Kassel and Basel, 1954–) [*NBA*].

Yoshitake Kobayashi, *Die Notenschrift Johann Sebastian Bachs. Dokumentation ihrer Entwicklung, NBA* IX/2 (Kassel, 1989).

Melvin P. Unger, ed., *Handbook to Bach's Sacred Cantata Texts: An interlinear translation with reference guide to Biblical quotations and allusions* (Lanham, Md. and London, 1996).

Life and Works: General Literature

Johann Nikolaus Forkel, Über Johann Sebastian Bachs Leben, Kunst und Kunstwerke (Leipzig, 1802; Eng. trans.: *BR*, 294–356) [Forkel].

Carl Ludwig Hilgenfeldt, *Johann Sebastian Bachs Leben, Wirken und Werke. Ein Beitrag zur Kunstgeschichte des achtzehnten Jahrhunderts* (Leipzig, 1850; repr. 1978).

Carl Hermann Bitter, *Johann Sebastian Bach* (Berlin, 1865, enl. 2nd ed. 1881, repr. 1951).

Philipp Spitta, *Johann Sebastian Bach*, 2 vols. (Leipzig, 1873–80 Eng. trans.: London, 1884–85; repr. 1951) [Spitta].

Albert Schweitzer, *J. S. Bach* ([Paris, 1905], Leipzig, 1908) Eng. trans.: London 1911, repr. 1967.

Charles Sandford Terry, *Bach: A Biography* (London, 1928).

Werner Neumann, *Auf den Lebenswegen Johann Sebastian Bachs* (Berlin, 1953).

Karl Geiringer, *Johann Sebastian Bach* (New York, 1966).

Barbara Schwendowius and Wolfgang Dömling, eds., *Johann Sebastian Bach. Zeit, Leben, Wirken* (Kassel, 1976). Eng. trans.: New Haven 1978.

Hans-Joachim Schulze, "Über die 'unvermeidlichen Lücken' in Bachs Lebensbeschreibung,"
    Bachforschung und Bachinterpretation heute: Bachfest-Symposium Marburg 1978, 32ff.

Malcolm Boyd, *Bach* (London, 1983).

Christoph Wolff, "New Perspectives on Bach Biography," *Bach: Essays on His Life and Music*
    (Cambridge, Mass 1991): 3–13.

Alberto Basso, *Frau Musika: La vita e le opere di J. S. Bach*, 2 vols. (Turin, 1979–83).

Walter Emery and Christoph Wolff, "Johann Sebastian Bach," *The Bach Family*, ed. Christoph Wolff
    (London & New York, 1983): 44–237.

Robert L. Marshall, *The Music of Johann Sebastian Bach: The Sources, the Style, the Significance*
    (New York, 1989).

Christoph Wolff, *Bach: Essays on His Life and Music* (Cambridge, Mass., 1991, ²1993).

———, ed. "Johann Sebastian Bach," in *Die Bach–Familie* (Stuttgart, 1993): 60–286 [rev. trans. of
    Emery–Wolff, 1983].

Martin Petzoldt, *Bachstätten aufsuchen* (Leipzig, 1992).

BIOGRAPHICAL AND HISTORICAL STUDIES

Hermann Wäschke, "Die Hofkapelle in Cöthen unter Joh. Seb. Bach," *Zerbster Jahrbuch* 3 (1907): 31ff.

Conrad Freyse, *Eisenacher Dokumente um Sebastian Bach* (Leipzig, 1933).

Georg Mentz, "Weimarische Staats- und Regentengeschichte vom Westfälischen Frieden bis zum
    Regierungsantritt Carl Augusts," *Carl August, Darstellungen und Briefe zur Geschichte des
    Weimarischen Fürstenhauses und Landes*, vol. 1, ed. Erich Marcks and Willy Andreas (Jena,
    1936).

Conrad Freyse, "Das Bach-Haus zu Eisenach," *BJ* 36 (1939): 66ff.; 37 (1940–48): 152ff.

Gustav Fock, *Der junge Bach in Lüneburg* (Hamburg, 1950).

Reinhold Jauernig, "Johann Sebastian Bach in Weimar," in *Johann Sebastian Bach in Thüringen*,
    ed. Hans Pischner et al. (Weimar, 1950): 49ff.

Fritz Wiegand, *J. S. Bach und seine Verwandten in Arnstadt* (Arnstadt, 1950).

Friedrich Smend, *Bach in Köthen* (Berlin, 1951; Eng. trans.: St. Louis, 1985).

Hans Löffler, "Die Schüler Joh. Seb. Bachs," *BJ* 40 (1953): 5–28.

Wolfgang Lidke, *Das Musikleben in Weimar von 1683 bis 1735* (Weimar, [1954]).

Ernst König, "Die Hofkapelle des Fürsten Leopold zu Anhalt-Köthen," *BJ* 46 (1959): 160–67.

Friedrich Blume, "Outlines of a New Picture of Bach," *Music and Letters* 44 (1963): 214ff.

Rolf Dammann, *Der Musikbegriff im deutschen Barock* (Cologne, 1967; 2nd ed. 1984).

Hans-Joachim Schulze, "J.S. Bach's Concerto-Arrangements for Organ—Studies or Commissioned
    Works?," *Organ Yearbook* 3 (1972): 4–13.

Martin Ruhnke, "Das italienische Rezitativ bei den deutschen Komponisten des Spätbarock," *Analecta
    musicologica* 17 (1976): 79–120.

Friedhelm Krummacher, *Die Choralbearbeitung in der protestantischen Figuralmusik zwischen
    Praetorius und Bach* (Kassel, 1978).

Herbert Zimpel, "Der Streit zwischen Reformierten und Lutheranern in Köthen während Bachs
    Amtszeit," *BJ* 65 (1979): 97–106.

George Stauffer, *The Organ Preludes of J.S. Bach* (Ann Arbor, Mich., 1980).

Peter Williams, *The Organ Music of J.S. Bach* 3 vols. (Cambridge, Mass., 1980–84).

Hans-Joachim Schulze, "'Aus einem Capellmeister ein Cantor zu werden . . .'—Fragen an Bachs
    Köthener Schaffensjahre," *Cöthener Bach-Hefte* 1 (Cöthen, [1981]): 4ff.

Christoph Wolff, "'The Extraordinary Perfections of the Hon. Court Composer': An Inquiry into the
    Individuality of Bach's Music" [1983], *Bach: Essays on His Life and Music* (Cambridge, 1991):
    391–97.

Hans–Joachim Schulze, *Studien zur Bach–Überlieferung im 18. Jahrhundert* (Leipzig, 1984).

———, "Historische Wahrheit statt Legende: Zur Präzisierung unseres Bach-Bildes," *Musik und
    Gesellschaft* 35 (1985): 123ff.

Markus Schiffner, "Johann Sebastian Bach in Arnstadt," *Beiträge zur Bachforschung* 4 (1985): 5ff.

Hans Rudolf Jung, *Johann Sebastian Bach in Weimar 1708 bis 1717, Tradition und Gegenwart,* Weimarer Schriften, vol. 16 (Weimar, 1985).

Günther Hoppe, "Köthener politische, ökonomische und höfische Verhältnisse als Schaffensbedingungen Bachs (Teil 1)," *Cöthener Bach-Hefte* 4 (Cöthen, 1986): 12ff.

Ulrich Siegele, "Johann Sebastian Bachs und Fürst Leopolds Auffassungen über das Hofkapellmeisteramt," *Cöthener Bach-Hefte* 4 (Cöthen, 1986): 5ff.

H. Peter Ernst, "Joh. Seb. Bachs Wirken am ehemaligen Mühlhäuser Augustinerinnenkloster und das Schicksal seiner Wender-Orgel," *BJ* (1987): 75ff.

Markus Schiffner, "Die Arnstädter Hofkapelle—regionales Zentrum der Musikpflege im historischen und zeitgenössischen Umfeld des jungen Bach," *Beiträge zur Bachforschung,* VI (1988): 37ff.

Andreas Glöckner, "Gründe für Johann Sebastian Bachs Weggang von Weimar," *Bericht über die Wissenschaftliche Konferenz Leipzig 1985* (Leipzig, 1988): 137ff.

Günther Hoppe, "Köthener Kammerrechnungen—Köthener Hofparteien: Zum Hintergrund der Hofkapellmeisterzeit Johann Sebastian Bachs," *Bericht über die Wissenschaftliche Konferenz Leipzig 1985* (Leipzig, 1988): 145ff.

Christoph Wolff, "Buxtehude, Bach, and Seventeenth-Century Music in Retrospect," *Bach: Essays on His Life and Music* (Cambridge, Mass., 1991): 41–55.

———, "Bach and Johann Adam Reinken: A Context for the Early Works," *Bach: Essays on His Life and Music,* 56–71.

———, "Chronology and Style in the Early Works: A Background for the Orgel-Büchlein," *Bach: Essays on His Life and Music,* 297–305.

———, "The Organ in Bach's Cantatas," *Bach: Essays on His Life and Music,* 317–23.

Christine Kröhner, "Kantoren und Kantorate in Mühlhausen am Beginn des 18. Jahrhunderts," *Struktur, Funktion und Bedeutung des deutschen protestantischen Kantorats vom 16. bis 18. Jahrhundert* (Oschersleben, 1995).

Heller, Karl and Schulze, Hans-Joachim, eds., *Das Frühwerk Johann Sebastian Bachs* [Colloquium, University of Rostock, 1990] (Köln, 1995).

Russell Stinson, "The Compositional History of Bach's Orgelbüchlein Reconsidered," *Bach Perspectives,* I (Lincoln and London, 1995): 43–78.

Christoph Wolff, "J. S. Bach and the Legacy of the Seventeenth Century," *Bach Studies 2,* ed. Daniel R. Melamed (Cambridge, 1995): 192–201.

Küster, Konrad, *Der junge Bach* (Stuttgart, 1996).

Vocal Works: General Literature

Charles Sanford Terry, *Bach: the Cantatas and Oratorios* (London, 1925; repr. 1972).

Karl Ziebler, *Das Symbol in der Kirchenmusik Bachs* (Kassel, 1930).

Friedrich Blume, *Die evangelische Kirchenmusik* (Potsdam, 1931); 2nd rev. ed. as *Geschichte der evangelischen Kirchenmusik* (Kassel, 1965; Eng. trans.: New York, 1974).

Arnold Schering, "Kleine Bachstudien," *BJ* 30 (1933): 30ff.

Werner Neumann, *J. S. Bachs Chorfuge* (Leipzig, 1938; 2nd ed. 1950).

Hans-Heinrich Unger, *Die Beziehungen zwischen Musik und Rhetorik im 16.–18. Jahrhundert* (Würzburg, 1941).

Arnold Schmitz, *Die Bildlichkeit der wortgebundenen Musik J. S. Bachs* (Mainz, 1950, repr. 1980).

Alfred Dürr, "Zur Chronologie der Leipziger Vokalwerke J. S. Bachs," *BJ* 44 (1957): 5ff.; pub. separately, rev. (Kassel, 1976).

Emil Platen, *Untersuchungen zur Struktur der chorischen Choralbearbeitung Johann Sebastian Bachs* (diss., Bonn, 1959).

Werner Neumann, "Über Ausmass und Wesen des Bachschen Parodieverfahrens," *BJ* 51 (1965): 63ff.

Doris Finke-Hecklinger, *Tanzcharaktere in Johann Sebastian Bachs Vokalmusik* (Trossingen, 1970).

Robert L. Marshall, *The Compositional Process of J. S. Bach: A Study of the Autograph Scores of the Vocal Works* (Princeton, 1972).

Ulrich Siegele, "Bachs Endzweck einer regulierten und Entwurf einer wohlbestallten Kirchenmusik," in *Festschrift G. von Dadelsen* (Stuttgart, 1978): 313ff.

Christoph Wolff, " 'Intricate Kirchen-Stücke' und 'Dresdener Liederchen' Bach und die
Instrumentalisierung der Vokalmusik," *Johann Sebastian Bach und der süddeutsche Raum.
Aspekte der Wirkungsgeschichte Bach,* ed. Hans-Joachim Schulze and Christoph Wolff
(Regensburg, 1991): 19-23.

Andreas Glöckner, "Neue Spuren zu Bachs 'Weimarer' Passion," *Leipziger Beiträge zur Bach-
Forschung* 1 (1995): S. 33ff.

Christoph Wolff, "Pachelbel, Buxtehude und die weitere Einfluß–Sphäre des jungen Bach,"
Das Frühwerk Johann Sebastian Bachs (Köln, 1995): 21–32.

Jean–Claude Zehnder, "Zu Bachs Stilentwicklung in der Mühlhäuser und Weimarer Zeit,"
Das Frühwerk Johann Sebastian Bachs (Köln, 1995): 311–338.

Melamed, Daniel R.: *J. S. Bach and the German Motet* (Cambridge, 1995).

Cantatas: General and Pre-Leipzig Works

Rudolf Bunge, "Johann Sebastian Bachs Kapelle zu Cöthen und deren nachgelassene Instrumente,"
BJ 2 (1905): 14–47.

Bernhard Friedrich Richter, "Über die Schicksale der der Thomasschule zu Leipzig angehörenden
Kantaten Joh. Seb. Bachs," *BJ* 3 (1906): 43–73.

———, "Über Seb. Bachs Kantaten mit obligater Orgel," *BJ* 5 (1908): 49–63.

Rudolf Wustmann, "Sebastian Bachs Kirchenkantatentexte," *BJ* 7 (1910): 45–62.

———, *Joh. Seb. Bachs Kantatentexte* (Leipzig, 1913; 2nd ed. 1967).

Charles Sandford Terry, *Johann Sebastian Bach: Cantata Texts, Sacred and Secular* (London, 1926;
repr. 1964).

Arnold Schering, *Über Kantaten Johann Sebastian Bachs* (Leipzig, 1942; 3rd ed. 1950).

Werner Neumann, *Handbuch der Kantaten Johann Sebastian Bachs* (Leipzig, 1947; 3rd rev. ed. 1967;
4th ed. 1971).

Friedrich Smend, *Joh. Seb. Bach. Kirchen-Kantaten,* 6 vols. (Berlin, 1947–49; 2nd ed. 1966).

Alfred Dürr, "Zur Aufführungspraxis der Vor-Leipziger Kirchenkantaten J. S. Bachs," *Musik und
Kirche,* 20 (1950): 54ff.

———, "Über Kantatenformen in den geistlichen Dichtungen Salomon Francks," *Mf* 3 (1950): 18ff.

———, *Studien über die frühen Kantaten J. S. Bachs* (Leipzig, 1951; 2nd rev. ed. 1977).

Friedhelm Krummacher, "Die Tradition in Bachs vokalen Choralbearbeitungen," in *Bach-
Interpretationen,* ed. M. Geck (Göttingen, 1969): 29–56, 210–12.

Werner Neumann, ed, *Johann Sebastian Bach. Sämtliche Kantatentexte* (Leipzig, 1956, 2nd ed. 1967).

Luigi Ferdinando Tagliavini, *Studi sui testi delle cantate sacre di J. S. Bach* (Padua, 1956).

Hermann Melchert, *Das Rezitativ der Kirchenkantaten J. S. Bachs* (diss., Frankfurt a.M., 1958);
excerpt in *BJ* 45 (1958): 5–83.

Jack A. Westrup, *Bach Cantatas* (London, 1966).

Gerhard Herz, *J.S. Bach: Cantata No. 4 "Christ lag in Todesbanden,"* Norton Critical Scores
(New York, 1967).

———, "BWV 131: Bach's First Cantata," *Studies in Eighteenth-Century Music: A Tribute to Karl
Geiringer,* ed. H. C. Robbins Landon and Roger Chapman (London, 1970): 272–91.

Ferdinand Zander, *Die Dichter der Kantatentexte Johann Sebastian Bachs. Untersuchungen zu ihrer
Bestimmung* (diss., Cologne 1966); excerpt in *BJ* 54 (1968): 9–64.

Harald Streck, *Die Verskunst in den poetischen Texten zu den Kantaten J. S. Bachs* (Hamburg, 1971).

Alfred Dürr, *Die Kantaten von Johann Sebastian Bach* (Kassel, 1971).

Martin Geck, "Bachs Probestück," *Quellenstudien zur Musik: Wolfgang Schmieder zum 70. Geburtstag*
(Frankfurt-am-Main, 1972): 55ff.

Reinhard Gerlach, "Besetzung und Instrumentation der Kirchenkantaten J. S. Bachs und ihre
Bedingungen," *BJ* 59 (1973): 53–71.

Alfred Dürr, "Bachs Kantatentexte: Probleme und Aufgaben der Forschung," *Bach-Studien* 5 (1975):
63ff.

Christoph Wolff, "Bachs Leipziger Kantoratsprobe und die Aufführungsgeschichte der Kantate BWV 23," *BJ* 64 (1978): 78–94.

Z. Philip Ambrose, "'Weinen, Klagen, Sorgen, Zagen' und die antike Redekunst," *BJ* 66 (1980): 35–45.

Andreas Glöckner, "Zur Chronologie der Weimarer Kantaten Johann Sebastian Bachs," *BJ* 71 (1985): 159–64.

Alfred Dürr, *Die Kantaten von Johann Sebastian Bach mit ihren Texten* (Munich and Kassel, 5th ed., 1985).

Helmut Krausse, "Erdmann Neumeister und die Kantatentexte Johann Sebastian Bachs," *BJ* 72 (1986): 7–31.

Andreas Glöckner, "Anmerkungen zu Johann Sebastian Bachs Köthener Kantatenschaffen," in *Cöthener Bach-Hefte* 4 (Cöthen, 1986): 89ff.

Stephen Allan Crist, "Aria Forms in the Vocal Works of J. S. Bach, 1714–1724," (Ph. D. diss., Brandeis University, 1988).

Renate Steiger, "Actus tragicus und ars moriendi. Bachs Textvorlage für die Kantate 'Gottes Zeit ist die allebeste Zeit' (BWV 106)," *Musik und Kirche* 59 (1989): 11ff.

George J. Buelow, "Expressivity in the Accompanied Recitatives of Bach's Cantatas," *Bach Studies*, ed. Don O. Franklin (Cambridge, Mass., 1989): 18–35.

Friedhelm Krummacher, "Bachs frühe Kantaten im Kontext der Tradition," *Mf* 44 (1991): 9–32

Klaus Hofmann, "Neue Überlegungen zu Bachs Weimarer Kantaten-Kalender," *BJ* 79 (1993): 9–29.

Peter Wollny, "Bachs Bewerbung um die Organistenstelle an der Marienkirche zu Halle und ihr Kontext," *BJ* 80 (1994): 25–39.

Hans Grüß, "Bemerkungen zur Aufführungspraxis des Actus tragicus BWV 106", *Das Frühwerk Johann Sebastian Bachs*, ed. Karl Heller and Hans-Joachim Schulze (Köln, 1995): 280–289.

Yoshitake Kobayashi, "Quellenkundliche Überlegungen zur Chronologie der Weimarer Vokalwerke Bachs", *Das Frühwerk Johann Sebastian Bach* (Köln, 1995): 290–310.

Friedhelm Krummacher, "Traditionen der Choraltropierung in Bachs frühem Vokalwerk", *Das Frühwerk Johann Sebastian Bach* (Köln, 1995): 217–243.

Christoph Wolff: "'Die betrübte und wieder getröstete Seele': Zum Dialog–Charakter der Kantate 'Ich hatte viel Bekümmernis' BWV 21," BJ 1996: 139–145.

Joshua Rifkin: "From Weimar to Leipzig: Concertists and ripienists in Bach's 'Ich hatte viel Bekümmernis' ", *Early Music*, 24 (1996): 583–603.

INDEX
INDEX OF WORKS BY BACH

THE PRE-LEIPZIG CANTATAS; SURVEY

(r/M, W, C, L = repeat performances in
  Mühlhausen, Weimar, Cöthen, Leipzig
  years; r* substantially revised version)

Ach! ich sehe, itzt, da ich zur Hochzeit gehe
  (BWV 162)
  20th Sunday after Trinity, October 25,
  1716; r/L

Alles, was von Gott geboren (BWV 80a)
  Oculi Sunday, March 24, 1715 (?); r*/L

Ärgre dich, o Seele, nicht (BWV 186a)
  3rd Sunday in Advent, December 13,
  1716; r*/L

Aus der Tiefen rufe ich (BWV 131)
  Unspecified occasion, 1707–8

Barmherziges Herze der ewigen Liebe
  (BWV 185)
  4th Sunday after Trinity, July 14, 1715;
  r/W, L

Bereitet die Wege, bereitet die Bahn
  (BWV 132)
  4th Sunday in Advent, December 22,
  1715

Christen, ätzet diesen Tag (BWV 63)
  Christmas Day, 1714–15; r/L

Christ lag in Todesbanden (BWV 4)
  Easter Sunday (Mühlhausen organist
  audition?), April 24, 1707 (?); r/L

Der Herr denket an uns (BWV 196)
  Wedding, ca. 1707

Der Himmel lacht! die Erde jubilieret
  (BWV 31)
  Easter Sunday, April 21, 1715; r/L

Du wahrer Gott und Davids Sohn (BWV 23)
  Quinquagesima Sunday, (Leipzig
  audition) February 7, 1723; r/L

Erschallet, ihr Lieder (BWV 172)
  Whit Sunday, May 20, 1714 (?); r*/C, L

Gleichwie der Regen und Schnee (BWV 18)
  Sexagesima Sunday [1713–14]; r/L

Gottes Zeit ist die allerbeste Zeit (BWV 106)
  Funeral, ca. 1707–8

Gott ist mein König (BWV 71)
  Mühlhausen town council election,
  February 4, 1708; r/M

Herz und Mund und Tat und Leben
  (BWV 147a)
  4th Sunday in Advent, December 20,
  1716; r*/L

Himmelskönig sei willkommen (BWV 182)
  Palm Sunday (Annunciation), March 25,
  1714; r/W, r*/L

Ich hatte viel Bekümmernis (BWV 21)
  3rd Sunday after Trinity, June 17, 1714
  (Halle audition, December 1713?; "in ogni
  tempo"); r/W, C, L

Jesus nahm zu sich die Zwölfe (BWV 22)
  Quinquagesima Sunday, (Leipzig
  audition) February 7, 1723; r/L

Komm, du süße Todesstunde (BWV 161)
  16th Sunday after Trinity, September 27,
  1716 (?); r/L

Meine Seele soll Gott loben (BWV 223)
  Unspecified occasion, 1707–8

Mein Gott, wie lang, ach lange (BWV 155)
  2nd Suday after Epiphany, January 19,
  1716; r/L

Mein Herze schwimmt im Blut (BWV 199)
  11th Sunday after Trinity, August 12,
  1714 (?); r*/W, C, L

Nach dir, Herr, verlanget mich (BWV 150)
  Unspecified occasion, ca. 1706–7

Nun komm, der Heiden Heiland (BWV 61)
    1st Sunday in Advent, December 2, 1714;
    r/L

Nur jedem das Seine (BWV 163)
    23rd Sunday after Trinity, November 24,
    1715; r/L (?)

O heilges Geist- und Wasserbad (BWV 165)
    Trinity Sunday, June 16, 1715 (?); r/L

Tritt auf die Glaubensbahn (BWV 152)
    Sunday after Christmas, December 30,
    1714

Wachet! betet! betet! wachet! (BWV 70a)
    2nd Sunday in Advent, December 6, 1716;
    r*/L

Weinen, Klagen, Sorgen, Zagen (BWV 12)
    3rd Sunday after Easter, April 22, 1714;
    r/L

Widerstehe doch der Sünde (BWV 54)
    Oculi Sunday, March 4, 1714 (?); r/L

VOCAL WORKS (INCLUDING THE PRE-LEIPZIG CANTATAS)

BWV	BC	Title	page no.
4	A 54a	Christ lag in Todesbanden	8, 9, 11, 26, 56, 88, 104, 109–12, 127, 150–52, 156, 159, 166–68, 172, 174, 212
6	A 57	Bleib bei uns, denn es will Abend werden	17
7	A 177	Christ unser Herr zum Jordan kam	17
8	A 137a	Liebster Gott, wenn werd ich sterben	17
12	A 68	Weinen, Klagen, Sorgen, Zagen	8, 12, 15, 28, 66, 105, 118–19, 120, 150–51, 153, 160, 165, 167, 179, 208
18	A 44a	Gleichwie der Regen und Schnee	13, 14, 86, 105, 119, 120, 150–52, 164, 176, 182
21	A 99a–b	Ich hatte viel Bekümmernis	11–12, 14, 15, 17, 28, 72, 86, 90, 96, 105, 118, 127, 135, 150, 152–53, 156, 158–59, 166, 176, 182, 203, 208, 212
22	A 48	Jesus nahm zu sich die Zwölfe	17, 66, 148, 153, 161–62, 168
23	A 47a	Du wahrer Gott und Davids Sohn	17, 148, 153, 161–62, 168–69
28	A 20	Gottlob! Nun geht das Jahr zu Ende	120
31	A55a	Der Himmel lacht! die Erde jubilieret	12, 14, 105, 148, 150–53, 160, 165, 167, 181, 211
54	A 51	Widerstehe doch der Sünde	13, 23, 61, 96, 105, 118, 148, 152, 156, 179, 182
55	A 157	Ich armer Mensch, ich Sündenknecht	67
59	A 82	Wer mich liebet, der wird mein Wort halten	128
61	A 1	Nun komm, der Heiden Heiland	13–15, 23, 28, 105, 120, 151–52, 161, 167
63	A 8	Christen, ätzet diesen Tag	13, 15, 28, 107, 152–53, 160, 182
66a	G 4	Der Himmel dacht auf Anhalts Ruhm und Glück	15, 70
70a	A 4	Wachet! betet! betet! wachet!	13, 15, 107, 165
71	B 1	Gott ist mein König	9, 11, 23, 58, 85, 86, 90, 94, 104, 109, 113, 126, 145, 146, 148, 150–52, 156, 158–59, 167, 175, 179, 201
80a	A 52	Alles, was von Gott geboren	12, 15, 105, 165, 167, 180, 181
82	A 169a	Ich habe genung	128

Instrumental Works

INDEX OF NAMES

Picture Credits

Staatsbibliothek zu Berlin/Staatsbibliothek Preußischer Kulturbesitz: Page 175, 177, 187 and 202.
Collection Rob van der Hilst: Page XI-XIII, 2, 7, 10, 50, 60, 68, 71, 76, 87, 98-99, 108, 114, 151,
157, 161, 169, 180, 184, 201 and 209.
Collection Ton Koopman: Page 43, 54 and 149.
Collection Uitgeverij Uniepers Abcoude and various collections: Cover, Page II, 12-13, 15, 16, 18, 21,
25, 27, 30, 32, 34, 36, 39, 46, 48, 50, 57, 60, 62, 75, 78, 81, 84, 92, 95, 100, 103, 106, 111, 117,
121, 124, 142, 147, 151, 153, 154, 163, 166, 170, 173, 192, 205, 207 and 212.

CONTRIBUTORS

Andreas Glöckner, of the Bach-Archiv Leipzig, works for the *Neue Bach-Ausgabe*. His publications include *Die Musikpflege an der Leipziger Neukirche zur Zeit Johann Sebastian Bachs* (Leipzig, 1990).

Ton Koopman, professor of organ and harpsichord at the Royal Conservatory in the Hague, is director of the Amsterdam Baroque Orchestra and Choir. His publications include *Barokmuziek, theorie en praktijk* (Utrecht, 1985), *The Harpsichord in Dutch Art before 1800* (Zutphen, 1987), and a new edition of G. F. Handel's organ concertos (Wiesbaden: Breitkopf & Härtel, 1989–).

Ulrich Leisinger, Bach-Archiv Leipzig, works on the *Bach Repertorium* project at the Saxon Academy of Sciences. Among his publications are *Die Bach-Quellen der Forschungs- und Landesbibliothek Gotha* (Gotha, 1993) and *Leibniz-Reflexe in der deutschen Musiktheorie des 18. Jahrhunderts* (Würzburg, 1994).

Daniel R. Melamed is associate professor of the history of music at Yale University. He is the author of *Bach and the German Motet* (Cambridge, 1995).

Claus Oefner is director of the Bachhaus Eisenach. His writings include *Telemann in Eisenach* (Eisenach, 1980) and *Die Musikerfamilie Bach in Eisenach* (Eisenach, 1984).

Martin Petzoldt is professor of theology at the University of Leipzig and pastor at the Thomaskirche. Among his publications are *Ehre sei dir Gott gesungen: Bilder und Texte zu Bachs Leben als Christ und seinem Wirken für die Kirche*, with J. Petri (Berlin, 1988; 2/1990) and *Bachstätten aufsuchen* (Leipzig, 1992).

Hans-Joachim Schulze, director of the Bach-Archiv Leipzig and professor at the Hochschule für Musik "Felix Mendelssohn Bartholdy," serves on the editorial board of the *Neue Bach-Ausgabe*. His publications include *Studien zur Bach-Überlieferung im 18. Jahrhundert* (Leipzig, 1984) and *Bach-Compendium* (4 vols.), with C. Wolff (Leipzig, 1985–89).

George B. Stauffer is professor of music at the City University of New York and organist at St. Paul's Chapel of Columbia University. Among his writings are *The Organ Preludes of Johann Sebastian Bach* (Ann Arbor, 1980) and *Historical Organ Technique*, with G. Ritchie (Englewood Cliffs, N. J., 1993).

Christoph Wolff, professor of music and dean of the Graduate School of Arts and Sciences at Harvard University, serves on the editorial board of the *Neue Bach-Ausgabe*. His publications include the *Bach-Compendium* (4 vols.), with H.-J. Schulze (Leipzig, 1985–89); *Bach: Essays on His Life and Music* (Cambridge, 1991; pbk./1993), and *Die Bach-Familie* (Stuttgart, 1993).

Peter Wollny, of the Bach-Archiv Leipzig, works on the *Neue Bach-Ausgabe*. His writings include "Studies in the Music of Wilhelm Friedemann Bach" (diss., Harvard University, 1993).

J. S. BACH

THE COMPLETE SACRED AND SECULAR CANTATAS

TON KOOPMAN

AND
THE AMSTERDAM
BAROQUE ORCHESTRA & CHOIR

EXCLUSIVELY FOR ERATO DISQUES